A Sales Tax for Alberta

# A Sales Tax
# for Alberta

## Why and How

Edited by Robert L. Ascah

AU PRESS

Copyright © 2022 Robert L. Ascah
Published by AU Press, Athabasca University
1 University Drive, Athabasca, AB T9S 3A3

https://doi.org/10.15215/aupress/9781771992978.01

Cover design by Natalie Olsen, kisscutdesign.com
Printed and bound in Canada

Library and Archives Canada Cataloguing in Publication

Title: A sales tax for Alberta : why and how / edited by Robert L. Ascah.
Names: Ascah, Robert L. (Robert Laurence), 1954– editor.
Description: Includes bibliographical references.
Identifiers: Canadiana (print) 20220190291 | Canadiana (ebook) 20220190348
    | ISBN 9781771992978 (softcover) | ISBN 9781771992985 (PDF) |
    ISBN 9781771992992 (EPUB)
Subjects: LCSH: Sales tax—Alberta. | LCSH: Fiscal policy—Alberta.
Classification: LCC HJ5715.C22 A43 2022 | 336.2/713097123—dc23

We acknowledge the financial support of the Government of Canada through
the Canada Book Fund (CBF) for our publishing activities and the assistance
provided by the Government of Alberta through the Alberta Media Fund.

Canadä    Alberta
                    Government

# Contents

# Figures and Tables

## Figures

# Selected Abbreviations

The following terms are consistently abbreviated in this volume.

**CIT**  corporate income tax
**GDP**  gross domestic product
**GST**  goods and services tax
**HST**  harmonized sales tax
**NDP**  New Democratic Party
**PIT**  personal income tax
**PST**  provincial sales tax
**UCP**  United Conservative Party

# Foreword

Alberta is undergoing a painful economic transition, and this book is well positioned to inform some of the critical debates concerning the province's financial future. Until about 2013, Alberta's economy had been outperforming the rest of Canada's for so long that it seemed a given. In 2005, TD Economics reported that GDP per capita in the Calgary-Edmonton corridor was a "gigantic" 47 percent above the Canadian average, as well as substantially above the average in the United States.[1] By the end of 2011, and despite the lingering effects of the global financial crisis, weekly earnings in Alberta had risen 4.5 percent over the previous year and wholesale trade was up by 17.1 percent, while unemployment was the lowest in the country—even though Alberta's population had climbed over the past year at a rate 70 percent above the national average.[2]

The fall from these economic heights was dramatic. Alberta's GDP peaked in 2014, shrank over the next two years, recovered partially from 2017 to 2019, only to drop again in 2020 to a new low.[3] Calgary and Edmonton vied with St. John's, Newfoundland, for the cities with the worst unemployment rates in the country. Population growth slowed markedly as interprovincial migration turned negative.[4]

Provincial finances faced an equivalent upheaval. In the 2010–11 fiscal year, the Alberta government had no net debt, and its AAA credit rating was the best among Canada's provinces.[5] A decade later, the November 2020 fiscal update forecast an annual deficit of $21.3 billion. Total taxpayer-supported debt was expected to reach $97.4 billion by 2021 and soar to

$125 billion by 2023.[6] Predictably, the province's credit rating was repeatedly downgraded.[7]

As dramatic as they are, these changes are only the early stages of a much longer and more profound economic restructuring of the province. For years, successive Alberta governments have allowed the province's economy, politics, and self-identity to be tied to the ups and downs of the petroleum industry. At a peak, almost 40 percent of the province's economy was directly or indirectly dependent on this one industry.[8] But as the world has begun to shift away from petroleum in order to combat global warming, the economic foundations of Alberta have started to crumble. Not even the surge in oil prices in 2022 could lead to a boom in Alberta.

The truth is there has been a hole in the Alberta government's finances for nearly six decades. As Bob Ascah notes in chapter 3, in every fiscal year since 1965–66, the Alberta government has relied on natural resource revenues to balance its books. Those revenues are no longer large enough to continue plugging that hole, and as the debt increases, the hole gets bigger.

So the great political question in Alberta has become, How should the province balance its budget?

Alberta cannot realistically hope to balance its budget simply by cutting expenses. The financial gap is too large. As Mel McMillan demonstrates in chapter 5, for the Alberta government to balance its budget by 2022–23 through cuts alone, program spending would need to be reduced by 20 to 25 percent. This would lower program spending to levels not known in more than fifty years, which is unlikely to be politically, socially, or economically acceptable.

If cuts alone are not the answer, though, then new sources of revenue will need to be found. Where will this money come from? This book provides much of the answer. An essential part of the solution to Alberta's fiscal crisis is a sales tax.

The province has, of course, long prided itself for its low taxes and its lack of a sales tax. From 2001 to 2012, I served as an opposition member of the Alberta legislature, and every year the budget speech included an update on how much lower Alberta's taxes were than those in other provinces. "If Albertans and Alberta businesses were in any other province," the 2008 budget speech reminded us, "they would pay between about

$10 billion to $18 billion more in taxes, every single year."[9] Similarly, the 2011 budget speech announced that Albertans would pay at least $11 billion less in taxes that year than they would in any other province. The speech did not omit to mention the absence of a sales tax: "This government remains firmly committed to maintaining the lowest provincial tax regime in Canada—with low personal taxes, low corporate taxes, the lowest fuel taxes, the highest personal and spousal tax exemptions, no capital tax, no payroll tax—and no sales tax!"[10]

To put the point another way, the Alberta government has been choosing to sacrifice billions of dollars in income each year. In the face of today's fiscal crisis, Alberta's continuing commitment to extremely low taxes seems reckless. As McMillan points out, a provincial sales tax of only 5 percent—lower than that of any other province—would have provided about $5.3 billion to the Alberta treasury in 2019–20. The "Alberta Advantage" is proving to be a liability.

The people of Alberta face some hard choices. No one is ever eager to pay more taxes. But how many schools and hospitals will we be willing to close, how many nurses and police officers will we agree to lay off, how many roads and public buildings will we allow to deteriorate before we face current realities? We can sit back and watch Alberta's credit rating slowly decline until the province loses its capacity to borrow money in order to make ends meet. Or we can confront the need to bring our tax regime into better alignment with those in other jurisdictions.

That need is increasingly urgent, and the province cannot afford to go on dismissing the possibility of a sales tax. As this book makes clear, a moderate sales tax, combined with some measure of fiscal restraint, could put the province on sustainable financial ground while still enabling it to maintain its status as a low-tax jurisdiction. Chapter by chapter, the contributors to this book deliver an invaluable guide to the economic rationale for a sales tax in Alberta and to the issues surrounding the implementation of one.

A sales tax cannot and will not be the entire solution to the Alberta's fiscal crisis. Nor will any other single tactic. As the authors in this collection make abundantly clear, however, it is difficult to imagine a solution that would provide the province with a stable financial future that does not include the introduction of a sales tax.

Kevin Taft

## Notes

1   Sébastien Lavoie and Don Drummond, "An Update on the Economy of the Calgary-Edmonton Corridor: More Action Needed for the Tiger to Roar," TD Economics Topic Paper, 3 October 2005, https://www.td.com/document/PDF/economics/topic/td-economics-topic-sli005-corridor.pdf, 2.

2   *Weekly Economic Review*, 23 December 2011, Government of Alberta, available at https://open.alberta.ca/publications/weekly-economic-review-2011.

3   "Gross Domestic Product, Income-Based, Provincial and Territorial, Annual," Table 36-10-0221-01 (formerly CANSIM 384–0037), Statistics Canada, accessed 14 December 2020, https://www150.statcan.gc.ca/t1/tbl1/en/tv.action?pid=3610022101.

4   Alberta Treasury Board and Finance, *Population Projections: Alberta and Census Divisions, 2020–2046*, 28 August 2020 (Edmonton: Government of Alberta).

5   *Government of Alberta 2010–11 Annual Report: Consolidated Financial Statements* (Edmonton: Government of Alberta), 1, 88.

6   *2020–21 Mid-year Fiscal Update and Economic Statement, November 2020* (Edmonton: Government of Alberta), 3.

7   "Investor Relations," Government of Alberta, 2022, https://www.alberta.ca/investor-relations.aspx#toc-4, esp. Table 3.

8   "Alberta GDP Attributable to Oil and Gas Activity (Direct and Indirect) by Industry (2011)," slide from presentation by Toby Schneider, "Alberta: The Road to a Strong and Diversified Economy," 9 February 2017, Alberta Ministry of Economic Development and Trade.

9   *Budget 2008: The Right Plan for Today and Tomorrow*, Budget Speech, April 22, 2008 (Edmonton: Government of Alberta), 9.

10  *Budget 2011: Building a Better Alberta*, Budget Speech, February 24, 2011 (Edmonton: Government of Alberta), 5, 4.

# Acknowledgements

As this book was taking shape, I sought out the opinions of a wide array of Albertans on the subject of a sales tax. Some I interviewed, and many others shared their views in informal settings, but, regardless of the context in which they spoke, I am deeply grateful to all of them for their thoughts and candour. These are the people for whom this book is written—people whose lives are daily impacted by the state of the province's finances.

From the beginning, my wife, Linda, has been a constant ally, a wise critic, and a stalwart supporter—patient, forgiving, and willing to read whatever I threw her way. Glenn Rollans, of Brush Publishing, with whom I discussed earlier plans to write a fiscal history of the province, has continued to offer valuable counsel, and I am indebted to him for his knowledge and advice.

My former colleague Robert Bhatia has been an ongoing source of inspiration. As I groped my way through various iterations of the earlier fiscal history project, it was he who pointed me toward the issue of a sales tax and then encouraged me to move beyond the question of *why* Alberta should have a sales tax to consider *how* the provincial government might be persuaded to bring one in. I have also benefited from conversations with Al O'Brien, especially with regard to the qualitative difference between revenue from the sale of public assets, in the form of non-renewable resources, and revenue from taxes. His experience and insights have proved invaluable.

As goes without saying, I owe an enormous debt of gratitude to all the contributors to this volume, for their enthusiasm, their creative ideas, their wealth of knowledge, and their commitment both to this project and to Alberta's future. I am especially grateful to Trevor Harrison, for his constructively critical review of an earlier draft of the manuscript and for his willingness to write an afterword for the book, and to Kevin Taft, for sharing his perspectives in his foreword to the volume.

I must also extend my heartfelt thanks to two long-time friends, Virendra Gupta and Dale Moll, who provided helpful feedback on early drafts of various chapters. I am likewise grateful to the two anonymous peer readers of the manuscript for their thoughtful criticisms and suggestions, which have further enriched the volume. Assistance from Val Footz, Heather Close, and staff of the Alberta Legislature Library has also been especially valuable.

Last but not least, it has been my pleasure and good fortune to work with the team at Athabasca University Press. In particular, acquisitions editor Pamela Holway has been a consistent source of encouragement, intellectual engagement, and editorial guidance. I am grateful as well to Megan Hall, the press director, for her depth of understanding and clarity of sight, to Sergiy Kozakov, for his expert redrawing of the book's numerous charts and graphs, and to Mary Lou Roy, for her meticulous work as production editor. Perhaps above all, I am deeply indebted to Kay Rollans. Far more than a copyeditor, she worked to sharpen the focus of individual arguments and to give the book a stronger sense of forward motion, and I cannot thank her enough for her help.

Sadly, we live in an era of polarization, and Alberta's political culture is no exception. In the present atmosphere, open and informed debate around public policy issues has all but vanished. We also live in a time of growing precarity, as costs soar and incomes drop. At the same time, the province's fiscal health remains dependent on world oil prices, which continue to fluctuate unpredictably—while the government continues to compensate for shortfalls by cuts to public services.

In the face of the ongoing erosion their quality of life, Albertans have every right to be concerned about the future. But concern alone will not solve problems. It is my hope that this book will inform the public about the considerations underlying the issue of a sales tax—what it would accomplish and what the potential drawbacks are. It is my conviction that if we sincerely wish to hold government officials accountable for their actions or inactions, we must first form a clear picture of what is at stake.

# A Sales Tax
# for Alberta

# Introduction

Alberta is the only Canadian province that does not have a provincial sales tax (PST). For many Albertans, this is not only a point of pride, but an aspect of their identity. But at what cost? This book argues that it is time for Albertans and their political leaders to reconsider their anti-sales-tax stance and begin to integrate new revenue bases to ensure a more sustainable fiscal future.

Although the contributors to this collection span the political spectrum in Alberta, they all agree on one thing: Alberta needs a sales tax. Their reasons are simple. Some emphasize the brute economic merits of a sales tax. For instance, a sales tax is a stable source of revenue, especially when compared with royalties, personal income tax, and corporate income tax. The mechanisms of a sales tax are well known and understood. The cost to raise a dollar of sales tax is much lower than for other taxes, and sales taxes capture wealth and spending that other taxes miss. Others look at the social, moral, and environmental benefits of such a tax. A sales tax could help fund crucial public programs such as education and health care in the province in times of economic downturn, rather than subjecting them to devastating cuts. It could also support the province as the world turns toward a low-carbon future.

Taken together, this collection is a timely resource for politicians, policy analysts, and the general public. Its purpose is to support a broad, public, and informed discussion about the precarious reality of the Alberta government's finances and the role that a sales tax might play in stabilizing them. Each chapter is motivated by one or both of the book's central questions: First, why does Alberta need a sales tax? And second, if it does need one, how might Alberta's political leaders bring about its adoption?

# The "Whys" of Sales Tax

Sales tax has historically been one of the more fraught topics of political discussion in Alberta. The debate about instituting a sales tax has simmered for a very long time, especially in times of economic downturn. It is, however, often shuffled away and conveniently forgotten when Alberta's commodity-driven economy produces vast surpluses for Alberta Treasury.

The problem is, those surpluses come and go; we can't actually rely on commodity markets to always provide for us what we need. Most recently, the debate around a sales tax was reawakened by a steep drop in the price of oil and natural gas that began in 2014 and extended into 2016. Prices then began to recover, only to plummet again in 2020, in response to the COVID-19 crisis, and since then have climbed steadily to highs not seen in over a decade. This volatility is unsurprising: it mirrors similar patterns in earlier years, although with some exaggeration. As the latest bust-and-boom cycle illustrates, however, the price of oil remains highly unstable. Relatively short-term price rises will continue to confound Albertans and their political leaders into believing the vague promise that we can rely on the oil-and-gas fairy to show up and turn Alberta's fiscal fortunes around. This short-term thinking is challenged by the thorough analyses offered in these pages.

## *Alberta's Economic Structure and Fiscal Consequences*

Alberta's economy, in spite of having features of a diversified industrial-service economy, remains based on single-commodity production. Alberta has long been what Harold Innis ([1956] 1999, 385) termed a "peripheral economy," supplying staples to the metropolitan regions of the world. At one time, these staples were agricultural: wheat and other grains. Prices were determined generally by supply and demand factors affected by unpredictable weather, crop yield, and occasionally financial speculation. In other words, Alberta's finances were at the mercy of international commodity markets. Today, Alberta has different staple commodities: coal, bitumen, and natural gas. The prices of these are similarly set by international markets. This reliance on international markets tends to spell volatility for a commodity-based economy, for while there are many things that a government has within its control, commodity prices are not one of them.

Now here's the kicker: the Alberta government's revenue bases—that is, the sources from which it receives operational funds—are deeply tied to this volatile economy. The province relies on resource royalties and tax revenue from resource development corporations that operate in the province to fund its public programs. Alberta's government and Alberta citizens are therefore left at the mercy of price swings in oil and gas. Some of this volatility could be mitigated by a solid and consistent savings strategy, but this, too, is something that has been unfortunately lacking in the province. Alberta governments have consistently failed to set aside sufficient financial reserves to weather commodity downcycles without resorting to heavy external borrowing and, often, deep expenditure cuts.

### Ecological and Social Concerns in Alberta

Add to this the unequivocal evidence that burning fossil fuels is the primary cause of the climate crisis that we are now witnessing unfold in our back yards and around the world, and Alberta's fiscal problems become more complex.

Increasingly, governments, investors, and financial institutions are recognizing that oil and gas extraction will have to be phased out quickly in order to achieve the goals agreed on at the Glasgow 2021 climate summit. Initial steps have included new financial disclosure requirements for corporations' emissions and detailed plans to achieve net zero. As well, a range of institutions from central banks to pension funds, endowment funds, and insurance companies have already established divestment policies. The pressure to divest from fossil fuels is also being extended to large banks who have significant loans to the sector. All of this means that it will be increasingly difficult for fossil fuel firms to get the funding to expand production. Indeed, it is clear that Alberta's energy industry, especially oil sands producers, are facing the prospect of stranded assets alongside massive environmental liabilities.

This crisis is problematic for Alberta because of its overreliance on fossil fuel extraction in achieving fiscal balance and funding its day-to-day operations. Because of a trend towards lower oil prices, the Alberta government has already been running large deficits since the early 2010s just to keep basic public programs running—and sometimes not even that. At the same time, we can only expect global trends towards decarbonization to continue to grow as the climate crisis becomes an ever more present aspect of all of our lives. This means that the medium- and long-term prognosis for Alberta's finances will continue to grow dimmer unless the province begins to seriously look for alternative revenue sources.

Were Alberta less reliant on resource revenue, its budgeting would be less affected by fluctuations in the price of oil and the province would have more stable footing from which to face the coming changes in global markets. A sales tax, for reasons detailed in this volume, would seem to be an ideal candidate for creating that stability.

## The "Hows" of a Sales Tax

Even though many of these "whys" of a sales tax are privately accepted by politicians and many Alberta citizens, the biggest obstacle to actually implementing such a tax is Alberta's political culture, which is widely considered to be hostile to taxes. Politicians fear electoral defeat should they ever advocate for the tax, or even consider the idea in public. This leaves the "hows" of a sales tax for Alberta somewhat difficult to pin down. I suggest that to begin to understand how the public and their elected leaders might bring about the adoption of a sales tax, we must first understand how Albertans' attitudes towards taxes came to be.

### Political Development

Periodic attempts by government to raise or introduce new taxes have historically been met with fierce resistance in Alberta. It is this aspect of Alberta's political culture that makes politicians cringe at the thought of electoral retribution should they ever utter the words *sales tax*. Salient elements of this political culture include the myth of Alberta exceptionalism, founded on rugged individualism, resentment at government intrusion, a spirit of optimism, and a sense of victimhood towards central Canadian economic and political elites.

This exceptionalism has been expressed through political discourse in Alberta, which remains dominantly conservative. Opposition to public ownership, trust in market solutions, insistence on "small" government, and faith in capitalist production are beliefs reflected in mainstream media. A corollary to the idea of small government is the deep-seated belief that taxes should be low. This idea is founded on two assertions: first, that big government "wastes money"; and second, that low taxes encourage capital investment, which leads to employment and, ultimately, a rising standard of living. These perspectives and others like them have been the rallying cries for organizations like the Canadian Taxpayers Federation, once led by a young Jason Kenney. To "prove" their claims, they point to Alberta's gross domestic product per capita, a commonly used measure of well-being, which has historically been one of the highest in the world on average. While *proof* may be too strong a word in this context (as I argue in chapter 10), it is certainly true that Alberta's reliance on resource wealth has offered limited economic evidence to persuade Alberta voters to consider the potential future need of other revenue sources such as a sales tax. Recurrent booms are mistakenly interpreted as justification for continuing low levels of taxation. As the old bumper sticker from the 1980s proclaimed, "Give me another boom and I promise not to piss it away!"— the joke being that, even in the boomiest of times, Alberta's handling of oil revenue has not set the province up for a stable fiscal future.

With the election of Ralph Klein in 1993, antitaxation beliefs were concretized in government policies and branded as the "Alberta Tax Advantage." The Progressive Conservative brand has become so ubiquitous that even the New Democratic Party, elected to government in 2015, sang the praises of Alberta's low taxes while in office, and were extremely reluctant to address the subject of Alberta's deficit challenges.

## How to Change the Tides?

Given Alberta's political legacy around taxation, how can we begin to have a meaningful discussion about implementing much-needed new revenue sources? The problem deepens when we consider the toll that two years of COVID-19 and over six years of slow economic growth have had on political discourse in Alberta. Indeed, over the past two decades, liberal democracies around the world have experienced a disturbing trend of polarization between conservative, traditional, and individualistic voices, and voices concerned with income inequality, racial injustice, and environmental degradation.

The debate on a sales tax is fundamentally a debate about the appropriate roles that the public and private sectors should play in our lives, and about what each of these sectors can control. Is the existing size of the Alberta state optimal or should its size be reduced? Do government policies ensure Albertans are given a fair share of private industry profits in oil and gas, or does the oil and gas industry control government policy (Taft 2017; Urquhart 2018)? In terms of the tax itself, what are the fiscal objectives of a sales tax? Is a sales tax to be revenue neutral and used as a means of reducing existing taxes to boost private sector investment (Bazel and Mintz 2016; McKenzie 2000), or is its purpose to address large fiscal deficits and ensure the long-term financial sustainability of government to meet the public's demand for government services over the full commodity price cycle (Harrison 2016; Flanagan 2011)? There are no formulae that will spit out objective answers to these questions. Politicians and voters must decide. While econometric analyses of the tax's economic pros and cons should be fundamental aspects of these decisions, our answers will also be rooted in how we answer a moral question: What kind of Alberta do we want to build for ourselves and future generations?

## The Structure of the Book

The first two chapters of this collection examine Alberta's unique economic and political landscape. In chapter 1, I give a more detailed history of Alberta's political development from the province's beginnings to today. This history is intended to form a foundation for understanding why Alberta's unique political culture strongly resists taxation in general, and a sales tax in particular. In the short chapter 2 that follows, veteran provincial affairs columnist Graham Thomson provides some evidence of the political consequences of this antitax sentiment, recounting how various Alberta finance ministers have been remonstrated by premiers, the media, and the public over openly musing about a sales tax.

Chapters 3 and 4, both my own, lay out Alberta's fiscal dilemma and its roots in both revenue and spending policies. The dilemma, I argue, is a tension between the public's desire for high quality public services and excellent infrastructure on the one hand, and, on the other, Albertans' exceptional belief that, almost as a birthright, taxes must be kept low. In other words, the province needs to keep spending more money without raising more money through taxes. The key to understanding this dilemma, as I argue in chapter 4, is understanding that it is not a problem of either spending or revenue, but of the push-pull dynamic between the two. To address the dilemma, Alberta must stabilize its revenue base to reliably match the steadily growing need for public service spending.

The next few chapters build the case for a PST in Alberta. In chapter 5, Melville McMillan points out the secular decline in resource revenue over the past fifty years. Drawing on economic and financial projections developed by Trevor Tombe (2018), McMillan argues that Albertans' desire for quality public services will eventually force the Alberta government to recognize it cannot address the fiscal dilemma without a sales tax.

In chapter 6, Ergete Ferede presents a more technical analysis of the rationale for adopting a sales tax. Using historical data, Ferede examines the response of the various tax bases to the business cycle. Ferede concludes that Alberta's general sales tax base, harmonized with the federal goods and services tax, is far more stable than either personal or corporate income tax bases.

Elizabeth Smythe begins chapter 7 by positing that good public policy is policy that reduces socioeconomic inequalities and addresses climate change. Although she acknowledges the regressivity of sales tax—a particular concern of the political left—Smythe finds that the social benefits of a broadly based tax and that the stability of such a tax as a source of revenue outweigh the costs of Alberta's current fiscal strategies.

In chapter 8, Ian Glassford takes on the question of how a sales tax might be successfully integrated by drawing on his experience as the former chief financial officer of Servus Credit Union, a cooperative, Alberta-based financial institution. Glassford argues that voters have good reasons to be skeptical of governments' ability to responsibly handle their money, and this skepticism gets in the way of successfully implementing taxes that could ultimately benefit them. Because of this, governments, like credit unions, must prove to their members or voters that they will responsibly handle the money that has been entrusted to them. Glassford describes a theoretical framework of PST collection and savings based on the growth of gross domestic product. By transparently communicating such a framework and making themselves publicly accountable to following it, Glassford suggests that governments could earn voter trust around the issue of a sales tax.

Ken McKenzie, in chapter 9, uses his experience over several decades as a sales tax advocate and advisor to provincial governments to argues that the time is politically ripe for a sales tax to be introduced, hinting at the fact that politicians are followers of their constituents' political will. As conditions in Alberta continue to speed towards the need for a sales tax, political leaders, he says, would do well to get ahead of the coming "sales tax parade."

In the last chapter of the book, I build on some of this volume's key themes and explore how Alberta's economic, fiscal, environmental, and social outcomes are intertwined, and how a sales tax can help support a sustainable future in the province in all of these areas. I look, too, at how these "whys" of sales tax are connected to the "hows." Alberta's path to a new fiscal future requires stability in provincial finances, a clear transition plan to reduce its reliance on fossil fuels, and massive investments in public education about, and engagement on, the existential issues facing Alberta today.

If Alberta is destined to play a meaningful role in the Canadian and global economies, our political and financial leaders require a dramatic shift in their thinking around revenue, taxation, and, more specifically, the sales tax. This collection outlines many ways of answering the question of why a sales tax is necessary. The "hows" are, admittedly, more complicated. While the reader will find some suggestions in these pages, the "how" of sales tax remains an issue to be solved. At the moment, no major political party in Alberta wishes to talk about a sales tax. The media and public opinion polls have labelled a PST a "political suicide tax." This interpretation has remained unchallenged for too long. It is my hope that readers will see, through the work of this collection's contributors, that a sales tax for Alberta is not only necessary, but inevitable. Ultimately, it will be up to all of us to engage with the issue of sales tax and untangle how it should be implemented in this province.

## References

Ascah, Robert L. 2021. "Alberta's Public Debt: Entering the Third Crisis." Preprint, submitted July 2021. https://www.policyschool.ca/wp-content/uploads/2021/07/AF22_AB-Public-Debt_Ascah.pdf.

Bazel, Peter, and Jack Mintz. 2013. "Enhancing the Alberta Tax Advantage with a Harmonized Sales Tax." *University of Calgary School of Public Policy Publications* 6, no. 29. https://doi.org/10.11575/sppp.v6i0.42441.

Flanagan, Greg. 2011. *Fixing What's Broken: Fair and Sustainable Solutions to Alberta's Revenue Problems.* Edmonton: Parkland Institute. https://www.parklandinstitute.ca/fixing_whats_broken.

Harrison, Trevor. 2016. "No Alternative to a Sales Tax." *Lethbridge Herald*, 11 February 2016.

Innis, Harold. (1956) 1970. *The Fur Trade in Canada.* Rev. ed. Reprint, Toronto: University of Toronto Press.

McKenzie, Kenneth. J. 2000. *Replacing the Alberta Personal Income Tax with a Sales Tax: Not Heresy but Good Economic Sense.* Calgary: Canada West Foundation.

Taft, Kevin. 2017. *Oil's Deep State: How the Petroleum Industry Undermines Democracy and Stops Action on Global Warming—in Alberta, and in Ottawa.* Toronto: Lorimer.

Tombe, Trevor. 2018. "Alberta's Long-Term Fiscal Future." *University of Calgary School of Public Policy Publications* 11, no. 31. https://doi.org/10.11575/sppp.v11i0.52965.

Urquhart, Ian. 2018. *Costly Fix: Power, Politics, and Nature in the Tar Sands.* Toronto: University of Toronto Press.

PART I

# No Sales Tax!

Alberta's Political and
Fiscal Environment

# 1  Alberta Exceptionalism and Taxation as Affront

*Robert L. Ascah*

"No Sales Tax!" This has been the promise of Alberta politicians for roughly the past eighty years, ever since the province's first, and highly unpopular, experiment with taxing goods ended not long after it began in 1936. But the lack of a sales tax in the province has also become a point of pride for Albertans, a mark of distinction that confirms their special status. This "Alberta exceptionalism"—Albertans' sense of themselves as rugged individuals to whom ordinary rules do not apply—has long found expression in a serious distaste for taxes in general and a sales tax in particular. Contemporary debates around the possible introduction of a sales tax thus emerge from a rocky but well-established fiscal history informed by Albertans' conviction that they deserve to receive public services such as education and health care but shouldn't have to pay for them. This chapter sets out to explore some of the roots of this still prevalent point of view in an effort to frame it within its broader historical context.

## Alberta's Self-Image

Albertans understand themselves to be different than other Canadians—to be rougher, tougher, and more industrious. To be special. Since before it became a province in 1905, Alberta has been known as a place of singularly majestic mountains and towering ambitions, of vast plains and boundless opportunities for whosoever was willing to put in the work. Aritha van Herk's (2001) *Mavericks: An Incorrigible History of Alberta* recounts some of these tales of adversity, sacrifice, and hard work in the early days of western settlement. These are not stories of oil and railway barons, but of men and women whose sweat built the province's early roadways, coal mines, and sod houses—stories of gritty labourers whose doggedness earned them their survival. These stories of hardship and sacrifice, hard work and perseverance have been passed down through several generations of Albertans, instilling in them the conviction that prosperity was the result of *individual* initiative, not collective, government-orchestrated policies and programs.

Closely related to these narratives of individual triumph is Albertans' insistence on their right to independence, both from one another and from regulatory meddling. C. B. Macpherson (1953, 11–20), for instance, characterized Alberta's class structure up to the 1950s as dominated by independent—that is, discrete—commodity producers. Alberta's rural residents were accustomed to functioning autonomously. While they still relied on government for basic services such as schooling, roads, telephone lines, irrigation canals, and so on, in the end they made their own decisions. This safeguarding of individual autonomy is reflected in the strongly libertarian attitudes commonplace in the province today. Take, for example, the resistance of some Albertans to wearing face masks and getting vaccinated during the COVID-19 pandemic. Even at the cost of endangering others, many Albertans do not like to be told what to do, least of all by government.

Flowing from this embrace of rugged individualism and a fierce independence is a third manifestation of Alberta exceptionalism: a sense of collective victimhood at the hands of federal government policy, central Canadian manufacturing, and central Canadian financial interests. Almost from the moment Alberta became a province, Albertan farmers harboured an antagonism toward central Canada's commercial control over shipping and banking—an anger that propelled the United Farmers of Alberta (UFA) to victory in the 1921 provincial election. Attitudes did not improve with the August 1935 election victory of William Aberhart's Social Credit government, which attempted to pass legislation that would limit federal control over the licensing of banks and credit arrangements. Social Credit politicians at the time declared Alberta to be "at war" with Ottawa. More than banks and credit, this "war" was, and continues to be, about Ottawa's power over the development of Alberta's natural resources—power that the province views as the theft of its wealth, harming Alberta to benefit the rest of the country.

This ongoing sense of victimhood is also manifest in Jason Kenney's United Conservative Party (UCP), elected to government in 2019. Take Kenney's Fair Deal Panel, for example, the mission of which, according to the Government of Alberta website, was to consult Albertans "on strategies to secure a fair deal in the Canadian federation and advance our vital economic interests." Predictably, the panel's final report, delivered in May 2020, was a survey of the outrage of those Albertans who feel that Ottawa mistreats their province. The embers of old grievances about the structure of Confederation, including equalization payments, federal regulatory policies, parliamentary representation, and federal spending in provincial jurisdictions, are continually fanned into flame.

From Alberta's early days, these three factors—individualism, independence, and victimization, whether perceived or real—combined to forge a unique sense of identity within the province. In 1935, with the election of Aberhart's populist Social Credit government, Canada was forced to contend with Alberta exceptionalism. Exceptionalism again flourished in 1973 when the Organization of the Petroleum Exporting Countries (OPEC), headed by Saudi Arabia, instituted an oil embargo that tripled oil prices virtually overnight, making Alberta suddenly wealthy. Federal-provincial conflict over the division of the economic rents[1] from higher commodity prices reinforced Alberta's sense of victimhood, sporadically fanning the flames of an independence movement.

Oil wealth led to a frantic period of state building that again included fostering unrealistic expectations for provincial government infrastructure and services throughout the province. Government largesse flowed, eliminating municipal debt, fully funding (for a time) public pension plans, building rural hospitals, expanding highways—all while lowering taxes. The Alberta Heritage Savings Trust Fund was another example of Alberta's exceptional capacity to save for future generations, and would become pride of place for many Conservative politicians decades after its founding. This largesse also fuelled a strong sense of pride in many Albertans.

Two unprompted examples of this sense of specialness or exceptionalism came up in interviews I conducted on the subject of a sales tax for Alberta.[2] The first comment was made by author, retired financial planner, former banker, and fellow Albertan Inez Dyer:

> I go back to Saskatchewan a lot [. . .] and you could feel that—"You guys, you go on the big trips, and you do this, and you do that, and you don't have to have a sales tax because the money is just floating in from the oil all the time." There's a resentment there, and it does make you feel kind of special. [. . .] We don't have a sales tax—and it's because of the oil. [. . .] I'm sort of proud of that. (interview with author, 7 December 2018)

The second comment was made by Conner Peta, a graduate student in political science at the University of Alberta:

> I remember in school social studies that you're told, "We're a 'have' province. Alberta has oil. Then there are all these 'have-not' provinces. They have taxes." I think a giant shift would have to occur for that political culture to change. The whole notion of the Alberta Advantage will have to disappear before a sales tax [could be implemented]. [. . .] A provincial sales tax could be interpreted as a policy of the have-nots. (interview with author, 29 November 2018)

While these comments represent only two individual opinions, they lend credence to the idea that, even today, Alberta's political culture is characterized by an insider belief that there is something exceptional about this province. This belief is a key barrier to even discussing the possibility of implementing a sales tax for the province.

## The Development of Alberta's Tax Aversion

Alberta's period of expansion from 1905 to the Great Depression was supported by an optimism that, with individual hard work, the future would take care of itself. During this time, provincial government spending, especially on public infrastructure, grew rapidly. Both the Liberal (1905 to 1921) and the UFA (1921 to 1935) governments borrowed heavily to support a generally held belief in a limitless future. All types of public works projects—including irrigation canals, railways, public roads for the new automobile, rural electrification, and a public telephone system—were financed mainly by government debt sold in both the domestic and international markets (MacGregor et al. 1939).

As Harold Innis (1933, 64–65) pointed out, however, this rapid growth was pulled along by a sense of opportunity and ambition that ultimately risked exacting a high price on Albertans. Innis wrote, "expenditures made on the assumption that revenue will return from various directions has been responsible for the incurable and dangerous optimism which characterizes government effort. On the whole, public enterprises to which government contributes have introduced an element of uncertainty in the financial position of the government and a degree of unwholesome inelasticity." The truth of Innis's words was brought to bear in a Bank of Canada (1937, 34) study of Alberta's finances:

> By the end of 1922, Alberta had direct and guaranteed debt
> (on which it was paying interest or for which it later became liable)
> which was some 50 percent higher than in the much older province
> of Manitoba and more than twice as large as that of Saskatch-
> ewan, though Saskatchewan had a 30 percent larger population.
> Substantially more than half the Alberta total debt represented
> accumulated losses and deficits, or so-called assets which were
> proving a constant drain.

The unbounded optimism of the province's business and political communities resulted in loose financial management, wildly optimistic capital expansion projects, and poor judgment on how these projects would eventually contribute future revenue to the province. By the 1920s, the provincial government had racked up a heavy burden of debt, which the UFA government inherited when they came into office in 1921. Fortunately for the UFA, the 1920s were a period of strong agricultural commodity prices, which allowed the government to continue to spend freely and borrow money without increasing taxes. By the end of the 1920s, according to the Bank of Canada's (1937) analysis, per capita taxes in 1929 were *lower* than the 1921 level. As it pointed out, "the province could scarcely have expected a more favourable opportunity than that presented in the years 1925–29 to recoup itself from the rural areas for some of the large expenditures made on them. The opportunity was allowed to pass, and no reduction in the dead weight debt took place" (12). In this first period of economic growth, optimism for the future trumped good financial management. Taxation seemed unnecessary as the province's economic future would be even bigger and better—or so Albertans fervently believed. This first period ended, of course, with the province defaulting on its debt in April 1936. It was the first and remains the only Canadian province ever to have done so.

A year prior, in 1935, a new party came into power: Aberhart's Social Credit Party. Despite the 1936 default, the Social Credit administration continued its policy of keeping taxes low for the next thirty-five years. This approach to political management changed with the election in 1971 of a Progressive Conservative government led by Peter Lougheed. With the 1973 OPEC oil embargo and Alberta's resultant sudden wealth, Lougheed was able to rapidly expand and modernize the provincial state (Richards and Pratt 1979). After a skirmish with the oil and gas industry over royalties stemming from the rapid rise in world oil prices, the Progressive Conservative Association of Alberta realized that, for its full political and economic goals to be realized, it had to gain more complete control over resource management. Section 92A of the federal Constitution Act, 1982, answered the party's prayers, establishing exclusive provincial power over natural resources, including non-renewables such as oil.

Lougheed resigned from provincial politics in 1985—a well-timed exit that left his successor, Don Getty, to run the then highest-spending provincial government in the country. Although Alberta had virtually no debt when Getty took office, Alberta's economy was struggling with rising unemployment levels, crashing residential and real estate markets, collapsing financial institutions, and a lack of capital investment. More importantly, non-renewable resource royalties, which I will simply call resource revenue, fell dramatically as oil and natural gas prices plummeted from $40 per barrel in the early 1980s to $11 per barrel in July 1986. Various bailouts and ill-fated investment ventures resulted in a significant rise in debt and dissatisfaction among right-wing supporters of the Progressive Conservatives. Perhaps because of this already-smouldering dissatisfaction, and despite the province's desperate need for cash, taxes were not materially increased during this period. Since the Alberta government's capacity to borrow remained high, Getty chose to go into debt rather than raise taxes on Albertans. Unlike the Liberal and UFA administrations of the early twentieth century who borrowed to build the province, however, under Getty's Progressive Conservatives, government borrowing was employed almost exclusively to simply maintain existing government programs.

Enter Ralph Klein. Klein was elected leader of the Progressive Conservative Association and appointed premier in December 1992, after Getty retired. This signalled an entirely new fiscal direction for the province, specifically in terms of the ascendance of what is commonly referred to as neoliberal policies of austerity—that is, reducing government debt by cutting spending and, importantly, not increasing taxes. Conservative and even some Liberal politicians of the time could frequently be heard intoning the mantra "We have a spending problem," essentially blaming government deficits on bloated expenditures, not insufficient tax revenue. In 1992–93, government expenses totalled $17.6 billion while revenue stood at only $14.3 billion. By 1996–97, expenses had been trimmed to $14.2 billion, and revenue had grown to $16.7 billion (Kneebone and Wilkins 2016, 11). In short, the province had moved away from the debt accumulation that began under Getty and, in the space of five years under Klein, had begun generating a comfortable surplus. In the eyes of the conservative government, the correlation between the spending cuts and the elimination of the deficit was rock-solid proof that government spending had previously been out of control. Evidence suggests, however, that spending was far from the only factor in this economic about-face. Arguably, rebounding oil and natural gas prices in the late 1990s played a much more critical role in the budgetary shift from red to black (Government of Alberta 2003). Resource revenues rose from $2.2 billion in 1992–93 to $4.6 billion in 1999–2000.

Let's back up for a moment to better understand the Klein-era beliefs around taxation and spending. In 1990, a new force entered the field: the Canadian Taxpayers Federation. The Alberta chapter of the organization, led by the young Jason Kenney, effectively attacked Getty's government for gaffes committed in its twilight years, including the deeply unpopular, gold-plated MLA pension plan.[3] Thus was born a very effective mouthpiece reinforcing the message that "government is the problem, not the solution." It's easy to see how this belief fuelled the related conviction that taxes should continually decrease. If government spending is the issue—that is, if taxpayers can't trust government to responsibly spend their money—then why give them more money to waste? By the end of Ralph Klein's first term, the political assumptions around taxation had hardened. The only possible way that taxes could go was down. This conviction, coupled with the apparent success of the spending-cut experiment, laid the groundwork for a twenty-year policy of reducing corporate and personal income taxes while paying down debt. It was packaged and sold as the "Alberta Advantage." According to successive Progressive Conservative governments, it reduced taxation and low oil sands royalties, not rising oil prices worldwide, that were responsible for the prolonged boom that extended more or less uninterrupted from the early 2000s through to 2014.

To put it plainly, Alberta's political culture displays a hostility to taxes. The belief appears to be that taxes inhibit economic growth or simply contribute to a bloated bureaucracy. Its logic goes like this: Taxation is nothing more than citizens and corporations handing money over to government to waste. Alberta's exceptional wealth is a predictable result of the independent entrepreneurialism and individual hard work of Albertans. Taxes dampen this entrepreneurial spirit by taking away—and ultimately mismanaging—the fruits of its labour. Ipso facto, tax reductions spur economic growth. This deeply rooted political belief system has long discouraged Alberta politicians, regardless of their party affiliation, from uttering the words *sales tax*.

## The Story of Alberta's First (and Only) Sales Tax

The story of Alberta's first and only sales tax begins in 1929, when Alberta's overreliance on agricultural staple production had become endemic. Nearly 40 percent of provincial income was derived from the agriculture sector. With the collapse of equity prices on Wall Street and rising protectionism at the beginning of the Great Depression, deflationary pressures set in with a vengeance. The average price per bushel of wheat fell from $1.75 in 1928 to $0.32 in 1932. Grain farmers saw a staggering drop in their income, and the provincial government, because of the Alberta economy's heavy reliance on grains, seeds, and hay, saw a similar drop in its revenues. By 1933, farm receipts had dropped to one-quarter of their 1928 level, even though total production fell by only one-third. While other agricultural sectors also suffered, such losses were not as consequential as those experienced by single-commodity wheat producers. Persistently weak grain prices forced the federal Conservative government to find a band-aid solution: stockpiling wheat (Ascah 1999, 54).

A key worry in the 1930s was the ability of the farming community to make their loan payments. Farmers faced a crushing debt burden as grain prices plummeted and interest on their loans consumed one-quarter of their estimated expenses (Government of Alberta 1938, 196–97). They claimed that bank interest rates exceeded the legal maximum rate of interest at the time (7 percent) because of the practice of discounting farmers' promissory notes.[4] At the same time, threshing charges cut deeply into their incomes, reducing the total value received by farmers by more than half—a situation not unlike the predicament of oil producers in 2018 in the face of costly rail transportation. On top of such a dismal economic situation, Albertans were living in a peripheral economic region that did not produce manufactured goods. They thus paid dearly for tariff-protected central Canadian industry. The Rowell-Sirois Commission calculated that by 1931, the cost of tariff-protected manufactured goods had doubled in the province (Royal Commission on Dominion-Provincial Relations 1940, 159). It was the perfect storm.

Municipal and provincial finances were in disarray owing to the collapse in grain prices and resulting unemployment. In the larger cities of Edmonton and Calgary, finances were wobbling because of social relief costs, huge property tax arrears, and a shrinking revenue base caused by falling property assessments. School finances were no better. In 1934, over four hundred school districts were in default, with more than $265,000 in unpaid teachers' wages. The province's insufficient revenue base combined with the "dead weight" nature of the provincial government's debt (and of the debts of municipal governments, government entities such as Alberta Government Telephones, and other guaranteed entities such as irrigation districts and railways) led Albertans to thoroughly examine their provincial and municipal taxation systems.

### The Alberta Taxation Inquiry Board, 1933

The Alberta Taxation Inquiry Board was appointed in December 1933 under the UFA government. Chaired by Deputy Provincial Treasurer J. F. Percival, the board was charged with assessing the productivity of Alberta's current tax structure at both the provincial and municipal levels. Percival also examined the differential impact of taxation on various occupational groups and on urban and rural residents. The board gathered information from the business community, labour organizations, citizens groups, and manufacturers before submitting its report in November 1935, three months after the Social Credit Party swept to victory. The board recommended that the government boost taxation to the level of other provinces and impose a retail sales tax (Alberta Taxation Inquiry Board 1935, 138–40).

As the board's report observed, a sales tax has "the merit of reaching everyone in such a way that he [sic] is conscious of the fact that he is contributing to the cost of government, and there are many who hold that it contributes to good citizenship that people should know that they are paying for government" (138). The report further noted that a sales tax is "fiscally adequate or productive; it is elastic; simple and easily understood; it is flexible, and may be readily modified. Its equity, however, is open to debate as it bears disproportionately upon the income of the poorer classes, even though the rich may make large contributions through their expenditures upon luxuries. However, its productivity makes it attractive" (138).

A sales tax was, moreover, not a completely foreign concept. The federal government had implemented a sales tax in 1920. At its lowest, this tax was set at 1 percent; at the time of the Alberta Taxation Inquiry Board's report, it had reached a high of 6 percent. The report was further informed by the United States' experience with sales taxes. Like Alberta, state governments faced the difficult choice of either cutting expenditures on relief, education, and other services or seeking a new source of revenue. By the time the inquiry board issued its report, sixteen US states had levied sales taxes, yielding a total of $180 million. As the report noted, the "hostility to a general sales tax weakened when the proceeds are devoted to some desirable object such as unemployment relief, education, or the reduction of obnoxious property taxation" (139). The board's ultimate recommendations on a sales tax in Alberta were tentative: Alberta, it said, should cooperate with other provinces "in an effort to secure the right to enact a General Sales Tax Act" federally. It demurred, however, when it came to making recommendations for the province itself, suggesting that "further study be made as to the advisability of a provincial tax of this character" (146).

On 3 March 1936, Provincial Treasurer Charles Cockroft introduced the Social Credit government's first budget, which reflected many of the Alberta Taxation Inquiry Board's ideas and included a 2 percent PST. The tax immediately raised uncomfortable issues for the government, not least of which was the question of how more taxation would support additional "purchasing power" for Albertans—a key objective of the social credit theory on which the party was based. Opponents asked, "Would there be taxation relief for the poor?" and, "Beyond certain essential items, what other exemptions might be made to the tax?" Central to the question of whether or not the new tax would be accepted by the public was the question of whether the public would directly benefit from it, for example through progress in unemployment relief or municipal tax relief.

## The Ultimate Purchasers Tax Act, 1936

Alberta's Act to Impose Taxes on the Ultimate Purchasers of Certain Commodities for Raising Revenue for Provincial Purposes (SA 1936, c. 7)—better known as the Ultimate Purchasers Tax Act—was proclaimed on 30 April 1936. The act spelled out the methods of tax computation and collection, record-keeping requirements, ministerial investigative powers, and offences. Addressing the concerns of economists and opposition politicians, exemptions were put in place by regulations pursuant to the act. The provincial cabinet was delegated considerable administrative powers including the capacity to create more exemptions from the tax in certain geographical areas, exemptions for municipalities and schools, and registration of vendors to collect the tax on behalf of the government. Exemptions, recorded in the *Alberta Gazette*, included necessities such as milk, coal, bread, water, newspapers, tobacco, sugar, flour, electricity, seeds, farm machinery, and a laundry list of other foodstuffs, goods, and services (Government of Alberta 1936, 281–82).

Remarkably, the 2 percent PST came into effect on 1 May 1936, less than two months after the budget was introduced. However, political and business opposition dogged the tax from the very beginning. A week after the budget was tabled, Ernest Manning, then minister of trade and industry, argued that the collection of revenue "cannot be interpreted as decreasing purchasing power" (quoted in "Legislation on Sales Tax" 1936). Manning, it turns out, was not even talking about the sales tax, but defending a 1 percent increase in PIT. Still, the idea that any tax would *not* diminish purchasing power drew questions from the public about sales tax. Typical news headlines blared:

> "Heavy New Taxes for Province—Will Sales Tax Stimulate Spending Outside Province?" (*Edmonton Journal*, 3 March 1936)

> "Merchants See Trade Loss Likely Result—Sales Tax" (*Edmonton Journal*, 4 April 1936)

> "Trade 'Slowed' by Sales Levy, Merchants Say" (*Edmonton Journal*, 4 May 1936)

"Ice Cream Vendors Point to the Difficulty of the System"
(*Edmonton Journal*, 5 May 1936)

"New Sales Tax Means Trouble, Vendors' Plaint—Protests
Voiced" (*Edmonton Journal*, 5 May 1936)

"Confusion Seen over Sales Tax Claim Government Inspectors
Giving Different Rulings" (*Edmonton Journal*, 14 May 1936)

"Purchasers Refuse to Pay Sales Tax" (*Edmonton Journal*, 3
August 1936)

While the government sought to enact its ambitious program of social credit, much more was going on under Alberta's Legislature dome. Premier Aberhart faced a backbench insurgency, conflict with C. H. Douglas (the father of social credit theory), the debt default on 1 April 1936, and skirmishes with the federal government, the banks, and the province's legal community. This proved difficult to manage all at once. Throughout 1936, pressures kept building on Charles Cockcroft, then treasurer, to exempt other goods from the tax. In March 1937, the Aberhart government's second budget revealed the sales tax revenue was anticipated to fall $1 million short of the previously estimated $2 million. Cockcroft was eventually replaced by Solon Low who, in 1937, announced the sales tax would end on 1 September 1937. Going in the face of Manning's comments about taxes and purchasing power a year earlier, Mr. Low said to the *Edmonton Journal*: "Instead of paying the tax, the purchaser will be given a ticket which will read '50 cents paid.' In that way we are remitting to the general purchasing public the amount of the tax which they would have to pay under the sales tax act." By way of clarification, Mr. Low continued:

> The remission of the sales tax only removes something which,
> under pressure from finance, this government itself imposed.
> Nevertheless, those instructed in the technique of Douglas
> dynamics will immediately recognize signs of its inauguration.
> In its simpler aspect, of course, tax remission represents the first
> step necessary to the issue of a dividend—is, in fact, the issue of a

dividend; for a tax is a dividend in reverse. That is why it would be foolish to begin issuing money as dividends only to pull it in by a graduated and universally applied tax, such as the sales tax. ("Sales Tax Comes to End" 1937)

This mystifying explanation was a symptom of the difficulty all Social Credit ministers and MLAs had in explaining any policy related to the election promise of a social credit dividend of $25 per family. Low's juggling act did little to garner public confidence.

Although it was short lived, the PST raised $947,000 in 1937, or 13 percent of the government's revenue—a significant achievement. In fiscal 1938, over the five months that it remained in effect, the tax brought $601,000 into the province's coffers.

Then, suddenly, Alberta's short experiment with a sales tax was over. The province's unemployment rate was still around 20 percent, and many Albertans were destitute (Dominion Bureau of Statistics 1935, 828). Those who did have a source of income continually feared losing their jobs, losing their homesteads, or not being paid. With the world economic recovery still tepid, antipathy towards this PST would have been palpable. Given the province's perilous finances, internecine warfare in caucus, and grave uncertainty about the promised Social Credit dividend, it was quite understandable for the government to retreat and declare victory. Backing down from this tax appears to have been, in hindsight, an astute move for Aberhart's young government. Social Credit's longevity in power—from 1935 to 1971—seems to illustrate that an unpopular and misunderstood tax is something to avoid if you are gunning for re-election in Alberta.

It was twenty-five years before any politician had the nerve to seriously consider an Alberta sales tax again.

### The Manning Years, 1943–68

After Aberhart died in 1943, Ernest Manning took on the mantle of Social Credit leadership, and thus the premiership. By the late 1940s, the province was reaping the rewards of an oil boom. The boom continued until the early 1960s, when the world was hit with a global recession. Oil prices declined, as did investment. In November 1962, Premier Manning established a committee to conduct a "thorough study of public revenues and expenditures at both the provincial and local levels" (Public Expenditure and Revenue Study Committee 1965, iv). Accompanying the announcement was a policy statement by Manning that read:

> Having regards to the public concern engendered by steadily rising public expenditures resulting in an ever-increasing burden of taxation and debt, the government proposes to invite representatives of municipal government, school administration, business, agriculture and labour to join in a factual study of public expenditures and the manner in which they can best be controlled and financed having regards to the legitimate needs and best interests of the people of the province as a whole. (iv)

Included in the committee's terms of reference was the "examination of the incidence of taxation and other revenue sources to determine the most equitable method of obtaining revenues required to finance necessary public expenditures" (iv). Manning—who, by 1962, had served as premier for almost twenty years—exhibited a paternalistic concern about the need to control public spending, which was well in keeping with the austere approach that was already synonymous with good financial stewardship in the province (Brennan 2008).

In 1965, the committee submitted its report. In the area of taxation, it recommended that rates of taxation on gasoline, fuel oil, vehicle licenses, and personal income be raised "to cover approximately one-half of the anticipated budget deficit in the ensuing year" (Public Expenditure and Revenue Study Committee 1965, xix). The remaining portion of the deficit would be funded out of provincial liquidity and reserves. However, as a fallback measure, the committee also proposed that "at such time as it becomes evident that the additional revenue available from these taxes is not adequate to meet a substantial proportion of the deficit, consideration be given to the introduction of a retail sales tax" (xix).

Meanwhile, Alberta's fiscal situation continued to worsen. In 1966–67, the Alberta government incurred a budget deficit of $87 million. This rose to $99 million in 1967–68. Further deficits were expected in the following fiscal years. In early 1969, Alberta undertook its first public issuance of government debt since 1951, borrowing $30 million (O'Brien 1969, 1).

The committee had been chaired by Provincial Treasurer Anders Aalborg, with the Honourable Raymond Reierson as deputy chairman and the Honourable Harry Strom as the third cabinet minister. Aalborg held the office of provincial treasurer from 1964 to 1971. Decades later, Al O'Brien, who himself served as a deputy finance minister from 1984 to 1999, speculated about Aalborg's attitudes toward a sales tax: "I think that Anders Aalborg would have liked to have brought in [a sales tax] after the 1967 election. And for whatever reason, not least of which would have been Premier Manning's departure [in 1968], it was thought to be inevitable" (interview with author, 3 November 2018). According to O'Brien, the argument for a sales tax at the time included a desire to avoid unsustainable future increases in other taxes. No sales tax was, however, forthcoming in 1968. Another quarter century would pass before the issue once again found its way into the government's view.

## The Alberta Advantage: Conservatism and Fiscal Austerity

On 6 March 1995, Progressive Conservative MLA Jim Dinning, Premier Ralph Klein's provincial treasurer, introduced Bill 1, the proposed Alberta Taxpayer Protection Act. The June 1993 provincial election was a precursor to this referendum legislation. It is important to understand this bill's provenance, as it reveals how deft electoral management of the subject of a sales tax can create political winners and losers in Alberta—so let's back up for a moment.

Although Alberta was in 1993 a much more prosperous and populous province than in 1936, the 1980s and early 1990s had been difficult years for the Alberta economy and broad segments of the population. During the 1980s, the double whammy of falling oil prices and exceptionally high interest rates caused unemployment to rise from 3.3 percent in October 1980 to 12.7 percent in March 1983. By October 1989, the rate had fallen to 5.8 percent. By January 1992, however, it had crept back up to 10.3 percent (Statistics Canada 2021). The province experienced a brutal recession from

1982 to 1984 in which its real GDP fell by nearly 10 percent. The economy started growing again in the mid-1980s, only to be faced with a brutal real estate crash, exposing a legacy of weak regulation in financial institutions. As early as 1983, people whose home equity value was less than their mortgage simply walked away from their homes, often selling their property for a dollar (Nelson 1983).

Don Getty was in charge of dealing with this crash. As it wore on, numerous Alberta financial institutions failed, including significant portions of the credit union system, dashing hope of a recovery. Notable institutional failures included Northland Bank and Canadian Commercial Bank (both federally regulated), the North West Trust Company, and the Principal Group, an alliance of investment companies. As the economy flatlined between 1990 and 1992, the popularity of the Progressive Conservatives plummeted. Getty announced his retirement in September 1992.

In the ensuing leadership contest for the Progressive Conservative Association, premier-to-be Ralph Klein ran against Getty's record. With the support of Ken Kowalski, an influential rural MLA, Klein defeated the party establishment's preferred candidate Nancy Betkowski, Getty's former health minister. A key plank of Klein's platform, and a key distinction between him and Betkowski, was his opposition to Getty-era bailouts. According to Klein, Getty had aimed to support businesses by handpicking "winners" who turned out to be losers. Klein saw this strategy to be a waste of money and bad fiscal policy. Appealing to Albertans' sense of gritty independence, Klein sought instead to "get government out of the business of business," and thereby kickstart an economy led by entrepreneurs.

The 1993 election was to take place on 15 June. Leading up to the release of a pre-election budget, Klein and his treasurer, Jim Dinning, acted quickly to frame the fiscal debate. On 21 January, Dinning announced the appointment of the Financial Review Commission, headed by TransAlta Utility's former chair and director Marshall Williams. This commission, which reported back at the end of March 1993, had a mandate to investigate the province's financial situation and accounting practices. On the report's opening page, a heading announced that "The Need for Albertans to Support Change Is Urgent"—a message no doubt tailored to the upcoming election. It billed the annual deficit as "serious" and "getting worse." "We cannot support this level of spending," it declared. "We have spent our savings," and we can't "just go on borrowing." We must "act now" (Alberta Financial Review Commission 1993, 1–3). The report went on to call for more timely and effective financial reporting, improved accountability, better coordinated and more streamlined systems of oversight, and the more prudent use of loan guarantees.

The commission's report came out around the same time that Alberta Treasury held a budget roundtable. According to Paul Boothe, then an advisor to Alberta Treasury, the roundtable "confirmed, as no polling results could, the willingness of Albertans to make significant sacrifices" (Boothe 2002, 4). These sacrifices ended up being two years of government cuts to services and public sector employees. Still, there was some debate over the matter of raising taxes versus cutting spending. According to Al O'Brien, "six of the ten groups that reported [to the roundtable] either supported a sales tax or supported a temporary sales tax. Most of them said we need to bring in a sales tax to get rid of the deficit and stop the bleeding and then we should eliminate it." However, the Klein team managed to interpret this sales tax "wisdom," as O'Brien called it, as being about "spending cuts first" (interview with author, 3 November 2018)—an interpretation made plain in the workbook prepared for the roundtable, subsequently published as *Right on the Money* (Dinning and Wagner 1993).

Why so much emphasis on spending cuts? Federal politics of the time might give us a clue. After Prime Minister Brian Mulroney and his Conservative government implemented a federal goods and services tax (GST) in 1991, they made a historically dismal showing in the 1993 general election, losing all but two seats in Parliament. With the federal Conservative Party debacle going on in the background, O'Brien figured that Klein—like Aberhart before him—"was convinced that spending cuts and other, subtler, less controversial revenue increases were the way to go" (interview with author, 3 November 2018).

### The Klein Years Begin, 1993

In a classic Albertan showdown, the 1993 election saw Progressive Conservative leader Klein, a former mayor of Calgary, face off against Liberal leader Laurence Decore, a former mayor of Edmonton. The parties had remarkably similar platforms of fiscal restraint. Eight years of consecutive deficits under Getty had awakened Albertans of all stripes, as well as their new political leaders, to the need for meaningful fiscal action. Albertans who had followed the goings-on of the Alberta Treasury roundtable were bracing for service cuts. However, the Liberal and Progressive Conservative leaders were coy about the specifics of their fiscal plans beyond comforting the electorate that taxes would not rise.

A Liberal campaign pamphlet at the time advertised a plan for the "Next Alberta": "Cleaning Up the ME$$." The pamphlet proclaimed the urgent need to reduce the "horrendous" $24.5-billion debt, emphasizing that "reduced spending is the *best* way to go." Among other things, the Liberals promised to mandate balanced budgets, cut back fat MLA pensions, introduce departmental efficiency audits, and subject existing programs to periodic review. They also proposed selling the Heritage Fund to pay down the debt. These measures would be supplemented by the implementation of a "detailed economic plan," with a focus on technological innovation and support for small businesses, as well as a program designed to encourage rural entrepreneurs to create jobs. The Liberals further vowed to protect important programs like health and education and to "take the environment seriously," while also holding government more accountable to voters by, for example, enabling them to recall an MLA who is "not representing them well" (Alberta Liberal Party 1993).

The central feature of Klein's election platform was a four-year fiscal plan, laid out in May 1993. Like the Liberals, Klein's plan emphasized the urgent need for a new economic strategy—one that would eliminate the deficit without any increase in taxes. Again like the Liberals, the Progressive Conservatives were prepared to eliminate the MLA pension plan, a plank promoted by Jason Kenney's Canadian Taxpayers Federation. In stressing smaller government, the Conservatives promised more efficiencies and enhanced expenditure control. Other shared themes included the need to make the education system more "competitive," to "control health costs," to provide protection to seniors, to undertake measures "to help people get off social assistance," and to offer support for rural development.

Unlike the Liberals, however, Klein's four-year plan specifically pledged "No Sales Tax" (Progressive Conservative Association of Alberta 1993).

The silence of the Liberals on the sales tax was a key factor in the Progressive Conservatives winning fifty-one of the available eighty-three Legislative Assembly seats on 15 June 1993. The Liberals won the other thirty-two.

Soon after its election, the Klein government established the Alberta Tax Reform Commission, which issued its *Report to Albertans* in February 1994. Seemingly at odds with the Progressive Conservative Association's stance, the commission acknowledged that a sales tax would form part of an "ideal" mix of revenue in the future; however, it was unequivocal in its recommendation to not impose a sales tax "at this time," noting that "Albertans, and most Canadians, don't like sales taxes" (Alberta Tax Reform Commission 1994, 39). Before a sales tax could be introduced, the report said, the government must balance the budget. Even then, the commissioners said they could only support a sales tax if it would lead to a comparable reduction in personal and corporate income taxes—taxes that the commissioners regarded as disincentives to employment growth. Finally, the commission recommended that, even if those conditions were met, any proposed sales tax should be debated and subject to a referendum. In other words, the report's conclusion was pretty much an anti-sales-tax recommendation.

### The Alberta Taxpayer Protection Act, 1995

This brings us back to the 1995 Alberta Taxpayer Protection Act (SA 1995, c. A-37.8), a very brief (one-and-a-half-page) document that begins:

> WHEREAS the people of Alberta want to maintain the Alberta Advantage; and
>
> WHEREAS Alberta is the only province in Canada that does not have a general provincial sales tax; and
>
> WHEREAS a general provincial sales tax is not a desirable tax; and
>
> WHEREAS the opinion of the people of Alberta should be obtained directly before any legislation that levies a general provincial sales tax is introduced; [. . .]

Although the second recital—that is, the second "WHEREAS"—is factually correct, the other three recitals were opinions of the victors of the 1993 campaign. In the legislative debate that ensued around the bill, the Liberals were generally sympathetic to those fiscal messages. The claim that a sales tax was not a desirable tax was a value statement that reflected Albertans' aversion to taxes in general.

The act continues:

> THEREFORE HER MAJESTY, by and with the advice and consent of the Legislative Assembly of Alberta, enacts as follows:
>
> Referendum required
>
> 1. A member of the Executive Council may introduce in the Legislative Assembly a Bill that imposes a general provincial sales tax only if, before the introduction of the Bill, the Chief Electoral Officer announces the result of a referendum conducted under this Act on a question that relates to the imposition of the tax.
>
> Holding a referendum
>
> 2. The Lieutenant Governor in Council may order the holding of a referendum that relates to the imposition of a general provincial sales tax.
>
> Question to be asked
>
> 3. The question or questions to be put to the electors at a referendum held under this Act shall be determined by a resolution of the Legislative Assembly on the motion of a member of the Executive Council.
>
> Procedure
>
> 4(1). Sections 4 to 11 of the *Constitutional Referendum Act* apply to a referendum held under this Act.
>
> (2). An order under section 2 of this Act is deemed to be an order under section 1 of the *Constitutional Referendum Act* for the purposes of section 5 of that Act.[5]

In its fledgling state as Bill 1, Treasurer Jim Dinning told the Legislative Assembly that the Alberta Taxpayer Protection Act would be a pinnacle achievement of democratic government that would "call upon the people of this province to make the ultimate final decision" on a sales tax—a decision that he hoped would "never be made but could only be made with the full consent of the people of the province."[6]

The bill's introduction in the Legislature reaffirmed the government's pre-election commitments to reduce spending and reinforced a low-tax-policy environment by preventing future "tax-and-spend" governments from "picking Albertans' pockets."[7] It's interesting, then, that Bill 1 was introduced a full two years after the Progressive Conservatives' election. Perhaps Klein's government wished to hedge their bets, not knowing whether the provincial economy would begin to rebound in those first two years. In the end, it did. By 1995, an economic recovery was emerging and the government probably felt it could again rely solely on oil industry revenue to reduce the deficit.

Liberal finance critic Mike Percy rebutted Dinning's rhetorical flourishes by reminding him that he had endorsed Nancy Betkowski's, not Klein's, candidacy for the Progressive Conservative leadership in 1992. Betkowski's platform, unlike Klein's, had included the consideration of a sales tax. Percy also pointed to the government's own Alberta Tax Reform Commission, which Percy interpreted as having recommended a sales tax—a somewhat liberal interpretation of the commission's actual "not at this time" conclusions. Percy went on to question the rationale for allowing Albertans the right to vote on a sales tax but not on other standard government levies such as income taxes, user fees, or health-care premiums. After reviewing the advantages and disadvantages of a sales tax, Percy concluded: "The reality is that every tax has positive and negative features, and you can't single out a particular tax as undesirable . . . because all taxes by their nature are undesirable from the perspective of individuals who pay them."[8]

Peter Sekulic, another Liberal MLA, was supportive of the bill, but expressed concern about the more than 220 new user fee and license fee increases that had been levied since the Conservatives were elected in 1993, commenting that "what we've seen in this province is in fact taxation by regulation."[9] In other words, according to Sekulic, the Conservative government was simply hiding their tax increases under another name. As the debate continued on 8 March, another member of the Liberal opposition, Terry Kirkland, asserted that the Conservatives had stolen the referendum idea from the Liberals' 1993 election platform. He then went on to describe Bill 1 as "nothing more than a political trick" and "redundant," noting that it "certainly will not achieve anything that in fact won't be achieved with good government."[10]

Critiques aside, the Liberals were in a difficult position. How could they oppose a bill that gave back to voters the power to decide whether a particular tax could be imposed? How could they vote against a bill that was part of their pre-election policy? Well, the most compelling reason for voting against such a bill was that it was total poltroonery. Coming from a government that clearly had no intention of imposing a sales tax, Bill 1 pretended to, in the words of Liberal MLA Gary Dickson, "bind the hands of governments in the future."[11] Its actual ability to do this, however, was a myth: according to the doctrine of parliamentary sovereignty—which is generally accepted in Canada—any law enacted by one legislature can be repealed by a succeeding legislature. Even though Liberal MLAs largely supported the bill, then, Dickson and several others observed during the bill's second reading on 11 April 1995 that the legislation was purely symbolic. As Dickson put it, "I always have difficulty with the proposition, Mr. Speaker, that by legislation now we somehow pretend that we're going to elevate this to a level of some kind of a constitutional constraint."[12]

Liberal MLA Lance White made a similar comment. "One government doesn't bind all governments thereafter," adding that any belief to the contrary was "presumptuous."[13] White further pointed to the basic principle of representative democracy—namely, that elected leaders are expected to acquire a depth of knowledge and understanding that the broader public generally lacks and then make informed decisions on behalf of those they represent. "There is only one reason to support this Bill," he declared, "and that is because it looks good. If we want to simply look good and not act well, then I guess we'll have to support the Bill."[14]

Despite the Liberals' stated reservations—indeed, despite castigating it as "insidious" and, later, "cynical," "flawed," and a "charade"[15]—the bill passed its second reading on 11 April 1995 by a unanimous vote of 42 to 0. Interestingly, the Liberals proposed an amendment to the bill at the Committee of the Whole debate that would require personal tax increases to also be subject to a referendum; the amendment was defeated by a vote of 33 to 12.[16] Bill 1 received its third and final reading without a recorded vote on 11 May 1995, and was subsequently passed.

The passage of the Alberta Taxpayer Protection Act solidified the Progressive Conservative brand as *the* party of low taxes and economic prosperity. Increasing resource revenues throughout the 1990s and early 2000s created the illusion that the government's low taxes led to wealth and prosperity—an idea that was nurtured by the Klein government through its branding of the Alberta Advantage signifying Alberta's low corporate and personal taxes and the absence of a sales tax. But the idea that elected representatives under our Westminster system of government should push their responsibility to set tax policy back on the electorate—that is, the idea at the centre of the Alberta Taxpayer Protection Act—is debatable, to say the least. Nevertheless, this sleight of hand was accepted by an electorate more exercised about paying more tax than about preserving government services—and one that, crucially, was led to believe that low taxes, in Alberta's case anyway, were causally responsible for a thriving economy, bottomless resource revenues for the government, and abundant public services. The problem is, without the return of high natural gas prices, this illusion would not have worked.

## Alberta Exceptionalism in the Twenty-First Century

The subject of a sales tax, and the issue of provincial revenue sources, continued to be a highly charged third rail of Alberta politics during the final years of the Klein era. In 2002, a new financial commission report—this one from the Alberta Financial Management Commission, chaired by David Tuer[17]—was released. Entitled *Moving from Good to Great: Enhancing Alberta's Fiscal Framework*, this report effusively complimented the Klein government's "outstanding" financial management—but it also observed that government needed to reduce the province's reliance on resource revenues (Alberta Financial Management Commission 2002, 1, 4). Noting that nearly one-half of the provincial economy was associated directly or indirectly with the energy sector, the commission recommended that only "an appropriate and sustainable level of resource revenue be spent on an annual basis" (8).

Klein's successor, Ed Stelmach, appointed his own council in 2009: the Premier's Council for Economic Strategy, chaired by former federal cabinet minister David Emerson. Stelmach's challenge to the council was presented as follows:

- What must Albertans begin to do now to sustain prosperity through the next three decades and beyond?

- How can we ensure our children and grandchildren enjoy even greater opportunity than we have—that we hand future generations a legacy of "a better Alberta"?

- What will it take to make the Alberta of 2040 *the* place for creative and committed citizens to live, work, raise families, contribute to and enjoy society? (Premier's Council for Economic Strategy 2011, 2)

In their report, the council drew a bead on Alberta's vaunted tax advantage, saying that "the true Alberta Advantage is not the ability to create a low-tax environment by underwriting a significant portion of government services with funds received from the sale of energy assets. Rather, the advantage lies in the opportunity to use the proceeds from natural resource wealth to intentionally invest in shaping an economy that is much less dependent on natural resources" (96). In other words, the government should be an intelligent steward of the province's natural resource wealth, taking into account long-term economic and demographic trends.

Since 2002, Alberta government budgets have contained a graph illustrating what has been branded Alberta's Tax Advantage. These graphs illustrate how much more residents of the province would pay in taxes if the Alberta government taxed at the same rates as other provinces and had a sales tax. Seen in a different light, the graphs show how much predictable revenue the Alberta government is choosing to forego. The 2021–22

Tax Advantage graph is shown in figure 1.1. The numbers, when framed as individual savings, are impressive. When framed as lost revenue, they lead us to ask: Has the existence of this tax advantage served Albertans well? From the viewpoint of Stelmach's Premier's Council, the answer is "no." The government was simply selling off its natural resources and consuming the wealth immediately rather than investing for the future. That being the case, a further question—a moral one—is raised: When, if ever, will the Alberta government turn away from repeated spending cuts in response to volatile oil prices, and towards a more stable revenue mix? When, that is, will it prioritize predictable funding for crucial public programs over its obsession with maintaining its "tax advantage"?

This question remains open. Even with the 2015 election of Rachel Notley's NDP—the most left-leaning party with a chance of forming government in the province—Alberta exceptionalism and aversion to taxation remain solidly woven into the fabric of Alberta politics. Indeed, after coming to power, the NDP adopted the Alberta Advantage in its own provincial budget documents. If antitaxation can become firmly entrenched in NDP policy, it's reasonable to ask: How could any discussion of alternatives to spending cuts ever be broached in this province?

These episodes in Alberta's fiscal history confirm conventional political wisdom that taxes are "bad." This political myth-making partly explains why politicians even today do not wish to speak publicly on the merits, or even the disadvantages, of a sales tax. The words themselves are taboo.

Perhaps the introduction of a sales tax is not, in the eyes of an Alberta premier or finance minister, worth the complications of administering such a task or the reputational costs of politically defending it. As Al O'Brien told me, "It's a tough thing in a four-year period to address all these things at once. Premiers don't have a lot of time to develop and to think about how this [sales tax] would happen. Premiers don't have to raise money—it's not top of mind. And treasurers come and go, and a new treasurer has not, typically, thought about the revenue side" (interview with author, 7 November 2018).

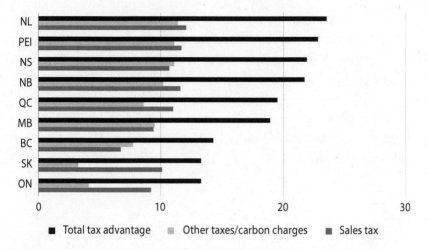

*Figure 1.1.* Alberta's Tax Advantage, 2021–22 ($ billions)

*Source*: Government of Alberta, *Budget 2021, Fiscal Plan*, 152, available from https://www.alberta.ca/budget-documents.aspx.

Certainly, there is an abundance of evidence that governing parties, not just in Alberta but in Canada as a whole, are punished when they introduce new taxes, as Mulroney's federal Conservatives were in 1993. However, the aversion to taxes is not universal, and may have more to do with the political culture of a certain time and place than anything else. Take, for example, the BC Liberals' attempt to mess with their province's sales tax during the October 2020 election campaign. According to one opinion piece by Gary Mason (2020), "cutting the PST in half, for a year or two, sounds like a reasonable temporary measure to give the economy a jolt. But eliminating it entirely for a year and then reducing to 3 percent for another year smacks of desperation. It's the Liberals looking for their own bridge-toll moment, a Hail Mary pass they pray changes the trajectory of the campaign." As it turned out, the BC Liberal gambit did not acquire traction; they lost the election and the PST remained as is. It's hard to imagine this happening one province to the east.

In the Alberta context, the Alberta Taxpayer Protection Act hardened the existing political establishment's resolve to maintain low taxes as a way of upholding the Social Credit and Progressive Conservative belief in private enterprise, free markets, and "small government." This rhetoric, of course, belies the fact that, by many measures, the Alberta government is, in fact, not a small government at all, nor has it been one since the early 1980s (MacKinnon 2003, 131). Despite efforts by the NDP to stabilize key programs like health care and education and to improve the progressivity of the PIT while in office, there remains a dogmatic consensus among major parties across the political spectrum that Alberta's "low tax advantage" is sacred.

## Notes

1   Economic rent is any payment to an owner of a factor of production (land, labour, or capital) in excess of the costs needed to bring that factor into production.

2   I conducted interviews in late 2018 with ten individuals, six of whom are quoted in this book. Two of these interviewees are Alberta residents with no detailed knowledge about Alberta's fiscal policies. One nonresident, former president of the Bank of Canada David Dodge, was selected because of his familiarity with Alberta fiscal policy through his work on two Alberta government assignments. The Alberta resident experts interviewed are two former deputy finance ministers (Al O'Brien and Robert Bhatia) and former leader of a Liberal official opposition (Kevin Taft).

3   Getty's MLA pension plan was modelled after the pension plan for members of Parliament and other provincial plans. Alberta's plan was a defined benefit plan, the pension entitlements of which were, like defined benefit pension plans in the public sector, indexed to inflation. However, the MLA pension plan entitled MLAs to a 4 percent pension entitlement for each year of service. This entitlement was more than twice that of most Canadian workers. On top of this, the MLA plan was noncontributory—that is, MLAs, unlike other public and private sector workers, did not have to pay into the fund in order to receive the pension. As a cherry on the cake, retiring MLAs could receive their pensions upon leaving public offices. This felt unfair to many Albertans, making pensions for politicians a lightning rod for discontent in the province.

4   A promissory note is a written promise to a money lender that the borrower will repay the money lent, plus interest accrued at an agreed-upon rate. When a promissory note is discounted, this means that the borrower receives the loan amount less a small sum, called a discount. In the context of 1930s

Alberta, if a farmer borrowed $100 at the legal maximum interest rate of 7 percent, they would receive a discounted amount—say, $97—but nonetheless have to pay back the loan plus interest on the full $100.

5   I am quoting here from the Alberta Taxpayer Protection Act as it stood before 23 July 2020, at which point it was amended slightly in accordance with the Referendum Act (SA 2020, c. 20), an amendment to the Constitutional Referendum Act (RSA 2000, c. C-25). The original Constitutional Referendum Act pertained solely to proposed changes to the Constitution of Canada. The 2020 amendment added several new sections that provided for referendums to be held in connection with non-constitutional issues. "Constitutional" was duly dropped from the title of the act, and section 4 of the Alberta Taxpayer Protection Act therefore now reads simply "Referendum Act."

6   Alberta, Legislative Assembly, *Hansard*, 23rd Leg., 3rd. Sess. (6 March 1995, afternoon sitting) at 356. Hereafter cited as *Alberta Hansard*. All references to debates in Alberta's Legislative Assembly will be cited in notes.

7   *Alberta Hansard* (6 March 1995, afternoon sitting) at 357.

8   *Alberta Hansard*, (6 March 1995, afternoon sitting) at 357–58.

9   *Alberta Hansard* (6 March 1995, afternoon sitting) at 360.

10  *Alberta Hansard* (7 March 1995, afternoon sitting) at 408–09.

11  *Alberta Hansard* (11 April 1995, evening sitting) at 1187.

12  *Alberta Hansard* (11 April 1995, evening sitting) at 1187.

13  *Alberta Hansard* (11 April 1995, evening sitting) at 1191. More than two decades later, Kevin Taft summed up the point rather nicely: "You can pass legislation like that until you're blue in the face, but it doesn't really change anything. Legislation can be changed at the stroke of a pen" (interview with author, 26 November 2019).

14  *Alberta Hansard* (11 April 1995, evening sitting) at 1192.

15  *Alberta Hansard* (11 April 1995, evening sitting) at 1181; *Alberta Hansard* (26 April 1995, evening sitting) at 1369, 1371.

16  *Alberta Hansard* (26 April 1995, evening sitting) at 1363–73.

17  David Tuer was an assistant deputy minister at Alberta Energy before joining Pan Canadian Petroleum in 1989, becoming president and CEO in 1994.

## References

Alberta Financial Management Commission. 2002. *Moving from Good to Great: Enhancing Alberta's Fiscal Framework*, chaired by David Tuer, 8 July 2002. Edmonton: Alberta Financial Management Commission.

Alberta Financial Review Commission. 1993. *Report to Albertans*, chaired
by Marshall Williams, 31 March 1993. Calgary: Alberta Financial Review
Commission.

Alberta Liberal Party. 1993. *The Next Alberta* [campaign poster]. Accessed
19 November 2018. https://www.poltext.org/sites/poltext.org/files/
plateformesV2/Alberta/AB_PL_1993_LIB.pdf.

Alberta Taxation Inquiry Board. 1935. *Report of the Alberta Taxation Inquiry Board
on Provincial and Municipal Taxation*, chaired by J. F. Percival. Edmonton:
Government of Alberta; King's Printer.

Alberta Tax Reform Commission. 1994. *A Report to Albertans*, chaired by Jack
Donald, February 1994. Edmonton: Alberta Tax Reform Commission.

Ascah, Robert L. 1999. *Politics and Public Debt: The Dominion, the Banks and
Alberta's Social Credit*. Edmonton: University of Alberta Press.

Bank of Canada. 1937. *Reports on the Financial Position of the Provinces of
Manitoba, Saskatchewan, and Alberta*. Ottawa: Bank of Canada.

Boothe, Paul. 2002. "Government Spending in Alberta." In *Alberta's Fiscal
Frontiers*, edited by Bev Dahlby, 1–18. Edmonton: Institute for Public
Economics, University of Alberta.

Brennan, Brian. 2008. *The Good Steward: The Ernest Manning Story*. Calgary:
Fifth House.

Dinning, Jim, and Norman Wagner. 1993. *Right on the Money: Alberta's Debt and
Deficit, 1993*. Edmonton: Alberta Treasury.

Dominion Bureau of Statistics. 1935. *Canada Year Book, 1934–35*. Ottawa: King's
Printer.

Government of Alberta. 1936. "Ultimate Purchasers Tax Act: Regulations."
*Alberta Gazette Part I* 32, no. 8 (30 April), 278–85.

———. 1938. *The Case for Alberta*. Edmonton: A. Shnitka, King's Printer.

———. 2003. *Fiscal Plan 2003–2006*. Available from https://open.alberta.ca/
publications/budget-2003-making-alberta-even-better.

Innis, Harold A. 1933. *Problems of Staple Production in Canada*. Toronto: Ryerson
Press.

Kneebone, Ronald, and Margarita Wilkins. 2016. "Canadian Provincial
Government Budget Data, 1980/81 to 2013/14." *Canadian Public Policy* 42,
no. 1 (March): 1–19. https://www.utpjournals.press/doi/pdf/10.3138/cpp
.2015-046.

"Legislation on Sales Tax Introduced." 1936. *Edmonton Bulletin*, 1 April 1936.

MacGregor, D. C., J. B. Rutherford, G. E. Britnell, and J. J. Deutsch. 1939. *National
Income: A Study Prepared for the Royal Commission on Dominion-Provincial
Relations*. Ottawa: King's Printer.

MacKinnon, Janice. 2003. *Minding the Public Purse: The Fiscal Crisis, Political Trade-offs, and Canada's Future*. Montréal and Kingston: McGill-Queen's University Press.

Macpherson, C. B. 1953. *Democracy in Alberta: The Theory and Practice of a Quasi-Party System*. Toronto: University of Toronto Press.

Mason, Gary. 2020. "BC Liberals' PST Gambit Is an Election Hail Mary." *Globe and Mail*, 30 September 2020. https://www.theglobeandmail.com/opinion/article-bc-liberals-pst-gambit-is-an-election-hail-mary/.

Nelson, Barry. 1983. "When Homes Sell for $1." *Maclean's*, 12 September 1983. https://archive.macleans.ca/article/1983/9/12/when-homes-sell-for-1.

O'Brien, Allison. 1969. "A Retail Sales Tax for Alberta: An Economic Evaluation of Alternative Structures." Master's thesis, University of Alberta.

Premier's Council for Economic Strategy. 2011. *Shaping Alberta's Future: Report of the Premier's Council for Economic Strategy*, chaired by David Emerson, May 2011. Available from https://open.alberta.ca/publications/report-of-the-premiers-council-for-economic-strategy.

Progressive Conservative Association of Alberta. 1993. *Our Plan for a Better Alberta* [campaign poster]. Accessed 19 November 2018.

Public Expenditure and Revenue Study Committee. 1965. *Public Expenditure and Revenue Study Committee: Complete and Final Report*, chaired by Anders Aalborg, 31 March 1965. Edmonton: The Committee.

Richards, John, and Larry Pratt. 1979. *Prairie Capitalism: Power and Influence in the New West*. Toronto: McClelland and Stewart.

Royal Commission on Dominion-Provincial Relations. 1940. *Canada: 1867–1939*. Vol. 1, *Report of the Royal Commission on Dominion-Provincial Relations*. Ottawa: King's Printer.

"Sales Tax Comes to End on Sept. 1, Low Announces." 1937. *Edmonton Journal*, 5 August 1937.

Statistics Canada. 2021. "Table 14-10-0287-01: Labour Force Characteristics, Monthly, Seasonally Adjusted and Trend-Cycle." Released 3 December 2021. https://doi.org/10.25318/1410028701-eng.

Van Herk, Aritha. 2001. *Mavericks: An Incorrigible History of Alberta*. Toronto: Penguin Canada.

# 2    The Political Suicide Tax?

*Graham Thomson*

It is the forbidden fruit of Alberta politics. And for a succession of finance ministers, it has proved to be something of a banana peel. They have stepped on it at their peril by musing about the possibility of introducing a PST. Ted Morton slipped on it in 2010; Lloyd Snelgrove, as Treasury Board president, in 2009. Other ministers did their own pratfalls, including municipal affairs minister Doug Griffiths who, during his career, stepped on this slippery subject so many times he should have worn a helmet to work.

A classic case in point was Ron Liepert, who, as finance minister in 2011, told reporters the idea of a PST had come up repeatedly during budget consultations with taxpayers. "In Alberta, we can't continue to rely on resource revenues and I think we should have that conversation sooner instead of later," Liepert said (quoted in Lamphier 2011). It was a measured, thoughtful response. But Liepert's caution was rewarded the following day with a front-page headline: "Sales Tax Back on Alberta's Agenda" (Lamphier 2011). That prompted Liepert to issue a written statement of "clarification," published as a news release under the impossible-to-misinterpret headline "No Provincial Sales Tax for Alberta." To make sure everybody understood, Liepert talked to reporters again. "I was asked about a sales tax in Alberta," he said. "My response was that the issue was raised at several of our round table discussions this month. Further,

I then stated it was a conversation Albertans needed to have sooner or later. I needed to be more clear in stating the conversation needed was about taxation in general" (Leipert 2011).

It is almost a rite of passage for Alberta finance ministers to muse about the possibility of a sales tax one day and then totally disown the idea the next. In 2010, it was Ted Morton who said the government would not introduce a sales tax for the time being. He also said, however, that "in the medium to long term, looking at all the options is a good idea" (quoted in D'Aliesio and Fekete 2010). This earned him his own front-page headline: "Sales Tax on Table in Alberta" (D'Aliesio and Fekete 2010). Morton then had to stand in the Legislature and say categorically that when it came to a sales tax, "the short answer is no, the medium answer is no, and the long answer is no."[1]

In 2009, Snelgrove did more than talk vaguely about a sales tax; he said a 5 percent tax could bring in as much as $8 billion a year to the treasury (Thomson 2009). This irritated Premier Ed Stelmach, who then sent a "very clear message" to his caucus declaring that the government was against not only a sales tax, but any tax increase of any kind. To underscore his point, Stelmach unilaterally scrapped a new tax hike on beer, wine, and liquor, costing the treasury $180 million in foregone revenue (Fekete 2009).

In early 2015, just ahead of the provincial election, then-premier Jim Prentice floated the idea of a sales tax: "I don't think Albertans generally advocate a sales tax, but I'm prepared to be educated and to hear from people" (quoted in Ibrahim 2015). At that time, the math looked neat, simple, and tempting as a way to solve a major fiscal problem. Prentice was predicting the provincial treasury would lose $7 billion over twelve months because of the depressed price of oil. Echoing Snelgrove's math from six years previously, government officials thought introducing a 5 percent sales tax would bring in about $7 billion (Ibrahim 2015). Problem solved. On paper, at least. But then the Prentice government opened up an online consultation, albeit cautiously, to see how Albertans thought the government should deal with the anticipated $7-billion drop in revenue. Some of the options included introducing a PST; raising PIT; raising CIT; reintroducing health-care premiums; and raising taxes on gasoline, cigarettes, or liquor (or all three). The public response to a PST was decidedly negative. Realizing he was getting himself in trouble by even floating the idea of a PST, Prentice immediately undercut the survey by declaring that any suggestion of a sales tax is "effectively" dead and "it would be unwise at this point to increase our corporate income tax" (quoted in Bennett 2015).

## A Complicated Relationship

A sales tax makes good sense, both economically and fiscally. Finance ministers know this. So do economists. Just about every economist who has studied the issue in Alberta has come to the conclusion that it's time the province introduced a PST. Groups as disparate as the Calgary Chamber of Commerce and the Parkland Institute have argued in favour of a PST. Jack Mintz (2011), founding director of the University of Calgary's School of Public Policy, delivered a lecture at the University of Alberta in which he advocated for a PST. Even the Premier's Council for Economic Strategy (2011) argued the province must stop using revenue from oil and natural gas to fund its day-to-day operations, and should cover those expenses through a revamped tax system including, potentially, a sales tax. Yet in Alberta, PST has come to mean "political suicide tax." The province even has a law in place—the Alberta Taxpayer Protection Act (SA 1995, c. A-37.8)—that dictates that the government must hold a referendum before introducing a sales tax. Why, then, do Alberta politicians have such a complicated relationship with PST?

Although the tax makes perfect sense in the ivory tower of academia, in the political arena the notion is—to put it mildly—problematic. Alberta politicians realize that adopting a consumption tax would be about as popular with voters as importing Norwegian rats into Alberta (a proudly rat-free province). What's more, the moment a government raises the notion of a PST, even in the most cautious terms, it is assailed by its opposition. As a result, Alberta politicians have, by and large, taken a simplistic, hands-off approach to even talking about a sales tax. This despite the fact that, if a government could ever survive its implementation, a sales tax might solve the provincial deficit and once and for all help smooth out the resource revenue rollercoaster ride that is Alberta's budgeting process. A sales tax must be to a finance minister what a neighbour's unsupervised swimming pool is to an eight-year-old child: an attractive nuisance, seductive but potentially fatal. Finance ministers can look but they aren't allowed to touch.

After she was elected premier in 2015, NDP leader Rachel Notley seemed willing, for a time, to buck this trend. In 2016, she dipped a toe into the PST swimming pool by saying she might be willing to talk about it in the 2019 election campaign. "We would have to in some fashion have a pretty upfront conversation with Albertans about the fiscal framework," said Notley. "I don't think, given the history of this province, that it would be respectful to voters to not talk to them about the issue if it was something that we were seriously looking at. I think that only makes sense" (quoted in Thomson 2016). However, by December 2018, after facing fierce opposition to the province's new carbon tax, Notley began to sound more like her Progressive Conservative forebears. Asked in a television interview with CBC News about her previous musings on a PST, Notley (2018) was definitive. "No, no, no—I haven't been talking about that," she said. "Now is not the time to bring something like that in."

Despite all this, some political parties in Alberta have, over the years, embraced the notion of a PST. In 2017, for example, Greg Clark, when he was still leader of the Alberta Party, said that "all options should be on the table" to increase government revenue, including looking at a sales tax. "I'm absolutely open to considering that," he said. "We can no longer afford to avoid difficult conversations or to rule anything out, even if it's politically unpopular" (quoted in Thomson 2017). Clark raised the notion of a dreaded PST for its shock value, if nothing else. He wanted to attract attention to the often-overlooked Alberta Party, apparently subscribing to Oscar Wilde's oft-cited dictum: "There is only one thing in the world worse than being talked about, and that is not being talked about" (Wilde [1890] 2015, 2).

## Provincial Survival Tax

After winning the 2019 provincial election and becoming premier of a UCP government, Jason Kenney offered a full-throated opposition to a PST, borrowing a mantra from the late former premier Ralph Klein: "We don't have a revenue problem, we have a spending problem." Like the many Conservative leaders before him, Kenney met the government's volatile revenue streams with cuts, cuts, and more cuts.

Then, in 2020, the COVID-19 pandemic began. The price of oil dropped so low as to go negative for a time. The province's deficit ballooned to a record $24 billion and the accumulated debt skyrocketed toward a record $100 billion. As Kenney pointed out repeatedly, Alberta was facing an economic crisis even greater than the Great Depression (see, e.g., "Premiers Seeking $70B" 2020). As it turns out, fiscal and economic distress can do funny things to hard-hitting Conservatives. The pressure on Kenney was so great it appeared to put a crack, however small, in his anti-PST armour. When asked point-blank whether it was time to introduce a PST, Kenney (2020) replied, predictably, "I do not believe that the right response in the midst of that economic crisis is to impose a new tax." But then he added a caveat: "Now, when we get through all of this, I've said to Albertans that there will be a fiscal reckoning. Our government had committed in our [election] platform to have a tax reform panel at some point during our mandate. So that will be a debate that Albertans will have in the future." For Kenney, any decision on a PST would have to be made by referendum, as per the Alberta Taxpayer Protection Act—but by admitting that such referendum was a possibility for the future, Kenney stopped short of slamming the door shut to a PST. In fact, it seems he may have even left it open a crack.

Some Conservatives—and stalwart ones at that—appear to agree with Kenney; a few have even advocated that the door be knocked down entirely. In an op-ed column during late summer 2020, former Wildrose Party leader Danielle Smith startled observers by calling for a fiscal overhaul of the government's finances. Unsurprisingly, she supported cuts to health care and education. Surprisingly—nay, *astoundingly*—she also advocated for a PST. "Yes, a provincial sales tax," she wrote. "Let's not kid ourselves about that, either" (Smith 2020).

The year 2020, with its pandemic and seemingly endless litany of bad news, sent an economic shockwave through Alberta that arguably rattled the province more than any other jurisdiction in Canada. In this economic climate, to label a PST as inherent political suicide is to take a decidedly defeatist point of view. As Kenney's and Smith's comments seem to suggest, political opinion is, once again, edging ever closer to publicly contemplating the merits of such a tax. What we need now is for the voting public to do the same. They could, for instance, mull over the fact that an Albertan PST comparable to that of, say, British Columbia, could generate, as Snelgrove calculated, more than $7 billion a year for Alberta—a detail that is available for all to see in the UCP government's own annual budget documents. The thing is, it is used there as a rhetorical tool to emphasize how fortunate Albertans are to live in a province with the lowest tax system in the country: $7 billion fortunate. Looked at from a different perspective, though, and the picture is less rosy. Without a PST, Alberta is passing up $7 billion a year in stable, predictable revenue. This revenue could solve many of the province's fiscal problems, not least among them avoiding fiscal catastrophe in tough economic times. The economic upheaval of 2020 has demonstrated the shortcomings of Alberta's current fiscal policy. In 2020, the federal government sent more money in transfers to Alberta than it collected from the province in taxes—the first time this has happened since the mid-1960s. More than this, Alberta saw the greatest per capita increase in federal spending of any province in the country (Dawson 2021).

Clearly, when the global economy goes haywire, resource revenues alone can't keep the province afloat. Perhaps now Alberta's political leaders will at last begin to look upon the PST as a life raft—not a "political suicide tax," but a "provincial survival tax."

## Note

1   Alberta Legislative Assembly, *Hansard*, 27th Leg., 3rd Sess. no. 36 (1 November 2010, afternoon sitting) at 1026.

## References

Bennett, Dean. 2015. "Corporate Tax Hike Not an Option for Fixing Budget Shortfall: Prentice." *Edmonton Journal*, 4 February 2015, A4.

D'Aliesio, Renata, and Jason Fekete. 2010. "Sales Tax on Table in Alberta." *Calgary Herald*, 26 August 2010, A1.

Dawson, Tyler. 2021. "For the First Time in More than 50 Years, Alberta Received More Money from Ottawa than It Sent." *National Post*, 10 November 2021.

https://nationalpost.com/news/politics/for-the-first-time-in-more-than-50
-years-alberta-received-more-money-from-ottawa-than-it-sent.

Feteke, Jason. 2009. "Premier Promises No Tax Hikes." *Calgary Herald*, 9 July
2009, A1, A4.

Ibrahim, Mariam. 2015. "Prentice Willing to Talk Sales Tax." *Edmonton Journal*, 14
January 2015, A1.

Kenney, Jason. 2020. "Coronavirus Outbreak: Now Is Not the Time to Impose
a New Tax: Kenney." Interview by Mercedes Stephenson. *The West Block*,
Global News, 3 May 2020. https://globalnews.ca/video/6896548/coronavirus
-outbreak-now-is-not-the-time-to-impose-a-new-tax-kenney/.

Lamphier, Gary. 2011. "Sales Tax Back on Alberta's Agenda." *Edmonton Journal*, 16
November 2011, A1.

Leipert, Ron. 2011. "No Provincial Sales Tax for Alberta." Government of Alberta
news release, 16 November 2011. https://www.alberta.ca/release.cfm?xID=
31530AD3A1B08-F761-A0C5-0A4DA0B8BD1F165A.

Mintz, Jack. 2011. "The VAT as Game-Changing Tax Policy in the US and Alberta
Contexts." Eric Hanson 17th Memorial Lecture, Institute for Public Economics,
University of Alberta, Edmonton, AB, 27 September 2011. https://era.library
.ualberta.ca/items/0e946ba7-d3db-49b4-93d5-405ef912603b.

Notley, Rachel. 2018. "Why There Won't Be an Alberta Sales Tax Any Time Soon,
and Who's to Blame for Provincial Pipeline Paralysis." Interview by Stephen
Hunt. *CBC News*, 18 December 2018. https://www.cbc.ca/news/canada/
calgary/rachel-notley-year-end-interview-pst-carbon-pricing-trans-mountain
-trudeau-1.4952511.

Premier's Council for Economic Strategy. 2011. *Shaping Alberta's Future: Report of
the Premier's Council for Economic Strategy*. Available from https://open.alberta
.ca/publications/report-of-the-premiers-council-for-economic-strategy.

"Premiers Seeking $70B for Health Care." 2020. *Calgary Herald*, 19 September
2020, NP3.

Smith, Danielle. 2020. "Alberta Needs to Hit Reset on Our Finances." *Edmonton
Journal*, 4 September 2020, A8.

Thomson, Graham. 2009. "Gov't Peddles Fear to Make Us Buy Cuts."
*Edmonton Journal*, 2 July 2009, A14.

———. 2016. "There's a Price for All of This Change." *Edmonton Journal*, 30 April
2016, B3.

———. 2017. "Alberta Party Makes Some Noise with Pitch on PST." *Edmonton
Journal*, 28 February 2017, A1–A2.

Wilde, Oscar. (1890) 2015. *The Picture of Dorian Gray*. Minneapolis, MN: Lerner
Publishing.

# 3    Alberta's Fiscal Dilemma

*Robert L. Ascah*

The people of Alberta have long grown accustomed to a relatively generous array of public services. In the early years of the province, these services were relatively simple—the provision of education, unemployment relief, and law enforcement, along with the construction and upkeep of roads, telephone lines, public buildings, and assorted public works. Since then, however, the range of government services has steadily expanded, partly in response to the growing complexity of modern life (Ascah 2013, 158–62). All of these services cost money. Albertans are not alone in expecting government services to keep pace with their needs but, Albertans do seem to be uniquely opposed to paying for those services through taxes. They seem allergic even to the mention of tax increases or new taxes—and to a sales tax, in particular. This, then, is Alberta's fiscal dilemma: how to respond to two contrary expectations on the part of voters: the first that services will expand and the second that taxes will remain low. In other words, how can the Alberta government spend more money without raising more money?

An answer to this question—one that still guides fiscal policy in the province today—arrived in 1947 when oil was discovered not far south of Edmonton, near the town of Leduc. The province soon found itself in possession of newfound wealth in the form of unanticipated royalties. It was not long before the government began to draw on this income instead of taxes to cover the cost of expanded and enhanced public services and other public projects. This trend continued during the recession in the early 1980s and then gradually became entrenched in Alberta's fiscal culture. As oil and gas industry executives and industry-friendly elected officials never fail to make clear, public infrastructure in Alberta is paid for in no small part by the energy sector. In other words, Alberta's long-standing, tax-averse fiscal policy makes the province dependent on oil and gas through thick and thin.

What does the Alberta government's heavy reliance on non-renewable resource royalties actually mean for the province? In part, it means unpredictability. The actual revenue generated by these royalties is highly unstable. As figure 3.1 illustrates, since the mid-1960s (when the data begins), the percentage of Alberta's own-source revenue[1] that comes from non-renewable resources has zigzagged from 70 percent to less than 10 percent, with the overall trend headed downward.

I am certainly not the first person to raise alarms about Alberta's volatile revenue problem. Way back in 2002, for example, L. S. Wilson published an important edited collection of essays exploring the topic: *Alberta's Volatile Government Revenues: Policies for the Long Run*. More recently, in an analysis of Alberta's long-term fiscal future, Trevor Tombe (2018, 26–28) explored the consequences that the province's reliance on such a highly volatile source of revenue has had on its capacity to repay debts, as measured by the ratio between its debt and its GDP. In a projection to the year 2040, Tombe finds that if Alberta continues with its customary revenue mix of low taxes and high dependence on non-renewable resource royalties, the range of possible future outcomes for its net debt-to-GDP ratio is very wide. Compared to Ontario, which lacks a similarly volatile component but does include a sales tax, Alberta's future is extremely difficult to predict. In short, the greater the stability of revenue sources, the more predictable future fiscal outcomes become.

The volatility of non-renewable resource revenue causes problems for Alberta's ability to plan for its future—but it is not the only factor that puts Alberta's fiscal future into question. This volatility is compounded by the manner in which the government has chosen to use non-renewable resource revenue. As Al O'Brien, a former deputy finance minister in

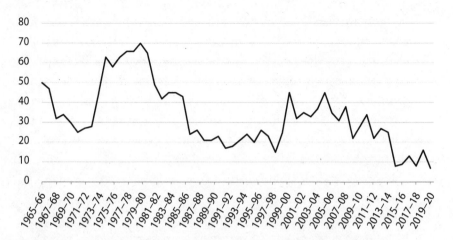

*Figure 3.1.* Non-renewable resource revenue as percentage of own-source revenue, 1965–66 to 2020–21

*Source*: Ronald Kneebone and Margarita Wilkins, "Canadian Provincial Government Budget Data—All Provinces Updated to 2019/20 and Some to 2020/21" (Excel spreadsheet), October 2021 version, available from University of Calgary School of Public Policy, "Research Data," http://www.policyschool.ca/publication-category/research-data/.

the provincial Department of Finance and Treasury, told me, "Royalty receipts are not revenue" (interview with author, 3 November 2018). O'Brien was making a distinction between non-renewable resource revenue and "ordinary" sources of government revenue such as taxes and other mandatory charges. Taxes are compulsory financial charges that governments impose on individuals, corporations, and other legal entities. Revenue from non-renewable resources is ultimately generated by royalties and other charges (variously known as bonuses, sales of Crown leases, and rentals and fees). Royalties are a percentage of a resource developer's profit that they pay to the resource owner (in this case Alberta). These royalties and other charges are paid in exchange for the right to develop and sell the resource. Unlike tax revenue, the royalties and charges that make up resource revenue are, for accounting purposes, akin to the sale of public assets—in this case, irreplaceable natural resources—to corporations, who then exploit them for one-time private profit.

From an accounting point of view, the difference between tax revenue and royalties is crucial. Let's look at a couple of simple examples. Say someone gives you $20. You now have $20 more than you had before. This example approximates tax revenue. Now say you buy a house for $200,000. You now have $200,000 less, but you own a house. Several years later, you sell the house for $180,000. The gross income from the sale is $180,000, but you haven't made $180,000. In fact, on a balance sheet, you've *lost* $20,000. On top of this, you no longer have a house. This second example approximates non-renewable resource revenue. This is because, first of all, non-renewable resource revenue is acquired through the sale of a resource that, once it's sold, it's gone. Like the sale of the house—and unlike taxes, which are paid every year, or forests, which can be renewed—non-renewable resource revenues, whether royalties, fees, or other charges, are not repeatable. Second, resource revenue is acquired through the sale of a resource that has a recorded value. For the purposes of budgeting, the Alberta government has treated non-renewable resource revenue like taxes by crediting them directly, in their whole amount, to the government's operating account, the General Revenue Fund. In essence, the government is selling off its finite assets and then burning off the cash. Accountants will tell you that the province should instead record the value of its non-renewable resources on its balance sheet. When the resources are sold, the sales should be recorded as simple exchanges of one asset for another: cash for access to exploit the resource. Unless there is a massive increase in the market value of the resource and the cash received was higher than the book value of the oil and gas reserves, *there is no revenue*, in an accounting sense, from this type of sale.

Yet for decades now, the Alberta government has used resource royalties to supplement a deficient flow of more reliable sources of revenue such as taxes and fees. It has used them, that is, as if they were repeatable, "ordinary" revenue. This is evident in the province's spending: the Alberta government has been spending 100-cent dollars to cover its expenditures, but taxpayers have been required to pay only 30 to 90 cents of these dollars, with resource revenues topping up the rest. Under its current fiscal strategy, if it didn't use non-renewable resource revenues in this way, the province would quickly accumulate debt.

## The Consequences of Volatile Revenue

What, then, are the consequences of treating revenue from non-renewables as if it were "ordinary" revenue? To O'Brien, the answer is simple: "We [the Alberta government] have been fooling you for decades. [. . .] We've never had a balanced budget since the Second World War" (interview with author, 3 November 2018). In other words, treating non-renewable resource revenue as ordinary, tax-based revenue does not a balanced budget make. Rather, it leads to the illusion of a balanced budget. Indeed, as figure 3.2 shows, Alberta has not once managed to balance its budget without the inclusion of revenue from non-renewable resources since the 1965–66 fiscal year.

For Albertans, to the extent that they are aware of it at all, this situation has proved comfortable because, even in the face of rising costs, it has so far allowed them to enjoy a high level of public services (to which they feel entitled) without having to pay more taxes—as though government revenues magically expand to meet the growing needs for public services. Despite compelling advice and analysis from experts such as Tombe and Wilson, and despite Alberta's recent boom-bust experience (2005 to 2021), revenue has not been growing at the rate of spending. Albertans' attitudes of tax aversion and self-entitlement have proved difficult to dislodge. Sound and sustainable fiscal policy remains elusive.

Periodically, Albertans' public services become vulnerable to the volatility of resource royalty revenues. Over the past three decades, we have seen how cutbacks to public spending during the Klein era and the UCP government's current efforts to freeze or reduce spending are consequences of steadily growing public expenditures being financed by variable revenue sources.

## Steadily Rising Expenditure and Volatile Revenue

For successive provincial governments, neither revenue nor spending can escape the volatility of the energy royalty rollercoaster. Typically, government officials working on budgets use the rule of thumb that budget increases should follow inflation and population growth.

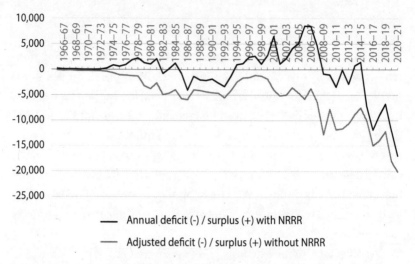

*Figure 3.2.* Alberta's annual deficit/surplus, 1965–66 to 2020–21, with and without non-renewable resource revenue ($ millions)

*Source*: Ronald Kneebone and Margarita Wilkins, "Canadian Provincial Government Budget Data—All Provinces Updated to 2019/20 and Some to 2020/21" (Excel spreadsheet), October 2021 version, available from University of Calgary School of Public Policy, "Research Data," http://www.policyschool.ca/publication-category/research-data/.

*Note*: This graph is in current dollars. Current dollars do not adjust for the effects of inflation; the dollars are current in the year spent. As the figure indicates, if we take away non-renewable resource revenue, the province has run a deficit since the 1965–66 fiscal year.

Ideally, government revenue should track in the same direction as spending—that is, growing steadily to yield balanced budgets over the long term. As we have seen, though, overall revenue is rather volatile because of its reliance to varying degrees on non-renewable resource revenue (Figure 3.1).

Successive efforts to wean the province off this rollercoaster have met stiff political resistance. The Alberta Financial Management Commission's (2002, 22) report *Moving from Good to Great: Enhancing Alberta's Fiscal Framework* drew attention to the "increasing dependence on non-sustainable resource revenues to fund core programs such as health and education." The report emphasized that "we can't count on resource revenue forever. It's time to plan now for the time when resource revenues decline" (48). The commission recommended that all revenue from non-renewables flow into the Heritage Fund, with a fixed amount then sent to the General Revenue Fund each year. This would enable the Heritage Fund to start growing again—something it hadn't done since 1987.[2] Legislation introduced after the commission's report set the annual maximum amount that could flow to the General Revenue Fund at $3.5 billion. However, as commodity prices rose in the years following the report, the amount to be transferred from the Heritage Fund to the General Revenue Fund was quickly raised to $4.75 billion in 2006 (Kneebone and Wilkins 2018, 7–8)—that is, as non-renewable resource revenue took an upward swing, policy was adjusted to allow for spending to increase as well. The revenue tail was wagging the spending dog. The government, in transition at that time from Ralph Klein to Ed Stelmach, restructured and renamed a variety of regulated funds, and created new funds and accounts—the Sustainability Fund, the Contingency Account, the Capital Account, the Operating Account, the Saving Account, the Debt Retirement Account. Spending and fiscal discipline eroded and financial legislation changed to accommodate the current needs of political leaders, making it difficult for analysts to understand where the money was coming from and where it was going (Ascah and Bhatia 2013).

What is easy enough to understand is that revenue drives spending: when revenue grows, spending grows, too. Figure 3.3 shows provincial government spending and revenue in Alberta since 1965. The area between the lines represents either deficits or surpluses. Both lines, predictably, slope upward. It is notable, however, that the revenue line is more jagged than that that of the spending line. The revenue line also features periodic decreases, whereas spending has only fallen once during the Klein era. The last two years shown in figure 3.3 are distorted because of the extraordinary COVID-19 spending and uncommonly high federal transfers.

Another notable feature is the fact that spending is driven up even when revenue increases are primarily the result of non-renewable resource revenue windfalls. This is seen in the late 1970s and in the mid-2000s. The message should be clear: without a source of revenue that

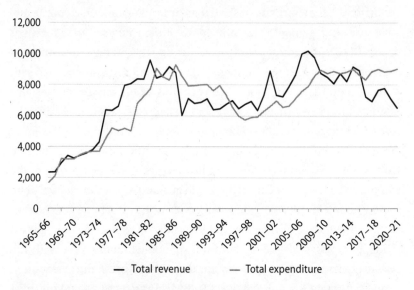

*Figure 3.3.* Government of Alberta revenue and expenditure, 1965–66 to 2020–21 ($ millions), adjusted for population and inflation

*Source*: Ronald Kneebone and Margarita Wilkins, "Canadian Provincial Government Budget Data—All Provinces Updated to 2019/20 and Some to 2020/21" (Excel spreadsheet), October 2021 version, available from University of Calgary School of Public Policy, "Research Data," http://www.policyschool.ca/publication-category/research-data/.

grows dependably along with population and the general economy, government spending is left to the mercy of the international markets that set the price for Alberta's main exports. This has meant unwanted cutbacks to government services and public sector employment when the economy is in a recession. This revenue-spending mismatch, characterized by unpredictable revenue streams and predictable spending needs, highlights the importance of matching *stable* revenue sources with the inexorable climb in the consumption and cost of government services. A more rational and sustainable approach to government finances in a commodity-dependent economy would be to stabilize revenue sources to meet the known funding needs of government programs. Matching stable revenue with public expenditures would provide more predictability for public sector workers, provincial agencies, businesses, government contractors, investors, bondholders, and taxpayers. Such a sustainable, long-term fiscal policy would eliminate the need for the types of abrupt changes to spending or revenue policies that define Alberta's current fiscal politics—changes that are deeply disruptive to all Albertans.

## What Can Governments Control?

Alberta's fiscal dilemma—how to spend more money without reliably making more money—is not just a matter of making the math work. It is a political problem at heart. Part of the problem lies in government policies and messaging that obscure what governments are and are not able to control in terms of their jurisdiction's finances and economy. Another part of the problem is that one of the solutions is to raise taxes—a move that makes politicians and their parties vulnerable to losing seats in a general election.

Most politicians believe their number-one job is to create or preserve employment for their constituents. Under Don Getty's Progressive Conservatives and Rachel Notley's New Democrats, this task was approached in an activist manner through royalty holidays, subsidies, and loan guarantees. Ralph Klein's government pursued the employment goal by creating a fiscal regime conducive to luring investment capital through low taxes, generous royalty policies, and limited regulation without picking economic winners and losers, as he understood Getty to have done. Both approaches shared the belief that through government policy, the province's fiscal capacity would ultimately be enhanced. Premier Jason Kenney and his Economic Recovery Council are adhering to the mantra that governments are somehow the sole creators of economic growth. Kenney has doubled down on his bet to rescue Alberta's beleaguered economy with more corporate tax cuts, a failed bet on the Keystone XL pipeline project, and higher infrastructure spending.

This belief that government policies are the main drivers of economic growth is not unique to Alberta. Governments throughout Canada's history have seen themselves as drivers of economic development, and in many ways they have been. The building of the Canadian Pacific Railway was literally a nation-building project. Similarly, TransCanada Pipelines and the St. Lawrence Seaway projects have been enterprises enjoying tacit government support or direct public investments (Kilbourn 1970). But in today's global investment world, governments must be careful they are not competing against each other as global corporations play one jurisdiction against another.[3]

These types of approaches risk being particularly misguided in Alberta in that they tend to reinforce dependency on non-renewable resource revenue by concentrating their incentives on the non-renewable resource extraction sector. Revenue from non-renewables is not just volatile; it also depends on private corporations to carry out the extraction and production. Continuing production therefore is dependent on the cash flow of these corporations, which in turn depends on two principal factors: oil and natural gas prices and continued capital investment to sustain and grow production. Oil and gas extraction and production are highly capital intensive and historically have relied on foreign capital. As *Alberta's Recovery Plan* (Government of Alberta 2020a, 2020b) confirms, Alberta's political and corporate leaders admit the province is essentially hostage to international and domestic finance capital:

> External sources of capital have become the largest source of investment into Alberta and a critical contributor to Alberta's economic growth. Much of the economic adversity experienced by Alberta since 2014 is tied to the flight of tens of billions of dollars of capital investment. To reverse this trend, and bring back job-creating investment, Alberta's government will create Invest Alberta, a dedicated investment promotion agency that will lead our investment attraction strategy in a new direction with better capital markets communications, proactive investment promotion targeting key companies and sectors, and concierge service for prospective investors seeking to navigate through regulatory and other hurdles. (Government of Alberta 2020a, 11)

In effect, Premier Kenney, his cabinet, and his Economic Recovery Council (headed by Jack Mintz) are admitting that Alberta does not have the homegrown capital to nurture economic growth.

A distinction between what is and is not actually financially and economically within the government's control is pertinent to political narratives and public discourse. Understanding the difference is particularly important when, as we often find, government-sponsored initiatives make promises beyond the limits of their control, and then predictably do not achieve their revenue goals. The absence of clarity about that for which the government can actually be held accountable is a major obstacle in the public's understanding of the province's fiscal circumstances. All too often, however, the media and opposition do not follow up on the failures of these untenable promises. It is, therefore, useful to be able to recognize such promises as fanciful from the beginning.

There are many significant economic, jurisdictional, and financial factors outside the control of the Alberta government. These include oil and natural gas prices; Canadian dollar exchange rates; interest rates; financial market returns; regulation of, among other things, interprovincial pipelines, banks, bankruptcy and insolvency, railways, and telecommunications; and equalization payments. Though not exhaustive, this list may well be enough to make a provincial politician feel helpless—What's the point? Why did I run for office? If we can't control these things, how can government effectively create a climate hospitable for capital investment and jobs? Instead of publicly acknowledging the helplessness around the many factors outside their control—including, notably, the price of oil—political leaders in Alberta tend to choose to *appear* in control, investing their energy in "fighting," in the name of their constituents, the external actors from whence these uncontrollable factors come, attempting to wrestle them into economic submission.

The energy that politicians put into these fights could instead be concentrated on using the tools at their disposal to manage the economic factors over which the government *does* have influence—for while the Alberta government cannot control the price of oil, it can influence policy outcomes in instances where its voice would legitimately be considered (for instance, Trans Mountain pipeline project). Beyond this, there remains a great deal that the provincial government can control on both its revenue and expenditure side. For instance, while the provincial government cannot control the price of oil, bitumen, and natural gas, it does have the power to establish royalty rates and dictate the pace and scale of oil sands development. Some other tools and factors at the Alberta government's disposal include the following:

- Health-care premiums
- Public sector salaries and benefits
- Appointment of senior officials, agency boards
- Operating programs
- Capital spending
- Debt management policies
- Investment policies
- Minimum wage
- Occupational health and safety
- Labour relations (except for federally regulated enterprises)
- Municipal affairs
- Energy and environmental regulation
- Revenue (PIT, CIT, and taxes and fees related to tobacco, alcohol, cannabis, gambling, fuel, carbon)

Here's the catch. The degree to which a government can actually control these things depends on it maintaining a strong mandate from the voting public. The political theatre of fighting factors that are outside of our control allows Albertans to maintain their sense of exceptionalism and entitlement, which they have come to take for granted. Catering to this exceptionalism does much to bolster a government's popularity and increase its chances of re-election. However, if a government were to spend more of its energy focussing on the factors within its control—for instance, by asking Albertans to pay more for or accept new taxes to fund the services they require—it would challenge this sense of exceptionalism. This would be very unpopular.

Alberta's fiscal dilemma is characterized by a chronic mismatch of steadily rising spending needs with volatile revenue caused by overreliance on non-renewable resource royalties. It is also characterized by another chronic issue: Alberta exceptionalism and a political hesitancy to challenge it. To ameliorate the first issue, political will, political capital, and political leadership must focus on managing key levers within the government's policy tool box. The main tools are controlling operating and capital spending, maximizing returns to the province from resource development (subject to strict environmental accountabilities), and setting appropriate revenue policy. However, without an open discussion of the trade-offs between voters' appetite for public services and their capacity and willingness to pay for these services, the fiscal dilemma will remain, and it will continue to fester. Without such a discussion, Alberta's government will continue to create the illusion of solving its fiscal dilemma with messianic promises on which it cannot deliver without the divine help of the global market gods. When that help is not forthcoming, politicians turn to reducing spending on public services and infrastructure instead of risking Albertans' wrath by speaking the word *tax*.

## Notes

1   Own-source revenue refers to revenue other than federal transfers.
2   The Alberta Heritage Savings Trust Fund was created in 1976 to save a portion of non-renewable resource revenue in order to benefit future generations of Albertans. It was based on the assumption that the provincial government needed to save money because revenue from non-renewables would decline over time as the resource was depleted. The transfer of resource revenues to the Heritage Fund was reduced from 30 percent to 15 percent in 1982–83 and eliminated entirely in 1987–88.
3   The example of Amazon "tendering" its second head office to the highest bidder is a recent example. This behaviour is often termed a "race to the bottom." See Wong (2018).

## References

Alberta Financial Management Commission. 2002. *Moving from Good to Great: Enhancing Alberta's Fiscal Framework*, chaired by David Tuer, 8 July 2002. Edmonton: Alberta Financial Management Commission.
Ascah, Robert L. 2013. "Savings of Non-Renewable Resource Revenue: Why Is It So Difficult? A Survey of Leaders' Opinions." In *Boom and Bust Again: Policy*

*Challenges for a Commodity-Based Economy*, edited by David L. Ryan, 151–98. Edmonton: University of Alberta Press.

Ascah, Robert L., and Robert Bhatia. 2013. "Does the Budget's New Math Add Up?" *Edmonton Journal*, 13 March 2013.

Government of Alberta. 2020a. *Alberta's Recovery Plan*, June 2020. Available from https://open.alberta.ca/publications/albertas-recovery-plan.

Government of Alberta. 2020b. *Alberta's Recovery Plan: Economic Statement*, June 2020. Edmonton: Government of Alberta. Available from https://open.alberta .ca/publications/albertas-recovery-plan.

Kilbourn, William. 1970. *Pipeline—TransCanada and the Great Debate: A History of Business and Politics*. Vancouver: Clarke, Irwin and Company.

Kneebone, Ronald, and Margarita Wilkins. 2018. "50 Years of Government of Alberta Budgeting." *University of Calgary School of Public Policy Publications* 11, no. 26. https://doi.org/10.11575/sppp.v11i0.53364.

Tombe, Trevor. 2018. "Alberta's Long-Term Fiscal Future." *University of Calgary School of Public Policy Publications* 11, no. 31. https://doi.org/10.11575/sppp .v11i0.52965.

Wilson, L. S., ed. 2002. *Alberta's Volatile Government Revenues: Policies for the Long Run*. Edmonton: Institute for Public Economics, University of Alberta.

Wong, Julia Carrie. 2018. "What Cities Offered Amazon: Helipads, Zoo Tickets, and a Street Named Alexa." *Guardian*, 15 November 2018. https://www .theguardian.com/technology/2018/nov/14/amazon-next-headquarters-losing -city-bids-what-offered.

# 4  The Revenue Push and Spending Pull

## A Double-Edged Look at the Source of Alberta's Fiscal Ills

*Robert L. Ascah*

The fiscal history of Alberta is a story of feast and famine dependent on the fortunes of a small number of commodities—largely grains, oil, bitumen, and natural gas (Ascah 2021). This overreliance has imperiled Alberta's financial health on a recurring basis, and yet the province doesn't seem to learn its lesson: relying so heavily on volatile revenue sources is a recipe for an unpredictable and unstable future. Successive governments have failed to intentionally shape a collective, sustainable future by remaining passively hostage not only to fluctuating prices of globally traded commodities but also to past governments' financial decisions to spend or save, to raise or lower taxes, or to borrow. Add to this the unrelenting evidence of international financial capital divesting its fossil fuel investments, and the problem deepens.

We and our political leaders have lived in near constant denial of the fragile state of Alberta's economy and public finances. As a result, Alberta's economic future is persistently clouded. How do we wake up from this denial? How do we clear the clouds away? In other words, where do we begin in solving Alberta's fiscal dilemma—with spending or revenue?

This chapter asks you, the reader, to delve into the numbers with me. My goal here is to examine the variability of the Alberta government's revenue and spending structures over fifty years to show that Alberta doesn't have a spending *or* revenue problem; it has a spending *and* revenue problem. I also examine Alberta's historical failure to save, and the implications of this on the province's current fiscal situation. By charting the key revenue sources and major spending areas of the Alberta government since the mid-1960s (adjusted for inflation and population) and running some simple statistical tests to compare long-term trends, I attempt to better understand where Alberta's economic woes lie, and how to fix them.

## Provincial Revenue

Figure 4.1 provides an overview of the sources of revenue over which the Alberta government has some control. The two major sources of revenue for the provincial government are non-renewable resource revenue and PIT. Although non-renewable resource revenue has dominated revenue sources since the mid-1960s and before, it is also the most volatile revenue source. This volatility is shown in figure 4.1 by the steep peaks and dips in the resource revenue line, which represent periods when the prices for oil and natural gas have had a significant impact on resource revenue. For example, we see sharp rises in the 1970s caused by the OPEC (Organization of the Petroleum Exporting Countries) embargo and Iranian revolution. Similarly, in the 2000s, resource revenue rose rapidly because of price increases, especially for natural gas, and because of growing production in the oil sands. Unlike volatile resource revenue, we see a relatively smooth, steady growth in PIT over time. CIT also shows growth that is relatively stable compared to resource revenue, though more variable than PIT and growing at a slower rate. PIT and CIT revenues were about equal in 1965; by 2020, CIT represented less than one-third of PIT revenue, adjusted for population growth and inflation. There is, of course, no line for a sales tax.

Figure 4.1 clearly shows the instability of non-renewable resource revenue. What is especially dramatic is the fact that non-renewable resource revenue exceeded PIT revenue from 1965–66 through to 1986–87. This

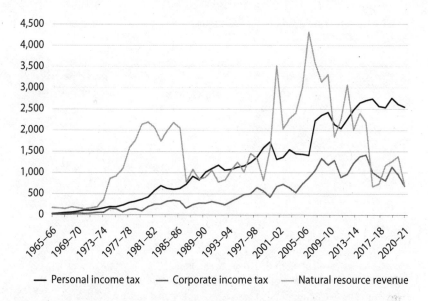

*Figure 4.1.* Major revenue sources per capita, 1965–66 to 2020–21 (2002 $ millions)

*Sources*: Ronald Kneebone and Margarita Wilkins, "Canadian Provincial Government Budget Data—All Provinces Updated to 2019/20 and Some to 2020/21" (Excel spreadsheet), October 2021 version, available from University of Calgary School of Public Policy, "Research Data," http://www.policyschool.ca/publication-category/research-data/; Statistics Canada, "Table 18-10-0005-01: Consumer Price Index, Annual Average, Not Seasonally Adjusted," released 20 January 2021, https://doi.org/10.25318/1810000501-eng; Statistics Canada, "Table: 17-10-0009-01: Population Estimates on July 1st, by Age and Sex," released 29 September 2021, https://doi.org/10.25318/1710000501-eng.

dominance resumed for a shorter period between 2000–01 and 2009–10. In other words, an unstable source of revenue exceeded personal tax revenues in thirty-seven of the past fifty-five fiscal years. At the turn of the millennium in particular, the resource revenue floodgates opened. It is this type of resource bounty that successive Alberta governments have banked on to pay for a significant portion of spending on public services and infrastructure and, at certain times, to reduce or at least not raise taxes.

Table 4.1 shows the results of measuring the volatility of each major revenue source for the fiscal years 1965–66 to 2020–21. The table shows the standard deviation measures for the full period between 1965 and

*Table 4.1.* Standard deviation of Alberta government revenue, 1965–66 to 2020–21

| Years | Personal income tax | Corporate income tax | Non-renewable resource revenue |
|---|---|---|---|
| 1965–66 to 1974–75 | 0.108 | 0.312 | 0.336 |
| 1975–76 to 1984–85 | 0.063 | 0.276 | 0.087 |
| 1985–86 to 1994–95 | 0.068 | 0.144 | 0.166 |
| 1995–96 to 2004–05 | 0.071 | 0.143 | 0.353 |
| 2005–06 to 2014–15 | 0.153 | 0.090 | 0.129 |
| 2011–12 to 2020–21 | 0.031 | 0.099 | 0.225 |
| | | | |
| 1965–66 to 2020–21 | 0.103 | 0.209 | 0.261 |

*Source*: Author's calculations based on Ronald Kneebone and Margarita Wilkins, "Canadian Provincial Government Budget Data—All Provinces Updated to 2019/20 and Some to 2020/21" (Excel spreadsheet), October 2021 version, available from University of Calgary School of Public Policy, "Research Data," http://www.policyschool.ca/publication-category/research-data/.

2021, as well as for seven ten-year slices within that period. Standard deviation is the degree by which each data point diverges from a data set's mean, or average, value. A low standard deviation measure indicates that the values within a single population sample tend to be close to the mean value of that sample; a high standard deviation indicates the opposite. Said differently, the lower the standard deviation, the lower the volatility of the numbers in a sample. In this case, those numbers are the annual changes, in percent, to Alberta's three major revenue sources: PIT, CIT, and non-renewable resource revenue. The data in in table 4.1 reveal that resource revenue, when considered across the full time period in question, is on average about 2.5 times more volatile than PIT and about 1.25 times more volatile than CIT.

This result is tied to the fact that many of the largest corporate taxpayers in Alberta are oil and gas companies whose profitability varies significantly over time with the prices of oil, bitumen, and natural gas, which are themselves, of course, very volatile.[1]

Generally unknown to most Albertans is another source of unstable revenue, unrelated to fluctuating oil and natural gas prices and oil patch activity: investment income. Amendments to the Alberta Heritage Savings Trust Fund Act (SA 1996, c. A-27.01) transitioned the fund's investment income from being mainly based on predictable interest payments to relying more on equities whose value can fluctuate dramatically. This change has produced greater volatility in the fund's earnings (see, for example, the dramatic dips in 2003–04 and 2009–10 in figure 4.2). Investment income—which, since 2008, has been heavily dependent on the success of AIMCo's (Alberta Investment Management Corporation) management of Heritage Fund assets—exposes Alberta's revenue structure to domestic and international bond, public equity, and private equity markets, as well as infrastructure and commercial real estate. While it might appear that investment income has stabilized since the 2008–09 financial crisis, AIMCo's management and board came in for significant criticism in April 2020 when *Institutional Investor* published a story about AIMCo's volatility-based trading strategy, which resulted in expected losses of approximately $2.1 billion to its clients, including the Heritage Fund (Orr 2020; Uebelein 2020).

It is also worthwhile looking at Alberta's revenue mix compared to those of other major Canadian provinces. Table 4.2 shows the significant differences in the revenue structure among Canada's largest provincial jurisdictions—Alberta, British Columbia, Ontario, and Québec—based on figures from the years 2019–20 or 2020–21. Alberta is an outlier in this group because of its resource revenue and the absence of a sales tax. Alberta is also an outlier when it comes to investment income, which is mainly earned through the Heritage Fund.

Notably, in 2020–21, Alberta derived a much higher proportion of its own-source revenue from PIT than in other years. This is because nonrenewable resource revenue in that fiscal year was low as a result of low oil and natural gas prices. As well, Alberta's enterprise revenue is normally closer to that of other provinces (which have significant hydroelectric power revenue) thanks in large part to the revenue from the Alberta Gaming, Liquor and Cannabis Commission and ATB Financial. However, a massive write-down at the government's North West Refining heavy oil upgrader in 2020–21 made Alberta's enterprise income negligible. Still, table 4.2 confirms Alberta's exceptionalism based on its resource wealth

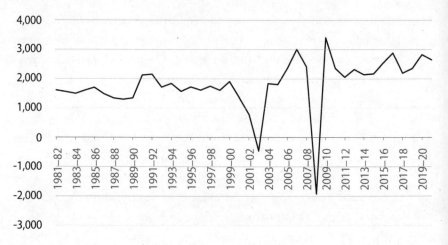

*Figure 4.2.* Investment income, 1981–82 to 2020–21 ($ millions)

*Sources*: Government of Alberta, "Historical Fiscal Summary" in *Annual Report: Government of Alberta 2020–21*, 12; Government of Alberta consolidated financial statements in annual reports (various years). All sources available from https://www .alberta.ca/government-and-ministry-annual-reports.aspx.

and its continuing political choice to rely on the sales of a non-renewable resource and investment income derived from setting some resource revenue aside. By presenting data from other provinces, I do not intend to show that these provinces are in better fiscal shape than Alberta. Rather, presenting this information is a means of illustrating that other provinces have policies that result in more balanced and broader sources of revenue, and Alberta politicians could consider these. Table 4.2 illustrates in particular how important the sales tax is for these other major provincial governments.

. As should be abundantly clear by now, Alberta does have a revenue problem—namely, that its revenue mix is unstable and highly dependent on the rise and fall of oil and gas prices. What's more, Alberta has been building this revenue problem into its legislation through changes such as those made to the Alberta Heritage Savings Trust Fund Act in 1996. Taken together, as the MacKinnon Report succinctly put it, this has made "budgeting in Alberta . . . challenging" (Blue Ribbon Panel on Alberta's Finances 2019, 12). As that report found, and as my analysis suggests, Alberta's revenue problem is structural. It has dogged the province since

Table 4.2. Revenue sources of selected provincial governments

| Percent of own-source revenue | Alberta | British Columbia | Ontario | Québec |
|---|---|---|---|---|
| Personal income tax | 35% | 23% | 26% | 37% |
| Corporate income tax | 9% | 10% | 12% | 9% |
| Sales tax | 0% | 16% | 21% | 23% |
| Other taxes | 16% | 21% | 20% | 9% |
| Resource revenue | 9% | 5% | 0% | 0% |
| Government enterprise | 0% | 8% | 5% | 5% |
| Investment income | 8% | 3% | 0% | 0% |
| Premiums, fees, and licenses | 12% | 9% | 9% | 5% |
| Other | 10% | 6% | 7% | 12% |
| Total own-source revenue | 100% | 100% | 100% | 100% |

Sources: Government of Alberta, *Annual Report: Government of Alberta 2020–21*, available from https://www.alberta.ca/government-and-ministry-annual-reports .aspx; Government of British Columbia, *Public Accounts 2020/21*, available from https://www2.gov.bc.ca/gov/content/governments/finances/public-accounts; Government of Ontario, *Public Accounts of Ontario: Annual Report and Consolidated Financial Statements 2020–2021*, available from https://www.ontario.ca/page/public -accounts-ontario-2020-21; Gouvernement du Québec, *Consolidated Financial Statements of the Gouvernement du Québec*, vol. 1, *Public Accounts 2019–2020*, http:// www.finances.gouv.qc.ca/documents/Comptespublics/fr/CPTFR_vol1-2019-2020 .pdf.

at least the mid-1960s. But revenue is only one side of the coin. Just because we do have a revenue problem doesn't mean we don't have a spending problem.

## Provincial Expenditure

Let's take a closer look at the Alberta government's major spending functions using the same analytical tool employed earlier: standard deviation. Figure 4.3 represents the same 1965–66 to 2020–21 time period used in figure 4.1, and illustrates in part the Klein-era reductions in spending between 1993 and 1996. These spending cuts targeted capital spending and departmental operating expenditures outside the health, education, and social services budgets. The figure also shows the explosion of

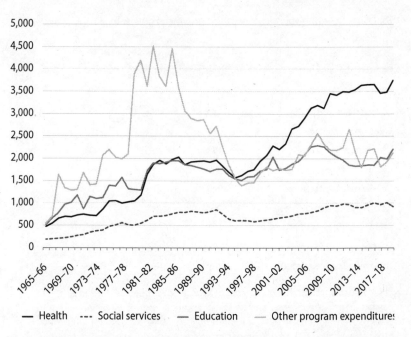

5,000
4,500
4,000
3,500
3,000
2,500
2,000
1,500
1,000
500
0

1965–66   1969–70   1973–74   1977–78   1981–82   1985–86   1989–90   1993–94   1997–98   2001–02   2005–06   2009–10   2013–14   2017–18

— Health   --- Social services   — Education   — Other program expenditure:

*Figure 4.3.* Major expenditures per capita, 1965–66 to 2020–21 (2002 $ millions)

*Sources*: Ronald Kneebone and Margarita Wilkins, "Canadian Provincial Government Budget Data—All Provinces Updated to 2019/20 and Some to 2020/21" (Excel spreadsheet), October 2021 version, available from University of Calgary School of Public Policy, "Research Data," http://www.policyschool.ca/publication-category/research-data/; Statistics Canada, "Table 18-10-0005-01: Consumer Price Index, Annual Average, Not Seasonally Adjusted," released 20 January 2021, https://doi.org/10.25318/1810000501-eng; Statistics Canada, "Table: 17-10-0009-01: Population Estimates on July 1st, by Age and Sex," released 29 September 2021, https://doi.org/10.25318/1710000501-eng.

spending in the health care sector relative to other sectors such as education and social services since 2000. What distinguishes spending patterns from revenue patterns are the relatively minor year-to-year changes in spending in each major expenditure envelope. Changes are especially muted in social services and education spending.

Table 4.3 shows the standard deviation calculations for the province's expenditure over the whole fifty-five-year period and for ten-year slices therein. The table shows that "other program expenditures" are the

*Table 4.3.* Standard deviation of Alberta government expenditure, 1965–66 to 2020–21

| Years | Health | Social services | Education | Other program expenditures |
|---|---|---|---|---|
| 1965–66 to 1974–75 | 0.080 | 0.058 | 0.106 | 0.381 |
| 1975–76 to 1984–85 | 0.109 | 0.044 | 0.103 | 0.232 |
| 1985–86 to 1994–95 | 0.029 | 0.042 | 0.023 | 0.066 |
| 1995–96 to 2004–05 | 0.036 | 0.015 | 0.050 | 0.053 |
| 2005–06 to 2014–15 | 0.032 | 0.025 | 0.025 | 0.069 |
| 2011–12 to 2020–21 | 0.016 | 0.026 | 0.030 | 0.078 |
| 1965–66 to 2020–21 | 0.069 | 0.0045 | 0.088 | 0.212 |

*Source*: Author's calculations based on Ronald Kneebone and Margarita Wilkins, "Canadian Provincial Government Budget Data—All Provinces Updated to 2019/20 and Some to 2020/21" (Excel spreadsheet), October 2021 version, available from University of Calgary School of Public Policy, "Research Data," http://www.policyschool.ca/publication-category/research-data/.

most volatile of the four major spending categories over the long term. It makes intuitive sense that the core programs of government—the health care, education, and social services ministries—would be less prone to wide fluctuations in spending because they are more likely to receive stable, predictable funding. Departments in the "other" category serve smaller population groups (e.g., farmers, business groups, construction firms) and are not considered core. Their pleas and requests for funding can be dismissed as less urgent or merely the products of self-interest, making them more prone to cutbacks. Such "other program expenditures" are therefore more discretionary—seen as more "optional"—than the core programs within the health, education, and social services ministries. Of these three less discretionary spending programs, social services have the least variation and education has the highest variation.

Table 4.4 compares the variability Alberta's major spending functions to that of its major revenue sources. The province's expenditures in its three core programs—health, education, and social services—are less

*Table 4.4.* Standard deviation of Alberta government revenue and expenditure, 1965–66 to 2020–21

| Expenditure | |
|---|---|
| Health | 0.069 |
| Social services | 0.045 |
| Education | 0.088 |
| Other program expenditures | 0.212 |
| **Revenue** | |
| Personal income tax | 0.103 |
| Corporate income tax | 0.209 |
| Nonrenewable resources | 0.261 |

*Source*: Author's calculations based on Ronald Kneebone and Margarita Wilkins, "Canadian Provincial Government Budget Data—All Provinces Updated to 2019/20 and Some to 2020/21" (Excel spreadsheet), October 2021 version, available from University of Calgary School of Public Policy, "Research Data," http://www.policyschool.ca/publication-category/research-data/.

variable than every major revenue source, and while "other" program spending is more volatile than PIT, it is less variable than both CIT and non-renewable resource revenue.

So, we know that Alberta's revenue is highly variable compared to its spending—but is Alberta's spending high? There is ample evidence to "prove" that, compared to other major province's, the answer to this question is "yes." However, one's ability to draw such a conclusion depends on the mathematical, comparative relationships selected and the time periods they analyze (McMillan 2015; Boessenkool and Eisen 2012; Boessenkool 2010; MacKinnon and Mintz 2017; Blue Ribbon Panel 2019; Ascah, Harrison, and Mueller 2019). In other words, while evidence exists, it is by no means definitive.

As with polling questions, the selection of facts and comparators cannot be assumed to be "value free." People have different points of view, and those points of view influence how they look at and look into certain questions. In the case of government spending, the inquiry may, for instance, be motivated by a desire to defend or reduce public sector employment, to raise or lower taxes, or to advocate for some other specific position.

Labour groups like to compare public spending to either GDP or personal disposable income. Business groups like to compare per capita spending and salaries of one provincial government to those of other provincial governments. Some analysts compare Alberta's spending levels against a provincial average; others prefer to compare Alberta spending or revenue with that of other major provinces (British Columbia, Ontario, and Québec) or against to Alberta's neighbours (Saskatchewan and British Columbia). It's easy to see how politicians could be confused by all the differing conclusions reached about the same spending or revenue numbers, but one thing is for sure: wages and spending have been spiralling upwards in Alberta for decades. Kevin Taft told me he expects that this will eventually "turn into a downward spiral. The wealth flowing into the private sector will start to decline, [which will] reduce the upward pressure on public sector wages." But this isn't necessarily a bad thing. Looking at comparative services between British Columbia and Alberta, Taft remarked, "I often ask myself if I go to British Columbia—Vancouver, Victoria, or whatever: Do I see perceptively worse public services there? The roads aren't worse, the cities are clean, the infrastructure's good. University of British Columbia and University of Victoria are excellent universities. Hospitals are good. You can run a province with lower spending and still do a very good job" (interview with author, 26 November 2018).

Experts delving into the jurisdictional comparisons soon discover that data availability, accounting peculiarities, time periods chosen, and widely varied government budget structures make it difficult to create meaningful longitudinal comparisons (Busby and Robson 2014; Kneebone and Wilkins 2016). Panel A of table 4.5 offers snapshot-in-time comparisons among Alberta, British Columbia, Ontario and, Québec for per capita spending based on 2019–20 and 2020–21 public accounts information.[2] Additional aggregate information is provided in panel B.

Table 4.5 confirms the view that Alberta spends more per capita compared to other major provinces—provinces with whom Alberta normally competes for investment and jobs.[3] However, one would be mistaken to think that the claim of cutting spending alone addresses the deeper question of Alberta's fiscal sustainability. Take, for instance, the claim that per capita spending in Alberta is too high because public sector wages have been historically, and unnecessarily, higher than the rest of the country (MacKinnon 2019, 44–50). Cut the wages, solve the spending problem, right?

Not necessarily—but this is not to say that the argument has no merit. One-half of operating spending goes to wages and benefits in Alberta. One reason typically given to justify high public sector wages is that Alberta's public sector employers must "compete" with Alberta's private sector, which is dominated by the high-paying oil and gas sector. Another often cited reason is that these high wages are necessary to compensate for higher costs of living in Alberta compared to other provinces. It is argued that these factors make it necessary to have higher public sector salaries to attract employees, including those from outside the province or country,

Table 4.5. Spending of selected provincial governments (current $)

| Panel A: Per capita spending of selected provinces, 2020–21 | | | | |
|---|---|---|---|---|
| Spending per capita | Alberta | British Columbia | Ontario | Québec (2019–20)* |
| Health[†] | 5,377 | 4,963 | 4,151 | 5,294 |
| Education | 3,198 | 2,897 | 2, 824 | 2,893 |
| Social services[†] | 1,339 | 1,510 | 1,177 | 1,237 |
| Agriculture, resource management, and economic development | 729 | 812 | 1,239 | 774 |
| General government | 637 | 759 | 299 | – |
| Protection of persons and property | 445 | 438 | 340 | 389 |
| Transportation, communications, and utilities | 341 | 651 | – | 582 |
| Regional planning and development | 557 | – | – | – |
| Recreation and culture | 72 | – | – | 192 |
| Environment | 187 | – | – | 676 |
| Housing | 63 | – | – | – |
| Debt servicing costs | 562 | 528 | 839 | 895 |
| Other | 90 | 551 | – | 399 |
| Total | 13,597 | 13,109 | 10,869 | 13,332 |

**Panel B: Total spending, population, and total per capita spending, 2020–21**

| Spending | Alberta | British Columbia | Ontario | Québec |
|---|---|---|---|---|
| Total spending ($ billions) | 60,099 | 67,624 | 181,297 | 114,364 |
| Population (1 July 2020) | 4,420,029 | 5,158,728 | 14,745,712 | 8,578,300 |
| Per capita total spending ($) | 13,597 | 13,109 | 12,295 | 13,332 |

*Sources*: Government of Alberta, *Annual Report: Government of Alberta 2020–21*, available from https://www.alberta.ca/government-and-ministry-annual-reports .aspx; Government of British Columbia, *Public Accounts 2020/21*, available from https://www2.gov.bc.ca/gov/content/governments/finances/public-accounts; Government of Ontario, *Public Accounts of Ontario: Annual Report and Consolidated Financial Statements 2020–2021*, available from https://www.ontario.ca/page/public -accounts-ontario-2020-21; Gouvernement du Québec, *Consolidated Financial Statements of the Gouvernement du Québec*, vol. 1, *Public Accounts 2019–2020*, http://www.finances.gouv.qc.ca/documents/Comptespublics/fr/CPTFR_vol1 -2019-2020.pdf; Statistics Canada, "Table 17-10-0009-01: Population Estimates on July 1st, by Age and Sex," released 29 September 2021, https://doi.org/10.25318/ 1710000501-eng.

\* 2020–21 per capita spending data were not available at time of writing for Québec; 2019–20 data has been used instead.

† The categories of health care and social services are combined in the Québec data. This combined data has been recorded in the "health" category for Québec. The social services category for Québec shows Ministry of Family spending.

to the public service. Arguments about high cost of living in Alberta tend, however, to ignore the absence of a sales tax, the absence of health-care premiums, lower marginal tax rates, and higher income tax exemption levels. In other words, these arguments tend to leave out the fact that Albertans pay very little in taxes compared to other major provinces. Add to this the fact that Alberta's housing costs today are lower than those in Vancouver, Toronto, Montréal, and Ottawa, and the cost-of-living argument is on thin ice. Perhaps Albertans in the public sector *are* paid too much.

Mueller (2019) disagrees. He has argued that while there are some areas where public sector pay appears to be disproportionately high (notably in municipalities), the "excess compensation" argument is overblown. Using real earnings for public administration, education, health care, and social assistance, Mueller has shown that while Alberta public sector workers' earnings relative to Ontario, British Columbia, and Québec have indeed been higher in the past, the difference as measured in 2018 has become much smaller (26–31). Moreover, while Alberta spending per capita is, in general, high relative to other provinces, the gap has been narrowing, in particular between Alberta, Québec, and British Columbia.

## A Spending or Revenue Problem?

While there are conflicting data on the sources and the extent of spending excesses, one cannot fairly say we do not have a spending problem. Rather, the straightforward answer to the conflicting data is that Alberta has both a spending and a revenue problem. Alberta's revenue is volatile and unpredictable. Its per capita spending, though much less volatile than its revenue, tends to be higher than that of other provinces.

The relative stability of spending is in large part due to the fact that spending is by and large more controllable than revenue. This is perhaps why spending is regarded by conservative governments as the source of the problem: it's easier to solve a problem over which you have control than one over which you don't. However, this doesn't mean the *need* for spending is easily controlled. In practical terms, spending proceeds incrementally as new programs are instituted to respond to new needs. Staff must be hired and operating rooms must be properly furnished. Citizens rely on government programs and expect services to be provided, often in unpredictable waves. Since users of government services vote, politicians must respond to demands that private sector organizations would reject unless they saw a financial benefit. In short, since spending cannot be adjusted dramatically from year to year without political consequences, it stands to reason that governments should have a revenue strategy that ensures a set of steady, predictable revenue sources to avoid cutting services and incurring the wrath of the citizenry.

Figure 4.4 maps Alberta's total per capita spending and revenue adjusted for inflation. The figure illustrates the volatile revenue streams Alberta governments have been unable to effectively manage. Rather than save a significant proportion of non-renewable resource revenue and grow the savings through reinvestment of earnings, successive

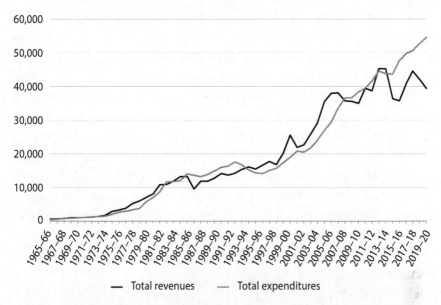

Figure 4.4. Alberta's total revenue and expenditure, 1965–66 to 2020–21 (current $ millions)

Source: Ronald Kneebone and Margarita Wilkins, "Canadian Provincial Government Budget Data—All Provinces Updated to 2019/20 and Some to 2020/21" (Excel spreadsheet), October 2021 version, available from University of Calgary School of Public Policy, "Research Data," http://www.policyschool.ca/publication-category/research-data/.

governments have chosen to build the province's financial foundation on the sands of a volatile revenue base, expensive government infrastructure, and program spending that is vulnerable to cuts when resource prices fall. Increases in revenue, usually the result of rising oil and gas prices, draw spending up, too. As resource revenue levels off, this higher spending produces budget deficits, creating fiscal pressures on provincial treasurers. This levelling-off of revenue is typically (though not always) followed by revenue declines, spending cuts, and rising debt.[4] As figure 4.4 shows, this pattern of revenue push / spending pull occurred in the late 1970s, the beginning of the 2000s, and briefly during the short Redford period from 2011 to 2014. Rising energy prices lead to a rush of funding requests as predictable as the spring thaw. As we used to say in Alberta Treasury, "When things go well, they go *really* well—when things are bad, they are *really* bad."

Figure 4.5 gives us another way of visualizing the push-pull dynamic of spending and revenue in Alberta. The graph shows the degree to which the change in Alberta's surplus or deficit (whether that change is positive or negative) is affected by a change in Alberta's revenue stream or spending structure (again, whether positive or negative) between 1965 and 2020. The predominance of the black bar in any given year records a period of either significant revenue decline or revenue increase. In Alberta, such decline or increase is principally associated with fluctuations in oil and/ or natural gas price changes. The predominance of a grey bar in any given year shows a period of spending pressure or spending reduction. Taken as a whole, figure 4.5 is a long-term picture of the degree to which Alberta's debt situation depends on revenue versus spending.

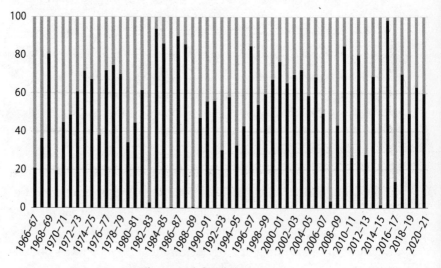

Figure 4.5. Percentage change in Alberta's deficit tied to revenue or expenditures, 1965–66 to 2020–21 (2002 $)

Source: Author's calculations using data from Ronald Kneebone and Margarita Wilkins, "Canadian Provincial Government Budget Data—All Provinces Updated to 2019/20 and Some to 2020/21" (Excel spreadsheet), October 2021 version, available from University of Calgary School of Public Policy, "Research Data," http://www.policyschool.ca/ publication-category/research-data/.

Fifty-four percent of the bar space shows changes in Alberta's deficit tied to revenue; the remaining 46 percent shows changes tied to expenditures. This is consistent with our finding above that revenue sources are more volatile than spending. But these percentages don't tell the whole story; they mask the cumulative dollar amounts at play over the full fifty-five-year period. Total year-to-year revenue changes (i.e., the absolute value of the increases and decreases) were $94.5 billion (59.3 percent) with expenditure changes totalling $64.8 billion (41.3 percent). These findings underline the critical importance that revenue plays in the overall dynamics of the province's income statement and balance sheet.

It's not, then, just a matter of understanding that we have both a spending and a revenue problem; it's a matter of understanding how these two problems are intertwined. Of course, electoral competition remains ideological and depends on political parties presenting simple, compelling narratives to differentiate their "visions" from those of other political parties. In some governments—for example, the Getty and Notley periods of 1985–92 and 2015–19, respectively—the answer was increasing spending. This led to accumulating deficits, increasing public debt, and, consequently, rising debt servicing costs. In the Stelmach-Prentice period (2006–15), drawdowns of the Stabilization/Contingency Account allowed the government to respond to spending pressure while ignoring the need for adjustments to spending and/or revenue. This drawdown in savings continued for a short time under the Notley administration as well, until these savings evaporated. At the time of writing, the UCP are in government. The combination of rising debt servicing costs and the public's aversion to debt and taxation has led the UCP to convey their "vision" by first freezing then cutting spending, notably on post-secondary education—this despite the fact that it is Alberta's volatile revenue sources that account for a majority of cases in which the province has moved between surplus and deficit. Around we go again in the push-pull dynamic of spending and revenue. We have seen this movie before, and they seem to just keep coming out with sequels.

The thing to note is that these simple, political narratives all have something in common: They're one-sided. Alberta's fiscal dilemma, however, is not. The problem runs much deeper than just spending or revenue, and thus cannot be solved by simplistic fixes that appeal to only one side of the issue. The way we have allowed our spending structure to be constantly dictated by our revenue mix is a systemic issue. Those who put forward simplistic platforms to address the issue, then, also have something in common: their willful ignorance of the endemic problems in Alberta's larger fiscal picture.

## Alberta's Savings Problem

On top of everything, when Alberta does run into tough times under its current fiscal policy structure (i.e., when its problem spending can't be covered by its problem revenue) it has a habit of spending its savings—that is, when it has any savings to spend. In 1976, Premier Lougheed introduced the Alberta Heritage Savings Trust Fund, a public savings account with the stated goal of saving a certain amount of oil and gas revenue for future generations. This is, in principle, a great idea, especially for a province that relies on volatile revenue. However, Alberta's fiscal propensity to spend was already too deeply entrenched for the Heritage Fund to really develop to its full potential. By 1982, Lougheed abandoned his vision of an intergenerational savings fund, adopting instead a "spend now, pay later" fiscal philosophy. This was accomplished by rebranding the Heritage Fund as a "rainy day" account—and it was raining just prior to the 1982 election. Consequently, the fund was used to finance significant increases in expenditure in 1982–83. For the first time, the government withdrew all investment income from the Heritage Fund, thereby preventing the fund from growing through reinvestment of earnings. Had Premier Lougheed left the investment income to compound without any further resource revenue deposits, my calculations show that the Heritage Fund would be worth something in the order of $260 billion today. Lougheed's new approach to mining the Heritage Fund to make up for revenue deficits rather than adjusting the province's revenue mix or spending structure was inherited by his successor, Don Getty, and later governments.

Between 1947 and 2020, according to data from the Canadian Association of Petroleum Producers, Alberta's oil and gas sector producers had cumulative revenue of $2.07 trillion.[5] In the same period, Alberta received $205 billion in royalties, for 10 percent return. These cumulative figures suggest Alberta could have accessed a bigger piece of the revenue but demurred from taking a larger share.[6] The biggest stumbling block to receiving a higher share has been the industry's case that unless royalties remained competitive, industry will not continue to invest. But even at this rate of return, if the Government of Alberta had continued to place 30 percent of its resource revenue in the Heritage Fund and keep all the reinvested earnings there, the fund would be worth over $400 billion today.[7]

More than just spending and revenue problems, then, Alberta has a two-part savings problem. On the one hand, because it relies so heavily on resource royalties to balance its budget—and because it keeps those royalties low—it doesn't contribute much to its savings in the first place. On the other hand, because of its general lack of fiscal discipline, the province never seems to leave its savings to accrue for very long. As a result—as we've seen with Kenney's UCP government—the province ends up essentially living from oil paycheque to oil paycheque and adjusting its spending in kind. Having inherited an unruly trinity of volatile revenue sources, a paltry sum of savings to address current budget needs, and an accounting policy that arguably overstates resource revenues, Kenney's government is back at the game of cutting spending in a time of need—what Finance Minister Travis Toews (2020) has called the "triple black swan event" of COVID-19, oil price correction, and an economic shutdown. The government is hoping against hope for its revenue luck to change.

As far as savings are concerned, I believe Alberta's savings project has failed to fulfill its original mandate of being an intergenerational savings account meant to meet the province's fiscal needs when the oil has run out. The Heritage Fund has provided flexibility for fiscal policy purposes, but its size is now less than one-third of Alberta's current spending. It may be a source of pride for some Albertans but if the Heritage Fund is no longer an intergenerational savings vehicle, it should be wound down.

## Solving the Dilemma

Fixing Alberta's fiscal dilemma requires a balanced approach that ensures that spending accomplishes its intended objectives and that there is a sufficient and stable revenue stream available to pay for government services. There is also a need to thoroughly examine revenue sources with a view to making a more resilient revenue stream, which essentially means making revenue more stable. And that entails looking at a sales tax.

A balanced approach is something new for Alberta—a whole new fiscal policy culture. Until now, this culture has been marked by an empty, binary debate about whether the province's fiscal challenges lie in a problem of spending or revenue, and a series of political sleights of hand that cloud the precarity of Alberta's fiscal situation. Fiscal policy during the Klein years was helped out by rising natural gas prices and the effects of very loose monetary policy of the early 2000s. The Kenney government has continued to stress its belief in cutting spending, maintaining low personal and corporate taxes, and trying to attract outside capital investment to the oil industry as the means of eradicating deficits. These strategies ignore the evidence presented in this chapter, which shows that revenue diversification to stabilize spending is at least as pressing an issue as lowering taxes and cutting spending. They also ignore urgent and unrelenting evidence that international financial capital is divesting from fossil fuels. The non-renewable resource that Alberta relies on so heavily as a revenue source may well disappear from the global market before oil dries up in the ground. Alberta governments will be forced to make difficult fiscal and economic choices in the very near term as climate change becomes an ever-greater factor in global investment decisions.

Alberta's fiscal solutions require a top-to-bottom review of its revenue, spending, and savings policies with the objective of ensuring fiscal stability and long-term fiscal sustainability. Alberta's public service has gone through enough feast-famine cycles already—it is time to reimagine a new future.

## Notes

1   An attachment to a 14 March 1980 memo from Deputy Provincial
     Treasurer A. F. Collins to Treasurer Lou Hyndman with the subject heading
     "Royalty Tax Credit Abuses" revealed that five companies paid 24 percent
     of gross tax collections, all of which were oil and gas corporations. Ten

corporations paid 36 percent of gross tax collections, all of them also oil and gas corporations. The situation today would likely be similar. See Lou Hyndman Papers, PR1986.0245, box 38, file 563, Provincial Archives of Alberta.

2   Public accounts are subject to an annual audit by the provincial auditor. The main differences between public accounts preparation are the results of exclusion or inclusion of entities such as government enterprises or provincial agencies such as universities and colleges.

3   The same conclusion is reached using other data sources. See, for example, the RBC Economics data used in Ascah, Harrison, and Mueller (2019).

4   Refer, for example, to the graph entitled "Reductions in Expenditures Lag Reductions in Revenue" (Premier's Council for Economic Strategy 2017, 98). This process is evident in the following periods: 1979–82, 1999–2002, 2005–2009, and 2012–14. Often, the periods end just around an election date.

5   The Canadian Association of Petroleum Producers compiles data at https://www.capp.ca/resources/statistics/. See, in particular, "Value of Producers' Sales: Alberta" and "Net Cash Expenditures of the Petroleum Industry: Alberta."

6   This did not include experimental crude and Alberta ethane until 1986. Oil sands include bitumen, but do not represent the true value of all synthetic crude oil.

7   In 1982–83, the deposit of 30 percent of non-renewable resource revenue to the Heritage Fund was reduced to 15 percent and then eliminated in 1987–88. There were extraordinary additions to the fund between 2005–06 to 2007–08 of $2.92 billion when natural gas prices were extraordinarily high. Since 1996–97, there has been $4.3 billion of investment income retained in the fund in an attempt to make it "inflation proof." See Government of Alberta (2021, 17–18).

## References

Ascah, Robert L. 2021. "Alberta's Public Debt: Entering the Third Crisis." Preprint, submitted July 2021. https://www.policyschool.ca/wp-content/uploads/2021/07/AF22_AB-Public-Debt_Ascah.pdf.

Ascah, Robert L., Trevor Harrison, and Richard Mueller. 2019. *Cutting Through the Blue Ribbon: A Balanced Look at Alberta's Finances*. Edmonton: Parkland Institute. https://www.parklandinstitute.ca/cutting_through_the_blue_ribbon.

Blue Ribbon Panel on Alberta's Finances. 2019. *Report and Recommendations: Blue Ribbon Panel on Alberta's Finances*, chaired by Janice MacKinnon,

August 2019. Available from https://open.alberta.ca/publications/report-and
-recommendations-blue-ribbon-panel-on-alberta-s-finances.

Boessenkool, Ken. 2010. "Does Alberta Have a Spending Problem?" *University of
Calgary School of Public Policy Publications* 2, no. 1. https://doi.org/10.11575/
sppp.v3i0.42347.

Boessenkool, Ken, and Ben Eisen. 2012. "Public Sector Wage Growth in Alberta."
*University of Calgary School of Public Policy Publications* 5, no. 1. https://doi
.org/10.11575/sppp.v5i0.42372.

Busby, C., and W. Robson. 2014. *Credibility on the (Bottom) Line: The Fiscal
Accountability of Canada's Senior Governments, 2013*. Commentary no. 404.
Toronto: C. D. Howe Institute.

Government of Alberta. 2021. *Alberta Heritage Savings Trust Fund: Annual Report
2020–21*. Edmonton: Government of Alberta. Available from https://open
.alberta.ca/publications/0702-9721.

MacKinnon, Janice, and Jack Mintz. 2017. "Putting the Alberta Budget on a New
Trajectory." *University of Calgary School of Public Policy Publications* 10, no. 26.
http://doi.org/10.11575/sppp.v10i0.42498.

McMillan, Melville. 2015. *Hard Math, Harder Choices: Alberta's Budget Reality*.
Edmonton: Parkland Institute. https://www.parklandinstitute.ca/hard_math
_harder_choices.

Orr, Leanna. 2020. "AIMCo's $3 billion Volatility Trading Blunder." *Institutional
Investor*, 21 April 2020.

Premier's Council for Economic Strategy. 2017. *Shaping Alberta's Future: Report
of the Premier's Council for Economic Strategy*, chaired by David Emerson, May
2011. Available from https://open.alberta.ca/dataset/report-of-the-premiers
-council-for-economic-strategy.

Toews, Travis. 2020. "First Quarter Fiscal Update and Annual Report." Alberta
Legislature. Recorded 27 August 2020. YouTube video. https://youtu.be/
yDdnmxWEv74.

Uebelein, Kevin. 2020. "A Message from Kevin Uebelein AIMCo Chief Executive
Officer." AIMCo.ca. https://www.aimco.ca/insights/a-message-from-the-ceo.

PART II

# The Least Painful Solution

Why a Sales Tax Makes Sense

# 5    Alberta Sales Tax

## An Inevitability and an Opportunity to Reset

*Melville McMillan*

Albertans are accustomed to enjoying quality public services and low taxes thanks to the substantial contributions that non-renewable resource revenues—which I will refer to simply as resource revenues—have made to the provincial budget. Those contributions, however, have decreased to a fraction of earlier levels—a drop in revenue that has left a substantial hole in the province's finances. Will resource revenues increase to close the budget gap and restore the Alberta Advantage? We can certainly hope for such a recovery but, despite the recent improvements, the prospects are uncertain and the projected magnitudes are insufficient to solve the problem in the long run.[1] In a low resource revenue environment, Albertans need to reassess their fiscal options.

The effective contributions of the provincial government's resource revenues to Alberta's households since 1972 are reported in figure 5.1. The graph shows the share of household incomes that the government's resource revenues would have comprised if, for example, they were paid out as "dividends" to Albertans. Of course, that was not done; the funds were actually retained by the province to finance public services and reduce the taxes paid by provincial taxpayers. However, by comparing resource revenues to household income in this way, we are able to look

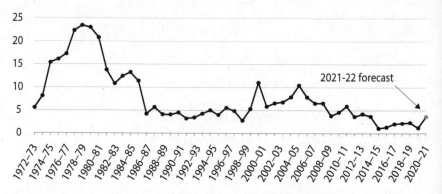

*Figure 5.1.* Non-renewable resource revenue as percentage of household incomes, 1972–73 to 2020–21 and 2021–22 forecast

*Source*: Non-renewable resource revenues are from Government of Alberta annual reports (various years), available from https://www.alberta.ca/government-and -ministry-annual-reports.aspx. Household incomes are from Statistics Canada (2021). Percentages are author's calculations.

at the impact of resource revenues in a way that accounts for population growth, inflation, and real income growth over time. Also, because citizens pay out of income for the bulk of public services through taxes and a variety of other levies (e.g., charges, fees, and licenses), comparison to household income serves to indicate the impacts of provincial government resource revenues on their net of tax income. In addition, household income is a major determinant of demand for public (as well as private) goods and services and, since wages and salaries make up the majority of household income and of government costs, it is also an indicator of the cost of providing public goods and services.[2]

Two features stand out in figure 5.1. First is that resource revenues are quite volatile, as the up and down movements of the graph demonstrate. This is a widely recognized fact. The second is that there has been a downward trend in resource revenues, which have failed to grow as fast as population and average household income. They have, therefore, become less able to contribute to government revenues. Until the 1985–86 fiscal year, resource revenues averaged 15.3 percent of household incomes. Over the next fourteen years, they averaged only 4.4 percent. For almost a decade at the beginning of the 2000s, they saw some recovery in their contribution, averaging 7.3 percent. When the global financial crisis hit in 2008–09, Alberta saw a drop in natural gas prices, due in part to the emergence of fracking technology and shifting locations of energy developments. This resulted in resource revenues dropping to 4.4 percent of household incomes. The collapse of oil prices in 2014 and 2015, and the resulting industry problems led to resource revenues dropping again, this time to an average of 1.8 percent of household incomes from 2015–16 to 2019–20. The COVID-19 crisis led to resource revenues falling to 1.2 percent of household income in the 2020–21 fiscal year. Importantly, figure 5.1 shows that resource revenues between 2015 and 2020 have been the lowest they've ever been relative to household incomes (and, just as importantly, to the government's budget) since 1973. However, oil and natural gas prices have increased markedly during 2021 and, as of August 2021, the provincial government's resource revenues for 2021–22 are projected to be more than three times the 2020–21 level (Government of Alberta 2021a). Nevertheless, that resource revenues will only amount to 3.8 percent of household income.

The impacts of these changes on provincial finances are substantial. While the longer story is interesting, the focus in this chapter is the period post-2000. As resource revenues improved following the turn of the century, the Alberta government accumulated a Sustainability/ Capital/Contingency Fund that reached $17 billion in 2007–08. Thereafter, those funds were drawn down to support government operating and capital expenditures. Borrowing grew during the recession, and the province ran a sequence of (typically small to modest) deficits until 2015–16, when another collapse of oil prices further negatively impacted the provincial budget. From 2015–16 on, deficits have been large and the extent of the province's borrowing has greatly expanded. The 2020 COVID-19 pandemic has created an additional fiscal shock. The 2020–21 deficit rose from a projected $7.3 billion to an actual $17 billion and the total taxpayer-supported debt reached $93 billion by the end of the 31 March 2021 fiscal year (Government of Alberta 2021a, 2021c). Illustrative of the deteriorating fiscal situation, the province's net financial assets have fallen from a positive $31.8 billion to a negative $59.5 billion since 2008–09—a decline of $91.4 billion, or $20,500 per capita at the 2021 population.

Will resource revenues recover and restore budget balance without further taxes or substantial expenditure reductions? Despite the 2021 improvement, the prospects are not optimistic. Projections appear in figure 5.2 for fiscal 2021–22 forward. To demonstrate the unpredictability of resource revenues, two projections appear for the years 2021–22 to 2026–27. The lower of the two is a projection I generated in the fall of 2020. At that time, the province had provided no post-COVID-19 budget projections or economic assumptions, so I generated projections of resource revenues and household incomes to 2026–27 from other sources.[3] Fiscal 2026 is the year that Trevor Tombe (2020) expects that the Alberta government would be able to balance its budget without increasing taxes, if it continues to freeze expenditures (excluding those related to COVID-19 and recovery from the pandemic) at $56 billion.

The upper line is the six-year projection based on the Government of Alberta's (2021a) projection that 2021–22 resource revenues will be $9.76 billion. At the time of writing, the province has not yet provided projections beyond 2021–22. Resource revenues might improve but, given that oil futures indicate that oil prices are expected to decline to

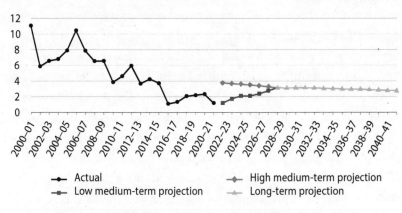

Figure 5.2. Non-renewable resource revenue (actual and projected) as percentage of household incomes, 2000–01 to 2040–41

Source: Projections from fiscal 2022 to fiscal 2026 are the author's own. Projections from fiscal 2027 on are based on Tombe (2018).

$65 per barrel over the next three years, resource revenues might not be sustained (ARC Energy Research Institute 2021). Given the uncertainty, I simply assume that resource revenues will continue to be $10 billion each year until 2026–27.

The two projections imply quite different medium-term futures, but both lead to the same end. The more optimistic forecast is positive in that it implies that Alberta avoids a slow resource revenue recovery and a prolonged period of exceptionally low resource revenues. However, both projections lead to Tombe's 2027–28 projection. At that time, resource revenues are expected to amount to 3.15 percent of household income—still well below pre-2015 levels. Hence, it appears unlikely that non-renewable resource revenues will recover to levels experienced during the first decade of the century when the economy boomed and provincial government budget surpluses were the norm.[4]

What about the long term? While resource revenues are notoriously difficult to predict, Trevor Tombe (2018) has ventured a look at Alberta's fiscal future to 2040. Figure 5.2 shows the predicted contributions of resource revenues relative to household incomes to 2040 using my projections from 2021–22 to 2026–27 and Tombe's projections from 2027–28 on. The graph also shows the percentages back to 2000, for comparison.[5] The projections assume that a restoration of the energy market and improved resource revenues would be accompanied by improvements in household incomes.

As figure 5.2 shows, the long-term projections for the contributions of resource revenues are rather gloomy. Resource revenues as a percentage of household incomes are not predicted to increase beyond the government's projected 2021–22 level of 3.8 percent. Indeed, under the more optimistic medium-term projections (which assume that resource revenues are steady at $10 billion per year to 2026–27), the percentage simply gradually declines to 2.8 percent in 2040–41. From 2027–28 to 2040–41, the average is only 3.0 percent. This is somewhat less than one-half the 6.4 percent average from 2000–01 to 2014–15 and about two-thirds of the average from 2009–10 to 2014–15, with the latter being a period during which the province was already experiencing fiscal problems. This long-term projection is even well below the 4.4 percent average experienced during the lows of the late 1980s and throughout the 1990s (see figure 5.1).

Thus, these projections suggest that growing resource revenues alone will not restore the fiscal comfort Alberta enjoyed before 2015–16.

Projections are uncertain and are the product of the underlying assumptions. As is typical, a range of assumptions were used in deriving the long-term projections presented here. The 2027–28 to 2040–41 projections reported in figure 5.2 are the average of eight specifications. Those eight are the result of Tombe's (2018) baseline and optimistic resource revenue projections in combination with four of my household income projections. It is also interesting to look at the range of outcomes that the set of specifications imply. That range is determined primarily by the difference in the assumptions about resource revenues.[6]

Figure 5.3 presents the high and low projections of resource revenues relative to household incomes for the years 2027–28 to 2040–41 along with, for perspective, the medium-term projections for the previous five years (as outlined in figure 5.2) and the actual levels from 2015–16 to 2020–21 (as outlined in figure 5.1). The low long-term projection line links to the low medium-term projection shown in figure 5.2 in 2027–28. The low long-term projection for 2027–28 is actually, at 2.84 percent, the highest level of that series. It then declines to 2.45 percent by 2040–41.

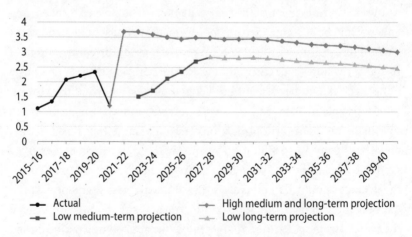

Figure 5.3. Non-renewable resource revenue (actual and projected) as percentage of household incomes, 2015–16 to 2040–41

Source: Long-term projections are based on Tombe (2018).

Over the thirteen-year long-term projection period, resource revenues average 2.68 percent of household incomes in the low projection scenario.

The high projection scenario looks rather different. It starts with the sharp increase in resource revenues projected in August 2021 for 2022–23, which are assumed to continue to 2026–27 (Government of Alberta 2021a). That medium-term projection transitions smoothly into the beginning of the long-term high projection in 2027–28, which is the beginning here of Tombe's optimistic projections. Though optimistic and being a considerable improvement from the six years of fiscal 2015 to fiscal 2020, the 3.5 percent level in 2027–28 is still modest compared to the percentages before fiscal 2015. In addition, while the percentage is projected to almost be maintained until 2031–32, it thereafter declines gradually to 3.0 percent in 2040–41. The average over the thirteen years is 3.29 percent.

The differences between the low and high projections are not dramatic. Indeed, they are probably disappointingly small, especially given that even the high estimate is only about half of the 6.4 percent level that resource revenues generated over the first fifteen years of the century prior to the 2015–16 recession. Hence, even if resource revenues considerably exceed baseline expectations, they will still be insufficient to generate enough provincial government revenues to match even the moderate, let alone the high, levels of the past. Hence, it appears that even in recovery Alberta will be facing an extended period of relatively low resource revenues. During this time, resource revenues will be unable to contribute nearly as generously to provincial budgets as they have previously.

It is possible that future resource revenues might exceed current expectations and, specifically, Tombe's (2018) projections post-2021–22. For one thing, as Tombe notes, his projections do not include (or do not fully include) the transition of oil sands projects from pre- to post-payout phases of the royalty system because of a lack of information. For another, Tombe is not the only one making projections. In 2017, the Canadian Energy Research Institute projected oil sands (bitumen) royalties to 2036 (Millington 2017, figure E7). Those estimates had royalties exceeding $20 billion in 2023. It's worth noting, however, that this amount was about twice the $10.4 billion that the province projected for that year in its "Path to Balance" in the 2018 budget (Government of Alberta 2018, 86).[7] More recently (although it does not include projections of government revenues), the Canadian Energy Research Institute also put forward a less rosy view, projecting oil sands production to 2039, with two of three scenarios allowing for setbacks in long-term output (Millington 2020a, 2020b).[8] Also, the US Energy Information Administration in its *Annual Energy Outlook 2020* reduced its nominal forecasts of West Texas Intermediate oil prices for the 2021 to 2040 time period by an average of $27.28, from a twenty-year average of $124.10 in 2018 to $96.81.[9] In its *Annual Energy Outlook 2021*, the Energy Information Administration's reference case projected oil prices returning to 2019 levels ($57 per barrel) after 2025. Clearly, projections can differ widely.[10] For consistency, the analysis here relies on Tombe's (2018) estimates.

What impact might lower resource revenues have upon provincial government expenditures in the absence of generating additional revenues (i.e., taxes) if the budget is to be balanced? The answer is substantial spending cuts. Since 2000, Alberta's program expenditures have averaged 21.7 percent of household incomes with little year-to-year variation. Resource revenues contributed an average of 6.4 percent of that 21.7 percent (or just under one-third) before 2015–16. If future resource revenues amount to 3.0 percent of household income rather than 6.4 percent, that implies a revenue gap of 3.4 percent of household income that must be met by expenditure reductions in order to balance the provincial budget. That decrease alone implies that a reduction of 15.7 percent in program expenditures is needed if additional revenues are not to be raised from other sources. However, larger debt requires that more interest also be paid, which means that, for the budget to be balanced, program expenditure must be reduced further. Using 2022–23 as an example, additional interest will increase the demand for funds by at least 1.0 percent of household income. Combined, the loss of resource revenues plus the higher interest costs would necessitate a 20.3 percent reduction in program spending (i.e., to 17.3 percent of household incomes) in order to balance the budget by 2022–23.

The UCP government laid out a plan in its October 2019 and February 2020 budgets to achieve budget balance in 2022–23 (Government of Alberta 2019, 2020b). Taking the findings of the MacKinnon Report as justification (Blue Ribbon Panel on Alberta's Finances 2019), the plan was (and still appears to be) to hold total expenses constant at approximately

$56 billion.[11] The COVID-19 crisis has upset those plans, but the subsequent budget documents and accompanying pronouncements suggest that post-2021–22, the expenditure freeze will effectively continue, though the timing of budget balance will be delayed (Government of Alberta 2020a; 2021a; 2021c, 7 para. 5).[12] Tombe (2020) predicts that this strategy could result in budget balance in 2026–27.

Overlooking the blip due to COVID-19 and recovery plan expenses in 2020–21 and 2021–22, what are the consequences of freezing total expenditures? That is, what would happen to the expenditures that fund public goods and services for Albertans if total expenses are held constant at approximately $56 billion until 2026–27? To answer these questions, we first have to account for the fact that population will continue to grow—specifically, from 4.43 million in 2020 to an estimated 4.76 million in 2026 (based upon Alberta's expected medium-term population growth path). Over that time, per capita program expenditures would decline from $12,576 to $10,832 (a nominal reduction of 14 percent). At the same time, we must consider that prices will continue to increase. Accounting for inflation, real per capita program expenditures would fall to $9,503 in 2020 dollars (a 24 percent drop). Household incomes will also change over the six years. Comparing program expenditures to predicted household incomes, the percentage would decline from 21.8 percent to 16.8 percent (a 23 percent drop). The consequences of balancing the budget by freezing total spending for a sustained period, then, are large reductions in real program expenditures and thus in the provincial services available to Alberta residents.

Given the current plans, how might Alberta's program spending compare with that in other provinces? Here, the comparison is limited to looking forward to 2023–24 because that is the year to which several provinces forecast revenues and expenditures.[13] Assuming that Alberta is back on its spending target path in 2023–24 and it and other provinces are past their pandemic-related expenditures, Alberta in 2023–24 plans to spend $12,191 per capita (in nominal dollars) on programs. Interestingly, this amount is essentially equal to British Columbia's planned expenditure of $12,361 per person in that year.[14] The comparison with British Columbia is of interest because it is one of the three "big" provinces with which the MacKinnon Report made comparisons, the others being Ontario and

Québec (Blue Ribbon Panel on Alberta's Finances 2019). Québec anticipates 2023–24 spending of $14,174 per person. There is no 2023–24 Ontario forecast in the November 2021 tables, but the Royal Bank of Canada September 2020 report recorded $10,231 per capita for 2022–23.[15] Thus, by 2023–24 Alberta would achieve program spending per person equal to the average per capita spending in the other three big provinces.[16] In addition, it is very likely that by 2026–27 the spending freeze will result in only Ontario spending less per capita than Alberta (and Alberta might even be lower than Ontario). Making interprovincial comparisons through the lens of household income provides further insight. Program spending as a percentage of household incomes in Alberta has been essentially equal to that in British Columbia and Ontario extending back to at least 2005–07 (McMillan 2018). Typically, program expenditures in Alberta (at about 21.7 percent) represent essentially the same share of household incomes as those in the two lowest-spending provinces. In the other seven provinces, the shares have been much larger, averaging 29.1 percent. Pursuing an expenditure freeze to 2026–27 would reduce Alberta's program expenditure share to 16.8 percent of household income, or about 20 percent lower than recent levels in British Columbia and Ontario.

How might Albertans respond to substantial reductions in provincial government expenditures and services in a persistent low-resource-revenue environment? If resource revenues materialize much as projected, and alternative revenues (e.g., expanded tax revenues) are not employed, anticipated real reductions in program expenditures in the order of 20 to 25 percent will be necessary to balance the budget.[17] The idea that Albertans will prefer reductions of this magnitude seems remote for various reasons. One reason is that such cuts would leave Alberta—a high-income (if not the highest-income) province and definitely the province with the lowest tax—at the bottom of the provincial spending ladder. Another is that Alberta tested low spending during the early Klein years when public program expenditures reached a low of 19 percent of household incomes in 1998–99, but that level was abandoned within two years to move closer to the 21.7 percent post-2000 average. The estimated budget-balancing cuts would reduce program expenditures to about 17 percent of household incomes, a level that Albertans have not experienced within the last fifty years at least. Currently, Albertans are being asked to absorb the entire reduction in resource revenues as a reduction in provincial services. Experience suggests that it is unlikely that, at least after adjusting fully to the alternatives, Albertans will prefer that option. Consumer theory supports the argument. A decrease in resource revenues effectively increases the tax price (or tax cost) of provincial services. Consumer behaviour suggests that when faced with a higher price of an important product in the budget, they normally reduce the consumption of that product somewhat but also reduce expenditures on other products to some degree. Not all of the cut is made to expenditures on the more expensive product. In the public finance context, this suggests that citizens will prefer some reduction in government goods and services in combination with some reduction in private goods and services—that is, some tax increase.

What might such a service reduction–tax increase trade-off look like? To illustrate, if Alberta was to levy a 5 percent harmonized sales tax (HST), which would be the lowest rate among all other provinces, it would generate revenue amounting to about 2.1 percent of household incomes. Of the 3.4 percent budget gap expected to be left by diminished future resource revenues, that amount would leave 1.3 percent (or just over one-third) to be met by reduced expenditure, and in turn reduced service.[18]

For a more specific example, consider an HST in the context of the 2019–20 fiscal year. A 5 percent HST in 2019–20 would have generated about $5.3 billion. That revenue would have reduced the budgeted deficit of $8.7 billion to $3.4 billion.[19] If the 5 percent HST had been combined with $3.4 billion in expenditure reductions—a 60:40 split of tax revenue to spending cuts—the budget would have been balanced. Even with $5.3 billion of additional tax revenue, Alberta would have maintained a significant tax advantage over every other province and, notably, a tax advantage of $8.2 billion over Ontario, the next-lowest-taxed province.[20] Yes, even with a 5 percent HST, Albertans would still have paid $8.2 billion less in taxes than if taxed under the Ontario system.

The already reduced and projected low contributions of resource revenues to the Alberta government will make the province's revenue base more similar to those of other provinces. Even if the medium-term improvement forecast offers some relief, the long-term picture is unchanged. In this situation, it is reasonable to expect that Alberta's tax structure will need to, and will, become more like those of the other provinces. Besides resource revenues, the obvious difference between Alberta and other provinces is Alberta's lack of a general sales tax. Also, pursuing alternative sources (such as PIT or CIT) for equivalent revenues appears generally economically and politically unappealing. Hence, when fiscally squeezed, an Alberta sales tax seems the logical and, indeed, the inevitable choice.

As demonstrated earlier, energy prices and government resource revenues are notoriously difficult to predict. Hence, resource revenues might exceed our expectations. If so, Albertans would be delighted. Although this possibility exists, we should still address the existing and projected budget gaps quickly through both tax and fiscal restraint measures to restore budget balance. This call to action has only been reinforced by the additional negative fiscal consequences of the COVID-19 crisis. Making the adjustments and, in particular, introducing a modest HST, would open neglected opportunities. The good fortune of unexpectedly large resource revenues resulting in unexpected surpluses would create an opportunity for Alberta to adopt a fiscal strategy supportive of a province richly endowed with resources but experiencing large resource revenue and economic volatility. Surpluses arising from any new, bountiful resource revenues should be allocated towards reducing provincial debt, accumulating a stabilization fund to avoid borrowing during cyclic downturns, augmenting the Alberta Heritage Savings Trust Fund to cover population increases and inflation (that is, maintaining it in real, per capita terms), and establishing a program to distribute earnings to Albertans should saving become adequate.[21] To put it plainly, should the province be so blessed as to realize resource revenues beyond those projected here, it should not relapse into devoting those revenues to expenditure increases and/or tax reductions. Instead, it should use them to reset its fiscal course and direct funds to a suite of (probably modest) savings alternatives.

The Alberta government's non-renewable resource revenues have shrunk in relative importance as they have failed to keep up with population growth, price change, and real income growth. Since 2015, these revenues have hovered at record lows. The sharp boost in resource revenues expected in 2021–22 will not solve Alberta's immediate fiscal problems and does not change the long-term prospects for significant recovery, which remain rather dim. Even favourable projections suggest that resource revenues will contribute to the province's revenue-generating capacity only one-half of what they did from 2000 to 2014. Although that represents a notable improvement from the one-quarter level experienced since 2015, the prospect is sobering. The province has a structural deficit problem from which resource revenues alone should not be expected to provide an escape. The current and the projected deterioration of resource revenues' contribution to provincial government coffers calls for a reorientation of fiscal policy. A review of the evidence indicates that Albertans can expect an expenditure cut of 20 percent or more and implies a level of services with which they are unlikely to be satisfied. Ultimately, while seeking some fiscal restraint, Albertans are expected to also choose some additional taxes. The HST is the logical revenue alternative and, if low resource revenues continue into the long term, it is the inevitable choice. A moderate HST plus moderate fiscal restraint can solve the budget gap problem and put Alberta on a sustainable (and budget-balancing) fiscal path, all while continuing to leave Alberta with a considerable tax advantage over all other provinces. Should the province be so fortunate as to see resource revenues exceed expectations, it would be an opportunity to reduce debt and to pursue revised fiscal policies aimed at maintaining stable public finances despite resource revenue volatility.

## Notes

1   This chapter was updated in November 2021. Since then, the provincial government's non-renewable resource revenues and projections for the near term increased more than the then available estimates. This means that the actual performance in 2021–22 and the near and mid-term projections reflect the optimistic estimates reported here (which would, in fact, be increased slightly). Despite that and although optimistic, those results are not especially encouraging. The longer-run projections are not impacted.

2   It is more common to compare government finances to GDP than to household income. However, in Alberta, GDP is considerably more volatile than household income. Furthermore, because of characteristics of GDP unique to Alberta, interprovincial comparisons based on GDP can be misleading (McMillan

2019b). For example, because of the importance of the oil and gas industry and related activities, GDP per capita and nongovernmental, nonresidential capital stock per person in Alberta are much larger than in other provinces. To illustrate, from 1990 to 2016, GDP per person in Alberta averaged 1.6 times that in the other provinces from Québec to British Columbia. Nongovernmental, nonresidential capital stock per person averaged 2.9 times larger. Hence, many interprovincial comparisons based on GDP (such as government revenues and expenditures) make Alberta levels appear relatively small when per capita figures are relatively large. For example, in recent years Alberta's government expenditure has been well below the ten-province average when compared to GDP while being average or above average in per capita terms.

3   For resource revenues, I relied heavily upon the predicted prices from the US Energy Information Administration's (2020) *Annual Energy Outlook* and its subsequent short-term forecasts, projected production volumes from the Canadian Energy Research Institute's reports (Millington 2020a, 2020b), and the Alberta government's experience with revenue collection. My forecasts of household income relied upon data from Statistics Canada (2021) and forecasts of primary household income from the Conference Board of Canada (2021) with adjustments reflecting relevant payments from the Government of Canada's (2020) "COVID-19 Economic Response Plan" (mostly Canada Emergency Response Benefit [CERB] payments).

4   Even if resource revenues equaled their 2005–06 to 2008–09 peak (when they averaged $12.4 billion), they would amount to only 4.7 percent of household income in 2021–22 and 3.9 percent by 2027–28.

5   I thank Professor Tombe for sharing his projection data with me. Tombe has not updated his 2018 projections but, given that the 2020 disruptions to the oil and gas markets may be considered mid-term, that may not be an issue.

6   To provide some background on the assumptions, note first that Tombe's (2018) baseline case was derived from National Energy Board predictions of production and prices and he considered that it generated conservative estimates. It estimated royalties of almost $17 billion in 2040–41 (or about $11 billion in 2018 dollars). His optimistic projection stemmed from the Government of Alberta (2018, 86) budget estimate of 2023–24 royalties of $10.4 billion (an amount $1.55 billion more than his baseline estimate for that year). His optimistic case projects royalties of nearly $20 billion in 2040–41. Second, I projected household incomes under four different sets of assumptions. The details need not be a concern as the alternatives have little impact on the projected shares.

7   In the Government of Alberta's (2020b) budget, the United Conservative government projected resource revenues to be $8.6 billion in 2022–23. In the 2021

budget (Government of Alberta 2021c) the 2022–23 forecast was $4.7 billion. The actual non-renewable resource revenue for 2020–21 was $3.1 billion but had been estimated to be as low as $1.2 billion.

8   The Canadian Energy Research Institute studies (Millington 2020a, 2020b) reflected the longer-term prices as forecast by the US Energy Information Administration's (2020) *Annual Energy Outlook*. The institute has subsequently issued more recent short-term price estimates.

9   A "nominal" forecast is one measured in current-year dollars rather than "real," inflation-adjusted dollars.

10  It is possible that new technological developments may generate or support a resurgence in the energy sector. For example, there is discussion of hydrogen production from hydrocarbons in Alberta contributing to a transition to clean(er) fuels. See, for example, see Government of Alberta (2021b).

11  The Blue Ribbon Panel on Alberta's Finances (2019), or MacKinnon Report, argued that Alberta's spending is high and should be reduced to a level comparable to that in (essentially) British Columbia and Ontario although Québec, a relatively high spending province, was also a comparator.

12  The Government of Alberta's (2021a) budget update makes no predictions beyond the 2021–22 fiscal year. However, it reports a $5.1 billion COVID-19 recovery plan expense in 2020–21 and forecasts $2.5 billion for that purpose in 2021–22 (the capital portions being largely achieved by accelerating future capital investment).

13  However, note that the projected program expenditures of $10,832 per person in 2026–27 would likely make Alberta the lowest spending of the ten provinces. Ontario, which has recently been the province with the lowest spending per person, spent $10,469 in 2019–20.

14  See the fiscal reference tables in Royal Bank of Canada (2021) for per capita program spending data.

15  The MacKinnon Report does not take into consideration factors that might contribute to the spending levels in Alberta and their impact on the services realized. Primary among those is the economic boom and its impacts on private and public sector costs. Note particularly that wages and salaries in Alberta have averaged 15 percent more than the ten-province average since 2000. Similarly, primary (i.e., market-derived) household incomes per person in Alberta have been and still are notably greater than in other provinces (although those in British Columbia are gaining). While post-2015–16 recession and the subsequent economic doldrums moderated the Alberta wage and income advantage, both are still greater in Alberta than in other provinces. In addition, infrastructure costs grew more rapidly in Alberta after 2000 than elsewhere, at least until 2015–16. Higher incomes and higher capital costs imply higher total costs,

meaning that a dollar of public expenditure in Alberta should not have been expected to translate into as much service as a dollar in other provinces.

16 Other than the fact that two of the three large-population provinces spent notably less per person than Alberta when the study was done, it is not obvious why the Blue Ribbon Panel on Alberta's Finances (2019) chose to restrict their comparisons to those three provinces and ignore the other six (especially Saskatchewan, which has experienced a boom-bust cycle parallel to Alberta's). In 2019–20, the nine-province average per capita program expenditure was $12,062, which is only slightly less than Alberta's $12,869 (RBC 2021). The per capita spending levels in Saskatchewan, Manitoba, and Québec ranged from $12,116 to $12,608 (only slightly less than Alberta). Alberta's total expenditure (i.e., including debt servicing costs) per person from 2000 to 2018 was 100.6 percent of (or effectively equal to) the ten-province average. For a broad discussion of Alberta's fiscal position, see McMillan (2019a).

17 Note that "balancing the budget" in this context is expected to still leave the province borrowing to finance a considerable portion of its capital expenditures. To cover both operating and capital outlays and avoid borrowing, additional cuts could be required.

18 It is interesting to note that the fiscal difficulties that Tombe (2018) projects are not caused by growth in program expenditures so much as they are caused by the relative deterioration of resource revenues and the growth of interest on public debt accrued from not addressing the budget imbalance. His projected program expenditures for the twenty-year post-2020 average are, by my calculations, 21 percent of household income—versus the 21.7 percent experienced since 2000—and reach a peak of 21.5 percent in 2040. The critical issue is to deal promptly with the budget imbalance.

19 I use the budgeted deficit as opposed to the actual deficit here because the actual $12.1 billion deficit reflected a large, one-time write off and was considered to be influenced by the impact of the COVID-19 pandemic. The $8.7 billion therefore better reflects the actual or structural fiscal situation with low resource revenues.

20 Besides Alberta's $13.4 billion 2019–20 tax advantage over Ontario (which amounts to about $3,024 per person), Alberta has a $14.6 billion advantage over British Columbia and a $21.2 billion advantage over Québec. For further information on Alberta's Tax Advantage, see the Tax Advantage graph in Alberta's 2019 budget (Government of Alberta 2019, 142) and the similar graphs published annually in the province's budgetary statements. Overall, taxes in Alberta are about 72 percent of the provincial average.

21 For a proposal on the distribution of earnings, see McMillan (2002).

# References

ARC Energy Research Institute. 2021. *ARC Energy Charts, US Crude Oil Futures*, 8 November 2021. https://www.arcenergyinstitute.com/wp-content/uploads/211108-Energy-Charts.pdf.

Blue Ribbon Panel on Alberta's Finances. 2019. *Report and Recommendations: Blue Ribbon Panel on Alberta's Finances*, chaired by Janice MacKinnon, August 2019. Available from https://open.alberta.ca/publications/report-and-recommendations-blue-ribbon-panel-on-alberta-s-finances.

Conference Board of Canada. 2021. *Provincial Outlook Long-Term Economic Forecast: Alberta—2020*. Available from https://www.conferenceboard.ca/e-Library/abstract.aspx?did=10583.

Government of Alberta. 2018. *Fiscal Plan, Budget 2018: A Recovery Built to Last*, February 2019. Edmonton: Government of Alberta. Available from https://open.alberta.ca/publications/budget-2018.

———. 2019. *Budget 2019, Fiscal Plan: A Plan for Jobs and the Economy*, 24 October 2019. Edmonton: Government of Alberta. Available from https://www.alberta.ca/budget-documents.aspx.

———. 2020a. *2020–21 First Quarter Fiscal Update and Economic Statement*, 27 August 2020. Edmonton: Government of Alberta. Available from https://open.alberta.ca/dataset/6042188.

———. 2020b. *Budget 2020, Fiscal Plan: A Plan for Jobs and the Economy*, 27 February 2020. Edmonton: Government of Alberta. Available from https://open.alberta.ca/dataset/budget-2020.

———. 2021a. *2021–22 First Quarter Fiscal Update and Economic Statement*, 31 August 2021. Edmonton: Government of Alberta. Available from https://open.alberta.ca/dataset/6042188.

———. 2021b. *Alberta Hydrogen Roadmap*, 5 November 2021. Edmonton: Government of Alberta. Available from https://open.alberta.ca/publications/alberta-hydrogen-roadmap.

———. 2021c. *Budget 2021, Fiscal Plan: Protecting Lives and Livelihoods, 2021–24*, 25 February 2021. Edmonton: Government of Alberta. Available from https://open.alberta.ca/publications/budget-2021.

Government of Canada. 2021. "COVID-19 Economic Response Plan." Last updated 23 November 2021. https://www.canada.ca/en/department-finance/economic-response-plan.html.

McMillan, Melville. 2002. "Maintaining the Alberta Advantage." In *Alberta's Volatile Government Revenues: Policies for the Long Run*, edited by L. S. Wilson, 129–48. Edmonton: Institute for Public Economics, University of Alberta.

———. 2018. "Alberta's Government Spending: How Big a Problem?" *University of Calgary School of Public Policy Publications* 11. https://doi.org/10.11575/sppp .v11i0.56994.

———. 2019a. "Deficit Free by 2023!" *Alberta Views*, 1 April 2019. https:// albertaviews.ca/deficit-free-2023/.

———. 2019b. "Provincial Public Infrastructure Spending and Financing in Alberta: Searching for a Better Course." University of Calgary School of Public Policy Publications 12, no. 10. https://doi.org/10.11575/sppp.v12i0.61782.

Millington, Dinara. 2017. *Canadian Oil Sands Supply Cost and Development Projects (2016–2036)*. Study no. 163, 9 February 2017. Calgary: Canadian Energy Research Institute. https://ceri.ca/assets/files/Study_163_Full_Report.pdf.

———. 2020a. *Canadian Crude Oil and Natural Gas Production and Emissions Outlook (2020–2039)*. Study no. 190, August 2020. Calgary: Canadian Energy Research Institute. https://ceri.ca/assets/files/Study_191_Full_Report.pdf.

———. 2020b. *Canadian Oil Sands Production and Emissions Outlook (2020–2039)*. Study no. 191, August 2020. Calgary: Canadian Energy Research Institute. https://ceri.ca/assets/files/Study_191_Full_Report.pdf.

Royal Bank of Canada. 2020. "Canadian Federal and Provincial Fiscal Tables." PowerPoint slides presented September 2020.

———. 2021. "Canadian Federal and Provincial Fiscal Tables." PowerPoint slides presented 5 November 2021. http://www.rbc.com/economics/economic -reports/pdf/canadian-fiscal/prov_fiscal.pdf.

Statistics Canada. 2021. "Table 36-10-0226-01: Household Sector, Selected Indicators, Provincial and Territorial." Released 9 November 2021. https://doi .org/10.25318/3610022601-eng.

Tombe, Trevor. 2018. "Alberta's Long-Term Fiscal Future." *University of Calgary School of Public Policy Publications* 11, no. 31. https://doi.org/10.11575/sppp .v11i0.52965.

———. 2020. "For Alberta, the Day of Fiscal Reckoning Has Arrived." *CBC News*, 28 April 2020. https://www.cbc.ca/news/canada/calgary/road-ahead-opinion -trevor-tombe-alberta-fiscal-reckoning-1.5546481.

US Energy Information Administration. 2020. *Annual Energy Outlook 2020*. Available from https://www.eia.gov/outlooks/archive/aeo20/.

———. 2021. *Annual Energy Outlook 2021*. Available from https://www.eia.gov/ outlooks/aeo/.

# 6    The Volatility of Alberta's Tax Bases

## Implications for Tax Policy Choices

*Ergete Ferede*

Over the last two decades, on average, the largest single source of revenue for Alberta's government comes from non-renewable resources when oil and natural gas prices are high, while PIT and CIT provide the second and third major sources of revenue for the government.[1] Resource-dependent economies such as Alberta rely heavily on resource revenue to fund their various public services and infrastructures. As a result, their budgets are often exposed to the vagaries of fluctuating world commodity prices. Previous analyses of Alberta's resource revenue volatility focus on finding ways to reduce the volatility of this type of revenue (Landon and Smith 2010). This chapter focusses instead on the crucial role that taxes can and do play in providing stability for government budget planning. Such a study is crucial for Alberta in particular, given its current economic and fiscal prospects.

The amount of tax revenue that a provincial government collects depends on both its tax rates and tax bases. A tax base is the income or consumption that is (or, the case of sales tax in Alberta, could be) liable to taxation. The three major tax bases I will be focussing on are CIT, PIT, and PST.[2] In the absence of tax rate changes, the stability of government tax revenue depends on how the tax bases respond to the business cycle. The business cycle refers to the fluctuations in output, or GDP. One main feature of business cycles is that most macroeconomic variables such as the various tax bases tend to fluctuate together. Thus, the business cycle poses an important challenge to policy makers and budget planners as it can have a significant effect on tax bases, and thus on government tax revenues.

The main objective of this chapter is to assess the volatility of Alberta's major tax bases by looking at how, exactly, they respond to the business cycle. Ultimately, the chapter aims to answer the question: Could the provincial government lessen the adverse impacts of revenue volatility by changing the tax mix?

## Taxation in Alberta

The Alberta government spends on various essential public services such as health care, education, infrastructure, social services, and so on. The sources of funds for these services come from tax revenue, non-renewable resource royalties, various fees, and federal grants. Between 1981 and 2016—the sample period used throughout this chapter—around two-thirds of Alberta's revenue come from taxes. The amount of tax revenue that the government can collect significantly depends on the overall performance of the economy. This is because the various tax bases tend to fluctuate with the economy.

Like other Canadian provinces, Alberta imposes CIT and PIT on tax bases that are generally consistent with the federal government's definition of tax bases. However, unlike all other provinces, Alberta does not levy a PST. Figure 6.1 shows the shares of own-source revenue (excluding resource revenue) accounted for by Alberta's various tax revenue sources, as well as those of Alberta's two neighbours, Saskatchewan and British Columbia, and for Ontario and Canada as a whole.[3] Aside from resource royalties and non-renewable resource revenue, PIT accounts for the largest share of Alberta's revenue over the period under consideration: about 32 percent. The comparable figures for British Columbia, Saskatchewan, and Ontario over the same period were 31, 36, and 33 percent, respectively.

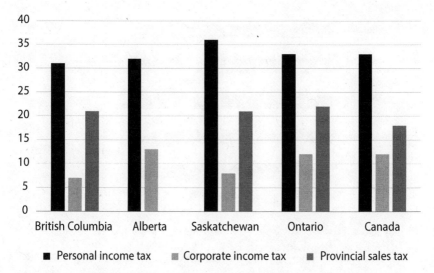

40
35
30
25
20
15
10
5
0

British Columbia    Alberta    Saskatchewan    Ontario    Canada

■ Personal income tax    ■ Corporate income tax    ■ Provincial sales tax

*Figure 6.1.* Tax revenue shares of selected provinces as percentage, 1981 to 2016

*Source*: Author's calculations using data from Ronald Kneebone and Margarita Wilkins, "Canadian Provincial Government Budget Data—All Provinces Updated to 2019/20 and Some to 2020/21" (Excel spreadsheet), October 2021 version, available from University of Calgary School of Public Policy, "Research Data," http://www.policyschool.ca/publication-category/research-data/.

CIT accounts for the second largest share of the province's tax revenue, averaging 13 percent over the 1981 to 2016 period—the highest in the country. The remaining 55 or so percent of Alberta's revenue over the same period comes from other own-source revenue such as investment income, net income from government business enterprises, and other revenue including premiums, fees, and licenses.

Figure 6.1 shows the average actual revenue accounted for by different taxes in Alberta and other selected provinces. This is, however only one way to understand potential variations in provincial governments' tax revenues. Another way is to look at tax bases. Figure 6.2 shows the per capita tax bases for Alberta and other selected provinces over the same sample period. Again, we include British Columbia, Saskatchewan, Ontario, and Canada as a whole for comparison purposes. As figure 6.2 shows, during the period under consideration, Alberta has the highest CIT and PIT bases per capita when compared to the other

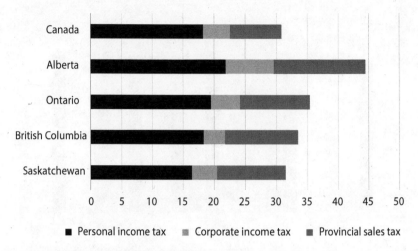

*Figure 6.2.* Tax bases per capita for selected provinces, 1981 to 2016 ($ thousands)

*Source*: Author's calculations using data obtained from Department of Finance, Canada, workbooks used in the calculation of equalization entitlements, provided at the author's request for data.

provinces and to the Canadian average. Alberta also has the largest PST base, even though the province does not currently levy a PST. Figure 6.2 thus suggests that Alberta has huge tax revenue potential, particularly if it taps into the hitherto unused PST base in the province.

It should be noted that tax bases are sensitive to tax rate changes. Thus, the government's tax rate choices impact tax revenue through both changes in the tax rate and their resulting effects on the tax base. Generally, an increase in a tax rate results in decrease of the tax base. Similarly, when governments lower tax rates, there will be more economic activity and the tax base can expand (Dahlby and Ferede 2012). The Alberta government introduced a flat-rate income tax system in 2001, which significantly lowered the progressivity of the PIT system in the province. Other things remaining the same, this change resulted in less volatility in PIT revenue. However, there are more factors than just tax rate that effect tax base changes, meaning that we cannot rely on tax rate changes alone to eliminate tax base volatility. It is important to see how tax bases vary over time. Since we are interested in assessing the volatility and responses of tax bases to the business cycle, it is better to look at how the tax bases evolve over time relative to the business cycle, measured in terms of fluctuations in GDP. Looking at tax bases as a percentage of GDP allows us to see the size of the tax base compared to the total GDP at a given time, as well as how the size of the tax base changes relative to GDP over time. Figure 6.3 shows the three tax bases as a share of GDP in Alberta over the sample period.

We can glean the following facts about Alberta's tax bases and GDP from figure 6.3. First, although there are temporary ups and downs, the tax bases are shown to be somewhat stable relative to GDP. Throughout the period under consideration, the share of the CIT base in GDP is the lowest. Prior to 1988, the PST base had the highest share. In 1988, there was a dramatic jump in the PIT base due to that year's major federal income tax reform, which eliminated several exemptions and deductions. As provincial tax rates were, at the time, given as a percentage of the federal rate, this reform significantly expanded the PIT base in every province, including Alberta. Consequently, since 1988, the PIT base has been higher than both PST and CIT bases.

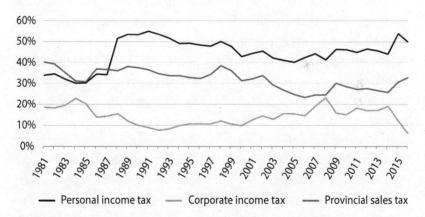

*Figure 6.3.* Alberta's tax bases as a share of GDP (percent), 1981 to 2016

*Sources*: Author's calculations using data obtained from Department of Finance, Canada, workbooks used in the calculation of equalization entitlements, provided at the author's request for data; Statistics Canada, "Table 36-10-0222-01: Gross Domestic Product, Expenditure-Based, Provincial and Territorial, Annual (× 1,000,000)," released 9 November 2021, https://doi.org/10.25318/3610022201-eng.

## The Relation of Tax Bases to Business Cycle in Alberta

This section assesses the volatility and co-movement of Alberta's tax bases and GDP during the business cycle.

### Tax Base Volatility

As is common in the literature, volatility is measured using the standard deviations of variables: the higher the standard deviation, the higher the volatility of the variable. To understand the volatility of Alberta's tax bases, however, we must look at them in relation to fluctuations in the province's GDP, or business cycle. These fluctuations—the cyclical component of the GDP—are called the "output gap": the deviation of an economy's actual GDP from its full potential GDP, or what it would achieve it if were producing at its full capacity. The output gap is not an observable variable and therefore must be estimated.

There are a number of different techniques we can use to filter the data in order to isolate the cyclical components of all of our variables of interest, including the estimated output gap. The specifics of how these calculations are carried out are not important here. The point is that each technique isolates the cyclical fluctuations in our variables in different ways, and thus sees them from different perspectives. The simplest of all these methods is log differencing, which simply uses the growth rates of GDP and the tax bases to assess how they fluctuate over time. Another strategy is log-quadratic detrending, which isolates the cyclical components in the data by removing the effects of changes in trend, or mean, over time. This method thus shows you *only* the fluctuations in the data, undistorted by trends.[4] Arguably, however, the most commonly used method of filtering these datasets is the Hodrick-Prescott (1997) technique, or HP filter. The HP filter involves using a sophisticated statistical procedure to isolate short-term fluctuations related to the business cycle, allowing us to see cyclical fluctuations separate from long-term trends.

In table 6.1, I use these techniques to filter Alberta's CIT, PIT, and PST base datasets over the sample period. I then calculate the standard deviations of this filtered data to shed light on their volatility from different perspectives. The results in table 6.1 show that, no matter how you filter the data,

CIT, PIT, and PST bases are more volatile than GDP, with the CIT base showing the highest volatility and the PST base showing the least volatility.

Knowing the standard deviations of these variables for the whole sample period gives us a quick glance at the general volatility of each repeated variable in the long term, but it doesn't allow us to look at this volatility in any detail. We may, for instance, want to know how the volatility of the tax bases evolve over time. To this end, figures 6.4 and 6.5 chart the standard deviations of each variable on an annual basis over the course of the sample period (using HP-filtered data, as this method is more commonly used in the literature). There are various ways of computing standard deviations for the purpose of assessing volatility. In figure 6.4, I use standard deviations computed using a rolling windows method. This method does not flatten out outlier data, and thus allows us to see in detail all of the spikes and dips of the business cycle over time. By contrast, the recursive or sliding window method, which I use in figure 6.5, is not influenced by the presence of outlier observations. It therefore provides a better picture of the general trends of Alberta's tax base volatility over time.

*Table 6.1.* Volatility of Alberta's tax bases and GDP, 1981 to 2016

| | Cyclical components measured using: | | |
|---|---|---|---|
| | Log differencing method | Log-quadratic detrending method | HP-filter method |
| Gross domestic product | 3.4 | 4.1 | 2.9 |
| Corporate income tax | 16.9 | 31.2 | 14.8 |
| Personal income tax | 9.6 | 14.4 | 8.7 |
| Provincial sales tax | 7.5 | 8.8 | 6.9 |

*Source*: Author's calculations using data obtained from Department of Finance, Canada, workbooks used in the calculation of equalization entitlements, provided at the author's request for data; Statistics Canada, "Table 36-10-0222-01: Gross Domestic Product, Expenditure-Based, Provincial and Territorial, Annual (× 1,000,000)," released 9 November 2021, https://doi.org/10.25318/3610022201-eng.

*Note*: Volatility is measured by standard deviation (in percent) of the variously calculated cyclical components of each variable.

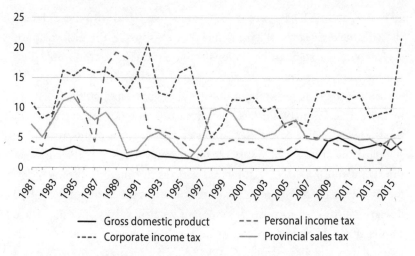

*Figure 6.4.* Volatility of Alberta's tax bases (five-year rolling window), 1981 to 2016

*Sources*: Author's calculations using data obtained from Department of Finance, Canada, workbooks used in the calculation of equalization entitlements, provided at the author's request for data; Statistics Canada, "Table 36-10-0222-01: Gross Domestic Product, Expenditure-Based, Provincial and Territorial, Annual (× 1,000,000)," released 9 November 2021, https://doi.org/10.25318/3610022201-eng.

*Note*: Volatility is measured by standard deviation (in percent) of the HP-filtered variables.

Again, higher standard deviation indicates higher volatility. As figures 6.4 and 6.5 show, while all the three major tax bases are generally more volatile than GDP, Alberta's CIT base shows the highest volatility and its sales tax base exhibits the lowest volatility. This is broadly consistent with the general perception that sales taxes are relatively more stable than other tax bases—yet Alberta, with its highly volatile resource revenues, is currently the only province in the country that does not rely on PST. These findings suggest that Alberta could benefit significantly in using sales tax bases as a reliable and stable government tax revenue source over the course of the business cycle.

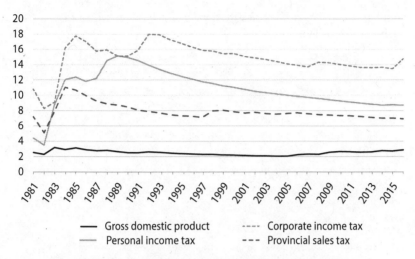

| | |
|---|---|
| —— Gross domestic product | ----- Corporate income tax |
| —— Personal income tax | --- Provincial sales tax |

*Figure 6.5.* Volatility of Alberta's tax bases (recursive window), 1981 to 2016

*Sources*: Author's calculations using data obtained from Department of Finance, Canada, workbooks used in the calculation of equalization entitlements, provided at the author's request for data; Statistics Canada, "Table 36-10-0222-01: Gross Domestic Product, Expenditure-Based, Provincial and Territorial, Annual (× 1,000,000)," released 9 November 2021, https://doi.org/10.25318/3610022201-eng.

*Note*: Volatility is measured by standard deviation (in percent) of the variables.

## Tax Base Co-movement

During the business cycle, many macroeconomic variables including tax bases tend to grow and decline together. In this section, I check whether the movement of our variables of interest are correlated. Co-movement among variables is often measured by the correlation coefficient: a numerical measure between −1 and +1 that describes the linear relationship between two variables. A strong correlation can either be positive or negative, with +1 describing a strong linear relationship in the same direction, −1 describing a strong linear relationship in opposite direction, and 0 describing the strongest possible disagreement. In the context of this study, I'm interested in whether there are positive correlations between the growth and decline of tax bases and the growth and decline of GDP. Table 6.2 presents the correlation coefficients of each tax base's movement with GDP movement. GDP itself is not presented in the table because

*Table 6.2.* Correlation of tax base movement with business cycle (GDP), Alberta, 1981 to 2016

| | Correlations computed based on: | | | |
|---|---|---|---|---|
| | *Growth rates of all variables* | *Output gap and tax base growth* | *HP-filtered GDP and tax base growth* | *All variables, HP-filtered* |
| Corporate income tax base | +0.50 | +0.50 | +0.36 | +0.37 |
| Personal income tax base | +0.30 | +0.24 | +0.41 | +0.26 |
| Provincial sales tax base | +0.01 | +0.15 | +0.35 | +0.11 |

*Source*: Author's calculations using data obtained from Department of Finance, Canada, workbooks used in the calculation of equalization entitlements, provided at the author's request for data; Statistics Canada, "Table 36-10-022-01: Gross Domestic Product, Expenditure-Based, Provincial and Territorial, Annual (× 1,000,000)," released 9 November 2021, https://doi.org/10.25318/3610022201-eng.

in such a comparison, the movement of GDP would have +1 correlation with itself.

The first three columns in table 6.2 describe "static correlation"—the correlation between the growth rate of tax bases with different ways of measuring the business cycle. The first column measures the correlation between the growth rates of tax bases with the growth rate of GDP. The second column shows the correlation coefficient between the growth rates of tax bases and the business cycle, this time measured by the output gap obtained through log-square detrending of GDP (Mendoza 1991). The third column shows the correlation coefficient between the growth rates of tax bases and the business cycle measured by the cyclical component of the HP-filtered GDP series. These correlations are consistent with the discussion of the volatility of tax bases and GDP that we already saw in table 6.1 and figures 6.4 and 6.5. All the tax bases show similar positive co-movement with the business cycle in these three scenarios.

The fourth column of table 6.2 shows the correlation coefficients for HP-filtered GDP and HP-filtered tax bases. When all variables are HP-filtered, their correlation is referred to as "dynamic correlation"

(Croux, Forni, and Reichlin 2001). The dynamic correlation measures the relationship between the cyclical or fluctuating components of all the variables of interest. Consequently, dynamic correlation provides a much better insight than static correlation into the co-movement of different variables. The fourth column of table 6.2 shows that there is a strong positive co-movement of the cyclical components of the three tax bases with GDP. The CIT base tends to show a much stronger dynamic co-movement with GDP. This implies, as is expected, that this tax base is an unstable source of revenue in the face of the boom-bust cycle. The dynamic co-movement of the PST base with GDP, on the other hand, appears to be much weaker, indicating its stability during the business cycle.[5]

Overall, table 6.2 shows that Alberta's tax bases are procyclical: they rise and fall as the economy goes through the boom-bust cycle. However, some tax bases are more sensitive to fluctuation in GDP than others. The CIT base is most affected by changes in the business cycle, followed by the PIT base, and then the PST base.

## Policy Implications

In broad terms, this analysis, based on data from Alberta, indicates that the province's CIT base has the highest volatility, and sales tax base the lowest. We also find that the CIT base is generally more responsive to the business cycle. This indicates that government tax revenue from such a base would be highly volatile during the boom-bust cycle in the province. Ultimately, this implies that when resource revenues are low, the revenue from CIT will also be low. This is not an insignificant finding for Alberta. As is well known, the Alberta government's revenue forecast is highly unpredictable because of the province's reliance on highly volatile non-renewable resource revenue. Because Alberta doesn't impose sales tax, it relies more heavily on CIT revenue than other provinces (see figure 6.2). However, because the CIT base is itself volatile relative to other tax bases, reliance on CIT serves to exacerbate Alberta's volatile revenue problem.

The opposite is true of the PST base: it is less volatile and less responsive to the business cycle than the other tax bases, and is thus a more reliable source of revenue during the boom-bust cycle. The PIT base falls somewhere in the middle. One policy implication of this for Alberta is clear: a revenue-neutral shift from CIT to PIT bases or (even better) to a sales tax base would lessen the volatility of the government's tax revenue sources.

In discussing the various ways of lessening the volatility of Alberta's revenue, Landon and Smith (2010) cite diversifying the province's tax bases to include sales tax base as one potential solution. However, the authors express their doubt about the effectiveness of this solution, arguing that the province relies heavily on non-renewable revenue sources, which are by nature very volatile. They conclude that the reduction in Alberta's revenue volatility that would ensue from introducing sales taxes would be minimal. The authors suggest the establishment of a resource revenue stabilization fund as the best remedy for Alberta's volatile revenue problem. While I agree with the importance of the use of such funds to smooth out volatile resource royalties, I believe it is a mistake to leave tax policies out of the discussion of possible solutions. Recurring volatility of the province's revenue requires looking at PST as an additional mechanism to combat revenue volatility. Take Norway as an example. People often refer to Norway as a resource-based economy that successfully manages its volatile oil revenue by using an oil revenue stabilization fund. However, it should be noted that Norway also relies on a value-added tax—a type of consumption tax that is similar to Canadian federal GST—of around 25 percent.

A change in Alberta's tax mix (say, through the introduction of sales tax) would have significant positive effects on the tax revenue stability of the province. Albertans would, for instance, benefit from reliance on a relatively less volatile tax base that would make budgeting and future government spending plans more predictable.[6] Generally, the less the province relies on a volatile tax base, the better. Optimal tax policy literature indicates that since the distortionary effects of taxes on society increase with the tax rate, the government needs to smooth tax rates over time.[7] Thus, if the province expands its tax bases by including PST, it will have a smoother tax policy in the face of business-cycle-triggered changes in tax bases.

The revenue potential of the province's PST base is substantial. In fact, the province could introduce the lowest sales tax rate in the country, thereby maintaining its low-tax "Alberta Advantage" and still collect significant tax revenue. For instance, in 2016, a 4 percent HST in Alberta—a sales tax rate lower than any province in the country—would have brought in about $3.9 billion in tax revenue.[8] This is important for the economy as a whole as the private sector can operate in a reasonably predictable tax policy environment.

Sales taxes are also attractive on economic growth and tax efficiency grounds (see McKenzie 2000; Dahlby 2012; Dahlby and Ferede 2012; and Ferede and Dahlby 2012). This change in the tax mix will have wider positive effects on the province's overall economic performance and thus total government tax revenue receipts. The resource sector could also be positively impacted by such tax changes as it could increase their international tax competitiveness with a reduction of, say, corporate (or personal) income tax rates.[9]

The implications of my analysis are broadly consistent with those of previous studies such as McKenzie (2000) and Bazel and Mintz (2013). It is, however, important to highlight some of the caveats of my results. In particular, this analysis does not look at the volatility of non-renewable resource revenues, which have on average accounted for the lion's share of the province's revenue. However, one thing is clear: the less the province relies on such a revenue source (say, by diversifying into PST), the less susceptible its budget would be to the boom-bust cycle. As well, this analysis focusses only on tax base volatility and the potential for the province to improve its revenue stability through changes in the tax mix. Of course, there are distributional effects associated with changing the tax mix that are important for society and policy makers. While beyond the scope of this chapter, some of these issues are addressed by Smythe in chapter 7 and Ascah in chapter 10 of this volume.

Still, in a nutshell, if the objective of the Alberta government is to have less volatile and more predictable tax revenue sources, then diversifying its tax bases to include PST looks like a promising option. Indeed, as of the time of writing, the Alberta government has hinted that it may consider a review of its revenue mix in light of historically high deficits. Given the provincial government's current fiscal position, I recommend that this review be completed post haste.

## Notes

1  According to my calculations using data Government of Alberta annual reports (various years), between 2000–01 and 2018–19, the average revenue shares from in Alberta were as follows: 17.3 percent from PIT, 5.3 percent from CIT, and 19 percent from non-renewable resource revenue.

2  While Alberta does not levy a provincial sales tax, it does have a sales tax base on which it could levy such a tax: all of the money spent on consumption in the province. Thus, a sales tax base exists in the province, but the tax rate on this base is 0 percent.

3  The PIT, CIT, and PST revenue shares are calculated as a share of each province's respective total own-source revenue excluding non-renewable resource revenue. In other words, non-renewable resource revenues and federal transfers are not included in the revenue share computations.

4  This method uses the trend and the square of the trend to isolate the cyclical component. In this method, the cyclical component is simply the residual obtained from the estimation of the log of each variable on trend and trend-squared.

5  An alternative way to assess the co-movement of tax bases with GDP is using a simple regression analysis. To this end, I have also investigated the response of the three tax bases to the business cycle using a simple empirical model. The analysis suggests that a one percentage point increase in GDP is associated with 1.93, 1.09, and 0.89 percentage point increase in CIT, PIT, and PST bases, respectively. These regression results are generally consistent with the correlation analyses, and they indicate that the CIT and PST bases exhibit the most and least responsiveness to the business cycle, respectively.

6  See Dahlby (2012), Dahlby and Ferede (2012), and Ferede and Dahlby (2012) for the potential economic efficiency gains from changing the tax base mix.

7  See, for example, Barro (1979).

8  Alberta's total sales tax base in 2016 was $96.8 billion. Thus, a 1 percent HST would bring in a revenue of about $0.968 billion for the government.

9  The United Conservative Party was elected in April 2019 partly on a promise of cutting the CIT rate from 12 percent to 8 percent over four years. This change was implemented in the Job Creation Tax Cut (Alberta Corporate Tax Amendment) Act in June 2019. In response to the COVID-19 pandemic,

the government accelerated the reduction of the CIT rate from 10 percent to 8 percent, effective 1 July 2020.

## References

Barro, Robert. 1979. "On the Determination of the Public Debt." *Journal of Political Economy* 87, no. 6: 940–71.

Bazel, Peter, and Jack Mintz. 2013. "Enhancing the Alberta Tax Advantage with a Harmonized Sales Tax." *University of Calgary School of Public Policy Publications* 6, no. 29. https://doi.org/10.11575/sppp.v6i0.42441.

Croux, Christophe, Mario Forni, and Lucrezia Reichlin. 2001. "A Measure of Co-movement for Economic Variables: Theory and Empirics." *Review of Economics and Statistics* 83, no. 2: 232–41.

Dahlby, Bev. 2012. "Reforming the Tax Mix in Canada." *University of Calgary School of Public Policy Publications* 5, no. 14. https://doi.org/10.11575/sppp.v5i0.42383.

Dahlby, Bev, and Ergete Ferede. 2012. "The Effects of Tax Rate Changes on Tax Bases and the Marginal Cost of Public Funds for Provincial Governments." *International Tax and Public Finance* 19: 844–83.

Ferede, Ergete, and Bev Dahlby. 2012. "The Impact of Tax Cuts on Economic Growth: Evidence from Canadian Provinces." *National Tax Journal* 65: 563–94.

Hodrick, Robert, and Edward Prescott. 1997. "Post-war Business Cycles: An Empirical Investigation." *Journal of Money, Credit, and Banking* 29: 1–16.

Kneebone, Ronald. 2015. "Mind the Gap: Dealing with Resource Revenue in Three Provinces." *University of Calgary School of Public Policy Publications* 8, no. 20. https://doi.org/10.11575/sppp.v8i0.42522.

Kneebone, Ronald, and Margarita Wilkins. 2016. "Canadian Provincial Government Budget Data 1980/81 to 2013/14." *Canadian Public Policy* 42, no. 1 (March): 1–19.

Landon, Stuart, and Constance E. Smith. 2010. "Energy Prices and Alberta Government Revenue Volatility." *C. D. Howe Institute Commentary* 13. https://ssrn.com/abstract=1719156.

McKenzie, Kenneth. J. 2000. *Replacing the Alberta Personal Income Tax with a Sales Tax: Not Heresy but Good Economic Sense*. Calgary: Canada West Foundation.

Mendoza, Enrique. 1991. "Real Business Cycles in a Small Open Economy." *American Economic Review* 81, no. 4: 797–818.

7      # Oil, Democracy, and Social Solidarity

## The Case for an Alberta Sales Tax

*Elizabeth Smythe*

The COVID-19 pandemic generated extraordinary challenges for governments and for communities. It has revealed and amplified the extent and impact of inequality in both health outcomes and livelihoods in Canada. The accompanying economic crisis has also posed enormous fiscal challenges for both federal and provincial governments. Nowhere has this been more evident than in Alberta, where an already weak economy was further buffeted by the collapse of oil prices and the soaring costs of dealing with the crisis. Even before the pandemic, the Alberta government faced tough choices in how to deal with its budgetary challenges due to weak oil prices and a recession. As we look ahead to the province's future, we need to look at how Alberta could rebuild its economy and society in a way that is more equal, democratic, environmentally sustainable, and just. I will argue that one element of accomplishing this is a revision of the province's tax policy that moves away from its dependence on non-renewable resource revenues and protects important programs such as education and health care from massive cuts made in the name of addressing revenue shortfalls and a growing deficit. Such cuts would further erode social solidarity—that is, our sense of interdependence as a community with a shared desire to enhance well-being and meet the needs of all. Major cuts to health and education—the two biggest programs in terms of Alberta's budget—hit the most vulnerable the hardest, as do cuts to other programs.

Such a revision of tax policy, for reasons I outline below, should include a PST. It should also, however, look to restore tax fairness, lessen inequality, and address the looming crisis of climate change. The social costs of income inequality have been well documented, as have the power imbalances that are created when income inequality levels are high—imbalances that ultimately erode democracy and undermine our sense of social solidarity as citizens. The environmental and human costs of climate change are, at this point, so abundantly clear that no one can seriously question the need for action. As matters currently stand, however, neither federal nor provincial policies promise adequate solutions to address these two very pressing problems.[1]

If we, as Albertans, were to succeed in meeting the challenges of climate change and income inequality, what would our province look like? It would have

- a diversified and sustainable economy that provides the province with stable sources of revenue, including a sales tax, thus allowing for reliable budget forecasting;
- an energy plan enabling a swift transition away from fossil fuels;
- public services and programs that support human health and well-being and promote social and economic equity; and
- a tax system and revenue stream that are not vulnerable to the boom-bust cycle and are distributionally fair.

Sadly, that is not the Alberta we have today. Why is that? In my view, if we, as socially conscious Albertans, wish to narrow the income gap and reduce our contribution to climate change, we must be willing to reconsider the sources of revenue on which the provincial government currently relies to fund policies and programs. I will argue that a PST, while not without its drawbacks, would offer a predictable source of revenue that could be used not only to fund the vital public services and programs on which Albertans rely, but also to help reduce the deficit and pay down the debt. More than this, by freeing the province from its historical dependence on the oil industry and royalty revenues, a sales tax would be a small step toward restoring democracy and would allow Alberta to develop a credible policy on climate change.

## The Problem: Volatile Oil Prices, Volatile Revenues

As figure 7.1 indicates, volatility is the norm with oil prices. Particularly since the latter half of 2014, we have seen gluts of oil on the market cause dramatic changes in the price of crude oil—plummeting, for instance, from well over $100 per barrel to under $30 by early 2015.

As figure 7.2 illustrates, the share of Alberta government revenues that derive from the exploitation of non-renewable resources is equally unstable. For example, the crash in oil prices that occurred in the fall

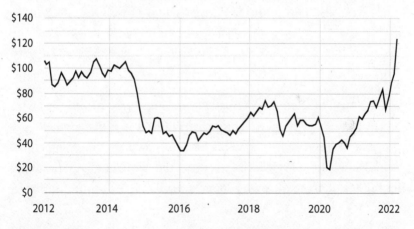

*Figure 7.1.* West Texas Intermediate crude oil prices per barrel, 2012 to March 2022 (US $)

*Source:* "Crude Oil Prices: 70 Year Historical Chart," Macrotrends, accessed 10 November 2021, https://www.macrotrends.net/1369/crude-oil-price-history-chart.

*Note:* West Texas Intermediate is a light crude oil that serves as a global benchmark reference price. Other oils are priced in relation to it, depending on their characteristics.

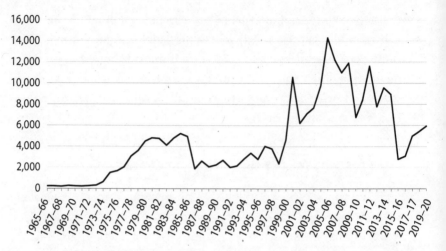

*Figure 7.2.* Alberta government revenue from non-renewable resources, 1965–66 to 2019–20 ($ millions)

*Sources*: Ronald Kneebone and Margarita Wilkins, "Canadian Provincial Government Budget Data—All Provinces Updated to 2019/20 and Some to 2020/21" (Excel spreadsheet), October 2021 version, available from University of Calgary School of Public Policy, "Research Data," http://www.policyschool.ca/publication-category/research-data/; Government of Alberta, *2019–20 Annual Report*, available from https://www.alberta.ca/government-and-ministry-annual-reports.aspx.

of 2014 was reflected in a dramatic drop in resource revenues to what journalist Robson Fletcher (2016) characterized as a "historic low." In a province so heavily invested in the fossil fuel industry, these sometimes radical fluctuations in global oil prices can thus have serious ramifications for the health of the Alberta economy overall.

## How Did We Get Here?

Comparative political scientists have been studying states where resource extraction has become the overwhelmingly dominant sector in the economy for years, noting the paradox that the huge wealth generated by production in most circumstances does not reduce poverty, increases inequality, and impedes the development of democracy. Sometimes called the oil curse, the development of petrostates is widely seen, as Taft (2017, 125) notes, in countries where the rapid expansion of resource sector production occurred in the context of weak state institutions.[2] Although historically this has not been the case in Alberta, there is persuasive evidence that the oil industry functions as a "deep state"—one in which power operates independently of overt political processes in accordance with its own agenda, such that the mechanisms of democracy no longer serve their purpose. In such a situation, the will of the people is overridden by other interests and the autonomy of government is compromised, producing what is sometimes called a "captive" state. In an economy that is heavily dependent on the oil industry, "the distinction between the government and the corporation gets blurred" (Taft 2017, 107).

The privileged position of capital in a liberal democracy and the structural power it gives corporations over public policy has long been recognized (Lindblom 1977). As Urquhart (2018) argues, this structural aspect of power has been accompanied by discursive power reflected in a set of ideas variously called "free market ideology," neoliberalism, or neoconservativism. These ideas have become, since the Reagan-Thatcher decades, a form of "market fundamentalism." Critics from George Soros to Joseph Stiglitz note proponents of neoliberalism have a quasi-religious faith in the unqualified benefits of unregulated markets (even in the absence of confirming evidence) and a zealous hostility to government intervention and regulation over the activities of for-profit corporations.

The dominance of market fundamentalism since the 1980s has been reflected in changes to tax regimes in many countries that belong to the OECD (Organisation for Economic Co-operation and Development), where there has been a marked shift away from progressive PIT and CIT and toward taxes based on consumption as major sources of government revenues. This accelerated in the 1990s because of changes to technology and trade agreements that further integrated global markets (Eggar, Nigai, and Strecker 2016). The result has been an enhanced mobility of capital and high-income individuals and a perception among governments that they must compete for investment. Not surprisingly, this has further resulted in a growing level of income inequality across many countries, including Canada (OECD 2011). The Conference Board of Canada (2012) ranked Canada twelfth out of seventeen comparable countries on inequality, giving it a score of C in addressing the issue.

In terms of the Alberta government, the petroleum sector, and its corporations, the shift to market fundamentalism is reflected in the contrast between the Lougheed era and subsequent Alberta governments. The Lougheed government showed some willingness to intervene in the economy and took the view that the province and its people owned the resource and should get a greater share of the economic rent. In addition, Lougheed's government legislated that a portion of non-renewable resource revenue should be put aside for future generations in the Alberta Heritage Savings Trust Fund, created in 1976. As a result, royalties on production were increased. In contrast, by the mid- to late 1990s, a much different regulatory and royalty regime had been put in place, which spurred the rapid expansion of the tar sands. These changes were accompanied by the introduction of a discourse of competitive tax regimes geared toward attracting and retaining corporate investment in Alberta. As Ralph Klein proclaimed in 1993, "Unlike some others, my government will not try to buy prosperity through higher taxes. Instead, it will build on Alberta's existing advantage of low taxes and its free enterprise spirit to develop the most competitive economy in North America. The government will strengthen the Alberta Advantage and sell it aggressively around the globe" (quoted in Eisen, Lafleur, and Palacios 2017, 5). Along with this new royalty regime came a set of tax changes, including a flat tax of 10 percent on personal income and the progressive reduction of the corporate tax rate from 15.5 percent in 2001 to 10 percent in 2006, where it remained until the lengthy Progressive Conservative reign ended in 2015. The Klein government tax changes, as Kathleen Lahey (2015) shows, not only contributed to increasing income inequality in Alberta overall but also widened the inequality gap in income between men and women. As figure 7.3 shows, as of 2014, Alberta had the highest level of income inequality of any province in Canada.

Non-renewable resource royalty rates have also proved difficult to increase. In addition, contributions of non-renewable resource revenues to the Heritage Fund stopped in 1987. Thus, as Taft (2017, 124) notes, royalties became "a politically addictive way to cut taxes and subsidize services"

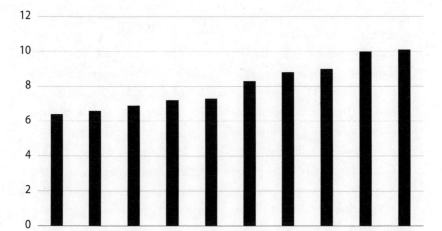

*Figure 7.3.* Provincial levels of income inequality (decile ratio), 2014

*Source*: Conference Board of Canada, "Income Inequality," accessed 15 March 2021, https://www.conferenceboard.ca/hcp/provincial/society/income-inequality .aspx. See the graph headed "Alberta and BC Have the Highest Income Inequality Using Data on Decile Ratios," which draws on raw data from Statistics Canada.

*Note*: These rankings are based on decile ratios for each province—that is, the ratio of the share of income garnered by the top decile of the population (the wealthiest 10 percent) to the share garnered by the bottommost decile.

in Alberta, but one that relied on narrow sources of revenue. Such a policy has proved to be disastrously volatile in the wake of the price-production war between Russia and Saudi Arabia and the economic impact of the COVID-19 pandemic. According to the Government of Alberta's (n.d.) regularly updated data, by April 2020, the price per barrel of West Texas Intermediate had dropped from US$63.86 in April 2019 to US$16.55, while Alberta's Western Canadian Select had plummeted in the same period to US$3.50 per barrel from US$53.25 the year before.

## Petro-, Captive, or Deep State: The Influence of the Oil Industry

Oil companies and organizations such as the Canadian Association of Petroleum Producers have had strong and growing influence, especially since the 1990s, over both provincial and federal government policies and regulations, even when governments shifted in a direction that appeared to be less sympathetic to the industry. As both Taft (2017) and Urquhart (2018) indicate, this power is manifested in aggressive lobbying (documented by Cayley-Daoust and Girard 2012), financial campaign contributions, and backroom influence at both the provincial and federal party levels. In addition, the industry accounts for a significant portion of Alberta's GDP and is a major employer with the mining, oil, and gas extraction industries accounting for 140,300 jobs in 2017 (Government of Alberta 2017). Still, oil and gas is by no means the largest employer even with the efforts of the industry lobby, and those sympathetic to it, to exaggerate the indirect employment effects (Barney 2017).

Alberta, as the owner of the non-renewable resource being extracted within its borders, has a stake in resource exploitation given that resource rents generate revenues for the government that, while unstable, are a significant source of income. This is unique to states where resource extraction dominates. In some such states, that income flows into the pockets and Swiss bank accounts of corrupt leaders or elites. In other cases, such as Alberta, it has allowed for lower levels of corporate and other income taxation; at the same time, with limited alternative revenue sources, it has created a government dependence on the industry and expanded levels of production. Reliance on this revenue and expanded production, given increasingly volatile oil prices, has directly transmitted the risk and uncertainty of oil price fluctuations onto the provincial budget and ultimately onto the funding of provincial programs and services.

Two instances of failed efforts to increase royalty rates in the past provide evidence of the influence of the industry over governments. The first occurred under the premiership of Ed Stelmach, a northern Alberta politician who replaced Ralph Klein as the leader of the Progressive

Conservatives in 2007. Stelmach pledged, as had most of his rival leadership candidates, to initiate a royalty review considering rising oil prices and criticisms, including from the Auditor General, that the province was failing to get its fair share. Despite an open and transparent review process and a panel that was knowledgeable and credible even to the oil industry, its fairly modest recommendations, which included creating an oil sands severance tax, were met with fierce opposition from the companies and the Canadian Association of Petroleum Producers. Together, they laid out a scenario of cutbacks to capital investment, slow growth, and major increases in unemployment. The government blinked and permitted a behind-closed-doors "consultation" with industry on the recommendations. The resulting changes were minimal. Along with corporate tax changes, this effort left the industry in a place as good as or better than where they were prior to the review. As Urquhart (2018, 194) observes, "perceptions of oil's growing scarcity, Alberta's political stability, a well-educated Canadian labour force, and the province's proximity to the American market" in 2007 should have provided leverage to extract a greater proportion of the economic rent, yet the government was unable to do so.

In the second case of failed royalty rate increases, the prospects for a significant change seemed likely with the 2015 election of an Alberta NDP government under Rachel Notley. As an opposition MLA to the previous government, Notley had sponsored a private member's bill to create a Resource Owners Rights Commission. Echoing the language of Lougheed, Notley's proposed commission would have involved broad representation of different groups and would have engaged in regular monitoring of the royalty regime. During the 2015 election campaign, however, Notley's position on this commission became increasingly ambiguous as the party gained momentum (Urquhart 2018). Post-election, the promise to review the royalty regime was implemented in the form of a one-shot royalty review. The review lacked transparency and reflected not the perspective of the owners of the resource but the impact of any royalty changes on the Alberta Advantage and on oil sands investment and competitiveness. Any serious commitment to overhauling the regime evaporated with the 2015 oil price crash. With a failure to raise royalty rates and tax changes that enhanced dependence on non-renewable resources, a case could be made that other sources of revenue needed to be found in the tax system. Raising taxes, however, has long been a politically fraught topic in Alberta.

## Has Tax Become a Four-Letter Word?

In their 2013 edited collection *Tax Is Not a Four-Letter Word*, Alex and Jordan Himmelfarb argue that, while citizens in general do not like taxes, historically there was a recognition among Canadians that taxes,

> however irksome, are the price we pay for civilization and a better future, for the privilege of living in Canada and the opportunities that provides. While there are legitimate disputes regarding how much tax and of what sort, we have generally accepted higher taxes as a way of funding valued public goods and services, redistributing income to avoid the worst excesses of inequality, and shaping the future to the extent we can. (Himmelfarb and Himmelfarb 2013, 1)

However, as the Himmelfarbs note, with the dominant discourse of market fundamentalism, "tax has gone from irritant to four-letter word, not to be uttered in public and certainly not to be discussed favourably in politics" (1). As part of this transformation, "the notion that taxes are somehow separate from the services and goods they buy is now a part of our political culture" (3). In addition, increasing levels of distrust of government in many liberal democracies, including Canada, has contributed to the negative view of taxation.

The discussion of taxation is part of a bigger conversation about the role of government and, in particular, questions of community, equality, fairness, and justice. Those wanting to shrink the role of government have used the discourse of keeping taxes low and cutting taxes to achieve that end, even though they may claim some other justification. A good example is the federal government 2008 cut of the GST rate from 7 percent (implemented in 1991) to 5 percent. While fulfilling a 2006 Conservative Party election promise, this cut had little or no support among economists or public finance experts. It led, however, to over $14 billion in foregone revenue annually, which put a major constraint on federal government spending.

The problem for those wanting to drastically shrink the size of government is that Canadians value many of the services governments provide, especially provincial government services such as health and education. Building on and encouraging distrust of government, the antitax movement has promulgated the "free lunch" version of tax cuts, which claims that more efficient spending and cutting can make up for all the lost revenue with no change to services by reducing the supposedly massive amount of waste present in current programs and expenditures. While disingenuous or deceptive at best, this painless vision of tax cuts has little basis in reality. Prior to elections, those seeking to cut taxes will make exaggerated claims about how much savings can be found in increasing efficiencies. Voters often find, however, that after elections, there is a real price to be paid for tax cuts, and that price is cutbacks to services and programs they value. This price tag is particularly steep for vulnerable populations who are especially reliant on these programs. As Himmelfarb and Himmelfarb (2013, 4) put it, "tax cuts based on the promise of ending the gravy train almost never find enough gravy."

Whether Alberta has a revenue problem or spending problem is a topic of sometimes heated debate (canvassed by Ascah in chapter 4 of this volume), and conclusions vary based on the measures and ratios one uses to determine debt loads and the provinces to which one compares Alberta (Graff-McRae and Hussey, 2016). The reality is that, because Alberta has relied on revenue from non-renewable resources to subsidize the cost of providing services, Albertans have been able to demand and receive services without having to cover their full costs through the taxes they pay. Without this resource revenue subsidy, citizens would be obliged to confront the true cost of these services, as well as the sizeable gap between the current costs of public services and the amount of alternative revenue sources available to fund them. It is unclear whether citizens would choose reducing services over raising taxes in these circumstances, but there is evidence to suggest that the prospect of major cuts to close the revenue gap might lead them to consider the possibility of finding other revenue sources. The impacts of the pandemic have made some of Alberta's fiscal challenges more visible to the public, which may be opening space for an honest conversation with citizens about possible solutions. Indeed, although a majority still oppose a PST, public opinion polling in 2020 reflects some shrinkage in this opposition (Labby 2020).

Research on public attitudes toward taxation in Canada also challenges the claim that raising taxes is political suicide for any government. As Frank Graves (2013) of EKOS Research Associates noted, the claim of citizens' across-the-board hostility to all taxes is a myth; in fact, the attitudes of Canadians toward taxation are much more complex. If taxes are linked to a positive public purpose—for instance, funding valued services or programs or reducing inequality especially by increasing taxes on the wealthy—they are viewed more positively (Fitzpatrick 2012).

There have been similar findings in Alberta. While polls in 2015 and 2017 reported that the majority of Albertans were opposed to a provincial carbon tax, Ian Hussey (2017) of the Parkland Institute found through public polling that if you link a tax to the idea of funding services that people value, you get a different result.[3] When respondents were asked directly about whether they support or opposed a carbon tax, 41 percent of Albertans supported it. However, when asked, "To what extent would you favour or oppose the Alberta carbon tax if you knew the funds were used to . . . invest in public health care and education[?]" support for the tax increased to 63 percent. In other words, people responded more positively to the carbon tax when the questions were worded in ways that linked the tax to various policies and programs that people valued. High levels of support were also found when the tax was linked to investments in public transit and renewable energy and was accompanied by rebates for lower and middle-income households (Hussey 2017, table 3).

The visibility of a tax also affects attitudes. Citizens tend to be more resistant to a highly visible tax, such as a sales tax. That being said, rebate programs targeting low-income households can often shift public views, as was the case with the federal government's carbon tax proposal. On 23 October 2018, Prime Minister Justin Trudeau announced that, to make sure the federal carbon tax is revenue neutral, 90 percent of the revenue collected in the four provinces without a provincial carbon tax would be returned to lower-income households within those provinces, while the remaining 10 percent would be divided between hospitals, schools, and other organizations.[4] Figure 7.4 illustrates the results of an Angus Reid Institute poll conducted shortly after the announcement of this plan, showing a national shift from opposition to the tax to support of it. The most dramatic shift was in Saskatchewan, where the government was in the process of challenging the carbon tax plan in court.

The poll also revealed a large generation gap between the 69 percent of younger respondents (eighteen to thirty-four years of age) who supported the plan, and the only 52 percent of older respondents (fifty-five years and older) who did. This may reflect differing generational attitudes about climate change. A subsequent poll just prior to the 2019 federal election revealed a majority of Canadians continued to see climate change as a priority, and 52 percent still moderately or strongly supported a carbon tax (though there were continuing regional gender and age divisions). Over 60 percent of those who opposed the tax, however, claimed that it was a "tax grab"—that is, an attempt to generate revenue without tying it to any particular public purpose (Angus Reid Institute 2019).

The argument that voters will reject parties or candidates that challenge the dominant discourse of tax cuts, small government, and balanced budgets was refuted by the results of the 2015 federal election, which was

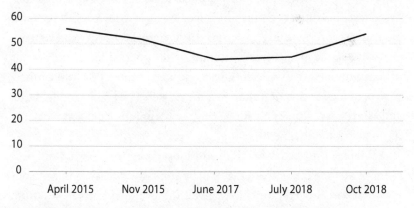

*Figure 7.4.* National support for federal carbon tax (percent), 2015 to 2018

*Source*: "Carbon Pricing: Rebate Announcement Tips Opinion in Favour of Federal Plan, Slim Majority Now Support It," Angus Reid Institute, 1 November 2018, http://angusreid.org/carbon-pricing-rebate/.

won by the Liberals, the only party to advocate running deficits to fund infrastructure spending. In the 2019 national election, deficits were a minor issue compared to leadership, climate change, and affordability, particularly of housing. Despite this, the leaders of the two major parties went back to the discourse of promising tax cuts, especially for the middle class, while they moved their commitments to balanced budgets further into the future. Neither party won either a majority of the popular votes or a majority of seats in the House of Commons—a reflection, perhaps, of the fact that voters' choices are not solely focussed on taxes and deficits, but are driven by a range of issues.

## Regressive Sales Taxes and the Corporate Agenda

Even if a case could be made for the need to increase taxes to fund important public services in Alberta, many of those who would support that approach would oppose a PST. Many on the left have a negative view of the move to fund government activities by taxing consumption. They cite two major reasons for this opposition. The first reason is that such taxes are regressive, falling more heavily on those with lower incomes. This is in contrast to, for example, a progressive income tax, where tax rates increase along with income. The second reason is that the use of consumption-based taxes has often been accompanied by a push to lower both personal income and corporate taxes. Such tax cuts benefit the wealthy and contribute to increasing inequality. Thus, some on the political left see advocates of consumption taxes—specifically, those who favour a PST while otherwise pressing for corporate and income tax cuts (see, for example, Bazel and Mintz 2013)—as simply furthering the corporate agenda in the name of global competitiveness.

While my preference would be for most revenue to come from progressive income taxes, there may still be some good reasons to consider a sales tax in Alberta, especially given the province's fiscal situation. First, Bird and Smart (2016) argue that the extent to which a sales tax is understood to be regressive depends largely on how the impact of the tax is measured, and that this impact has, by and large, been overstated. Second, such regressive impacts on lower-income taxpayers can be mitigated somewhat by creating refundable tax credits for lower-income taxpayers. Third, sales or value-added taxes like the federal GST provide very stable, predictable revenues that increase consistently over time, as the (pre-pandemic) data provided by the federal government indicate in table 7.1.

Moreover, a sales tax is less subject to avoidance since the tax is imposed on everyone at the retail level. It thus avoids some of the challenges of capturing tax revenues from wealthy individuals and corporations—challenges connected to globalization, capital mobility, and the enhanced influence of large corporations at all levels of government. The ability of the wealthy to avoid taxation by, for example, shifting profits and income to jurisdictions with low or no taxes increases the burden of funding services on less mobile taxpayers within a given jurisdiction. The OECD has led an effort to limit what it calls tax-based erosion and profit shifting through international agreements. However, the development of robust international rules and state cooperation to stop avoidance of these taxes is still limited. This has allowed tax havens to flourish, encouraged tax competition among jurisdictions to attract investment, and increased the challenge for states to capture these tax revenues. So, while those on the left rightly argue that fair taxation should include progressive taxation of income and higher levels of corporate taxation, a case can be made that, in the context

*Table 7.1.* Federal budget revenue projections, 2018

| Year | Outlook for budgetary revenue (GST in $ billions) |
|---|---|
| 2016–17 | 34.4 |
| 2017–18 | 36.5 |
| 2018–19 | 37.7 |
| 2019–20 | 39.2 |
| 2020–21 | 40.6 |
| 2021–22 | 42.0 |
| 2022–23 | 43.5 |

*Source*: Government of Canada, *Equality and Growth: A Strong Middle Class* (budget 2018), https://budget.gc.ca/2018/docs/plan/budget-2018-en.pdf. See table A2.7, "The Revenue Outlook."

of continuing income tax avoidance by the wealthy, a sales tax could broaden a government's range of revenue sources, lessen dependence on royalties, and help ensure predictable funding for important programs such as education and health care.

## Pipe Dreams, Pipelines, and Sunset Industries

In 2017, a *Globe and Mail* editorial asked: "How much longer can they [Albertans] afford to elect governments that fail to develop the kinds of stable revenue mechanisms—a sales tax or higher income taxes, notably—that can help smooth out the rough patches and keep the province moving forward in hard times?" ("Alberta Can't Rely" 2017). Alberta in 2020 was indeed in hard times as a result of oil price drops and the economic crisis connected to the COVID-19 pandemic. Since the beginning of the 2000s, as production especially in the tar sands expanded, many Albertans and their governments have been living in what Barney (2017, 85) calls "this imaginary country where jobs spring from the ground in great numbers and go on forever and the public coffers are always full of revenues generated by taxes and royalties." The volatility of oil prices and the industry's influence have been reflected in government policies that, depending on oil prices and royalty revenues, went from increasing spending to cutting spending, providing tax- and royalty-based inducements to the industry to continue investing and to increase production, and hoping higher oil prices would help balance the books.

In recent years, building new pipelines has become the imagined saviour of the Alberta economy. Even if pipelines could be built without great costs, both social and environmental, they would not solve the problems of oil price volatility and fluctuating revenues. While they would afford Alberta oil more access to markets, which might reduce the discount on the price of Western Canadian Select oil relative to the benchmark West Texas Intermediate price, the overall downward trends and volatility of global oil prices would still be there. Indeed, the COVID-19 pandemic has seen further drops in non-renewable resource revenue, weak demand for oil, and a provincial deficit ballooning to over $24 billion. The pandemic has also had the effect of increasing income inequality. In response to the crisis, the provincial government has talked ominously of a fiscal reckoning and possible cuts to critical programs such as Assured Income for the Severely Handicapped—a cut proposed in the fall of 2020, though the government backed down from major funding reductions to the program in the 2021 budget. Without a revenue rebalance to support public programs—specifically, one that includes a sales tax—cuts will continue to increase inequality, target the most vulnerable, and undermine social solidarity. While a PST would not be a panacea for all of the province's fiscal woes, it could help to address revenue shortfalls (as long as it is not accompanied by corporate and income tax cuts). It could also relieve pressures to cut spending on services that Albertans value and provide some space to open a public conversation about the future of Alberta in a post-carbon world. What Alberta needs is an honest conversation between political leaders and citizens about how we will fund our programs in the face of volatile oil prices. This conversation is now all the more urgent in the face of a looming climate crisis and pandemic-related deficits and debt which threaten the future of all Albertans.

## Notes

1    See, for example, chapter 6 in Martin Lukacs's (2019) *The Trudeau Formula: Seduction and Betrayal in an Age of Discontent*, entitled "How Justin Learned to Stop Worrying and Love the (Alberta Carbon) Bomb." In the case of climate change, Lukacs points out that, despite Prime Minister Trudeau's emissions reduction commitments in Paris in 2015, the Trudeau government purchased what was then the Kinder Morgan pipeline in 2018. Lukacs also draws attention to the very close relationship between the company lobbying for the Canadian Association of Petroleum Producers and the Liberal Party.

2    State institutions include the public service (departments) and government agencies, boards, and commissions that carry out mandates established by legislation and regulations.

3    Tony Coulson, of Environics, made a similar argument in 2016.

4    This refers only to the fuel portion of the tax, not to the levy on large carbon emitters. It is, of course, the fuel portion that is visible to ordinary taxpayers.

# References

"Alberta Can't Rely on Oil Revenues Forever. But It's Going to Try," editorial. 2017. *Globe and Mail,* 24 March 2017. https://www.theglobeandmail.com/ opinion/editorials/alberta-cant-rely-on-oil-revenues-forever-but-its-going-to -try/article34416940/.

Angus Reid Institute. 2019. "Balancing Act: Majorities Say Both Climate Action, Oil and Gas Growth Should Be Top Priorities for Next Government." *Angus Reid Institute* (blog), 5 September 2019. http://angusreid.org/election-2019 -climate-change/.

Barney, Darren. 2017. "Who We Are and What We Do: Canada as a Pipeline Nation." In *Petrocultures: Oil, Politics, Culture,* edited by Sheena Wilson, Adam Carlson, and Imre Szeman, 78–119. Montréal and Kingston: McGill-Queen's University Press.

Bazel, Peter, and Jack Mintz. 2013. "Enhancing the Alberta Tax Advantage with a Harmonized Sales Tax." *University of Calgary School of Public Policy Publications* 6, no. 29. https://doi.org/10.11575/sppp.v6i0.42441.

Bird, Richard, and Michael Smart. 2016. "Taxing Consumption in Canada: Rates, Revenues, and Redistribution." International Center for Public Policy working paper no. 16-05, Georgia State University, Atlanta, March 2016.

Cayley-Daoust, Daniel, and Richard Girard. 2012. "Big Oil's Oily Grasp: The Making of Canada as a Petro-State and How Oil Money Is Corrupting Canadian Politics." *Polaris Institute Publications,* 4 December 2012. https://www .polarisinstitute.org/big_oil_s_oily_grasp.

Conference Board of Canada. 2012. "International Ranking, Income Inequality." https://www.conferenceboard.ca/hcp/Details/society/income-inequality.aspx.

Coulson, Tony. 2016. "How to Sell Taxes to Canadians? Show Them Why They Should Care." *Globe and Mail,* 10 December 2016. https://www .theglobeandmail.com/report-on-business/rob-commentary/how-to-sell-taxes -to-canadians-show-them-why-they-should-care/article33288038/.

Egger, Peter, Sergai Nigai, and Norah Strecker. 2016. *The Taxing Deed of Globalization.* Discussion paper no. 11259. London, UK: Centre for Economic Policy Research. https://cepr.org/active/publications/discussion_papers/dp .php?dpno=11259#.

Eisen, Ben, Steve Lafleur, and Milagros Palacios. 2017. *The End of the Alberta Tax Advantage.* Vancouver: Fraser Institute. https://www.fraserinstitute.org/sites/ default/files/end-of-the-alberta-tax-advantage.pdf.

Fitzpatrick, Meagan. 2012. "Canadians OK with Higher Taxes to Fight Inequality." *CBC News,* 10 April 2012. https://www.cbc.ca/news/politics/canadians-ok -with-higher-taxes-to-fight-inequality-1.1171051.

Fletcher, Robson. 2016. "Alberta Resource Revenue Plunges to Historic Low." *CBC News*, 4 March 2016. https://www.cbc.ca/news/canada/calgary/resource-revenue-alberta-history-royalties-budgets-1.3474346.

Government of Alberta. 2017. *Alberta's Labour Market Highlights 2017*. Available from https://open.alberta.ca/publications/2368-9536.

———. n.d. "Oil Prices: Price per Barrel of WCS Oil in US Dollars." Alberta Economics Dashboard. Accessed 22 May 2020. https://economicdashboard.alberta.ca/OilPrice.

Graff-McRae Rebecca, and Ian Hussey. 2016. "Alberta's Immediate Concern is Limited Revenue, Not Debt." *Parkland Blog*, 19 April 2016. https://www.parklandinstitute.ca/albertas_immediate_concern_is_limited_revenue_not_debt.

Graves, Frank. 2013. "Canadian Public Opinion on Taxes" In *Tax Is Not a Four-Letter Word: A Different Take on Taxes in Canada*, edited by Alex Himmelfarb and Jordan Himmelfarb, 67–85. Waterloo: Wilfrid Laurier University Press.

Himmelfarb, Alex, and Jordan Himmelfarb. 2013. "Introduction." In *Tax Is Not a Four-Letter Word: A Different Take on Taxes in Canada*, edited by Alex Himmelfarb and Jordan Himmelfarb, 1–14. Waterloo: Wilfrid Laurier University Press.

Hussey, Ian. 2017. "Albertans Like the Carbon Tax When It's Tied to Enhancing Public Services." *Parkland Blog*, 11 April 2017. https://www.parklandinstitute.ca/albertans_like_the_carbon_tax_when_its_tied_to_enhancing_public_services.

Labby, Bryan. 2020. "Albertans Warming to Idea of a Provincial Sales Tax, According to Poll." *CBC News*, 12 June 2020. https://www.cbc.ca/news/canada/calgary/alberta-pst-opinion-poll-favour-oppose-1.5603707.

Lahey, Kathleen. 2015. *The Alberta Disadvantage: Gender, Taxation, and Income Inequality*. Edmonton: Parkland Institute. https://www.parklandinstitute.ca/the_alberta_disadvantage.

Lindblom, Charles. 1977. *Politics and Markets: The World's Political-Economic Systems*. New York: Basic Books.

Lukacs, Martin. 2019. *The Trudeau Formula: Seduction and Betrayal in an Age of Discontent*. Montréal: Black Rose Books.

OECD (Organisation for Economic Co-operation and Development). 2011. *Divided We Stand: Why Inequality Keeps Rising*. Paris: OECD Publishing. https://doi.org/10.1787/9789264119536-en.

Taft, Kevin. 2017. *Oil's Deep State: How the Petroleum Industry Undermines Democracy and Stops Action on Global Warming—in Alberta, and in Ottawa*. Toronto: Lorimer.

Urquhart, Ian. 2018. *Costly Fix: Power, Politics, and Nature in the Tar Sands*. Toronto: University of Toronto Press.

## PART III

# Suggestions for the Future

## How to Get a Sales Tax for Alberta

# 8    A Disciplined PST

*Ian Glassford*

"Your money, my passion." These words describe the risk in an agency relationship. The agent may choose to use money provided by others to fund their own interests. These interests may not be consistent with those of the funds' providers. Such a situation is offensive to Canadians' sense of fair play and trust, yet we see it all too often in both the private and public sectors. Indeed, it is very likely one of the root concerns and sources of distrust that make a PST a "political suicide tax" in Alberta. I propose that a sales tax is such a hard sell in Alberta is not just because Albertans don't like paying taxes, but because they have not been given a good reason to trust their governments with the extra tax revenue. How can Albertans be sure that a PST won't just be a way for governments to force Albertans to pay for outcomes they don't want and that wouldn't have otherwise made it into the province's budget?

To make it possible for Albertans to have a real dialogue about where a PST fits in addressing the province's revenue challenges—a dialogue that happens *with* Albertans, not *to* Albertans—work must be done to create more grassroots acceptance before an implementation is attempted. For some, the facts and statistics about Alberta's non-renewable resource revenue dependence and its fiscal challenges may be enough to convince them of the merits of a sales tax. The Alberta government has, for instance, seen annual resource revenue decline by more than 30 percent in four of the nineteen fiscal periods up to 2019–20 (Government of Alberta 2020), including a major decline in 2015–16 from which it has not recovered (figure 8.1). The repeated and ongoing disruptions of Alberta's non-renewable resource revenue provide strong evidence for the argument that is it time to explore more stable sources of funding for government expenditure. For many, however, such statistics don't address the core issues: the agency risk involved in increasing tax-based revenue and the mistrust many Albertans feel toward government spending.

Trust is not based on data, but on emotion, values, and principles. This does not, however, mean that mistrust is irrational. In fact, it has a foundation in reality: the "institutional imperative." Warren Buffet (1990) describes the institutional imperative in the business sector as follows: "Just as work expands to fill available time, corporate projects or acquisitions will materialize to soak up available funds." In other words, as revenue expands, so does the impulse to spend. The problem is that this spending is not necessarily consistent with what the shareholder or taxpayer was looking for or was initially promised. This issue is as true in government as it is in the corporate world, and plays into valid feelings of

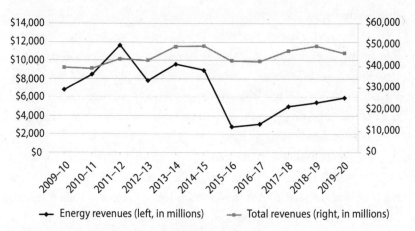

*Figure 8.1.* Alberta government revenues, 2009–10 to 2019–20 ($ millions)

*Sources*: Government of Alberta (2020); Government of Alberta annual reports (various years), available from www.alberta.ca/government-and-ministry-annual-reports.aspx.

mistrust that must be addressed. In the context of a sales tax, addressing issues of mistrust means speaking to and mitigating the concerns of those who oppose a sales tax. This must be as much a part of the conversation as providing the data that explains the pros and cons. If Alberta governments can't develop voter trust around issues of spending, a PST is likely dead in the water.

How can Alberta begin to build this all-important trust? I believe the answer is discipline. To gain public trust around sales tax, the government must prove that it has the discipline to responsibly and effectively spend sales tax revenues. In this regard, Alberta could use a role model—one with proven experience in applying transparent fiscal discipline policies to gain the trust of their stakeholders. I suggest that this role model may be found in the credit union world.

## The Credit Union: An Example of Effective Fiscal Discipline

My experience in financial management at Servus Credit Union, a member-owned financial cooperative, may provide some insight into how the Alberta government can build public trust and, ultimately, set the stage for a conversation about a sales tax. A credit union serves as a good role model for government in part because, in many ways, the tensions that exist in managing a credit union are very similar to those that exist in government:

- The owner/voter is also the customer. The people paying for the services are also those receiving them, with no third party taking profits in between.

- The owners/voters do not have a uniform set of needs. Often, what is desired by one group is opposed by the other.

- Governance is rooted in the principle of one vote per owner/voter. Power is democratic; it is not based on the size of owners'/voters' economic interests.[1]

- Credit unions and governments both have very wide mandates and are not profit-maximizing entities. Their mandate includes social, environmental, worker, community, and other directives.

I have found that it is possible, in a cooperative business, to gather general member support for spending of revenues that would have otherwise gone back to members, if four criteria can be satisfied:

1. **Real need.** There must be a real need for the spending that members can understand and to which they can relate.

2. **Fairness.** Members must believe that the funds that will be used to pay for this need will be raised equitably.

3. **Effectiveness.** Members must believe that the funds raised will be used to address the specified need and not spent on initiatives to which the members have not agreed.

4. **Efficiency.** Members must believe that the funds will be used efficiently to actually address the need, rather than being used to skirt around the issue and avoid making difficult cost management decisions.[2]

Like a cooperative business, government must garner support for its revenue and spending decisions. If a government truly intends to use the PST to stabilize revenues and support quality services rather than to fund excessive spending and avoid cost management, it could try applying these same credit union criteria. Let's look again at these four criteria, this time in terms of how the Alberta government could use them to guide its approach to a public conversation around sales tax:

1. **Real need.** Alberta would benefit from a stable source of revenue like a PST, particularly because non-renewable resource revenue is very volatile and appears to be on a long-term downward trend. A PST could improve Alberta's credit rating and, through this, its cost of debt. A PST could also be used as a counter-cyclical tool. This would reduce pressures on the government to raise taxes in an economic downturn and ensure funding for critical public programs. Framed with these ends in mind, Albertans might understand and relate to what a PST can do for them.

2. **Fairness.** Everyone has a different definition of "fair." Still, since a sales tax is functionally regressive (that is, it will represent a higher

percentage of the income of lower-income earners), introducing some form of refund for lower-net-worth individuals would likely help meet this criterion.

3. **Effectiveness.** Understandably, while people may agree with the rationale in item 1, most voters likely do not trust governments to use PST revenues for their stated purposes alone, whatever those may be. A framework like the one I propose later in this chapter could go a long way to showing that the government truly intends to (and has little choice but to) use PST revenues for promised purposes such as health and education. In good times, the government should be able to fund fundamental services without using all of its annual PST revenue. It can thus reduce the flow of PST into its operating budget in good times, constraining the amount of money available to it to spend on new projects and preserving funds for core services in bad times.

4. **Efficiency.** Buffet's institutional imperative makes it far too likely that increased revenue from the introduction of a PST will result in increased spending plans or avoidance of cost containment strategies unless a clear discipline model is in place. Establishing discipline around the use of PST funds by reducing their flow in good times and increasing it in bad times would force a certain amount of spending efficiency. With fewer available funds to soak up, government can constrain the institutional imperative: fewer available funds means less impulsive spending. Less revenue in good times also helps motivate cost-effective management of programs even when the economy is strong. Such a framework of fiscal discipline should provide some comfort to voters by showing them that adding PST revenues to the province's revenue mix would neither contribute to excessive spending when times are good nor higher income taxes when times are bad.

My proposal, then, is that, by establishing a numeric discipline model around when to use and when to save PST revenues—and, crucially, by communicating this model to Albertans—the Alberta government and the province's voters could actually begin to have a real conversation about a sales tax and how it can achieve what both parties want from it.

## A PST Fiscal Discipline and Stabilization Framework

Since 1980, average real GDP growth in Alberta has been approximately 2.6 percent. Between 2009 and 2020, however, growth has been negative in five fiscal periods (table 8.1), and Alberta has run deficits in all but one year (Statistics Canada 2021). If the intent of a PST is to help create more stable revenues, some might argue that eliminating the PST in better-than-average economic times—that is, times when growth is above 2.6 percent—and implementing it when the economy and government revenues fall would seem to be consistent with this goal. However, this type of implementation presents two problems: first, doing the PST hokey-pokey year by year would drive everyone up the wall; and second, applying a consumption tax in bad economic times, when consumers and the economy can least afford it, will do more harm than good. A better solution would be a commitment by the government to only take the PST into general revenues that are for spending when the economy is weak, and to allocate PST revenues into a segregated fund when the economy is strong. This would offset the need to raise taxes in economic downturns by creating a pool of revenues to fund that offset in economic upswings.

With a properly structured strategy, the government could restrain itself from succumbing to the institutional imperative. Doing this will require a certain amount of fiscal discipline. The system I propose here would give the Alberta government this discipline in the form of objective rules to follow regarding the use of PST revenue. The government will put some or all of its PST revenue into a reserve fund in good times and will give itself access to more than a typical year's PST revenue in bad times. This objectivity negates the need to argue about how to use revenue and avoids the problem of building spending habits in good times that can't be sustained over the long run. In my experience at Servus, this type of restriction actually made the job easier, in part because it was transparent to our board and all members of management. A set formula like the one

*Table 8.1.* Provincial sales tax (PST)-gross domestic product (GDP) discipline and stabilization framework

| Real GDP growth level in year *y* compared to year *x* growth | Percent of year *x* PST included in year *y* revenues | Allocation of PST revenue to/from reserve fund in year *y* | Year *y* general revenues |
|---|---|---|---|
| ≤ 1.5% | 150% | Amount equivalent to 50% of year *x* PST **taken from** reserve fund. | 100% of year *x* PST revenue is available to spend, along with the 50%-equivalent reserve fund allocation. |
| 1.51% to 2.3% | 100% | No allocation. | 100% of year *x* PST revenue is available to spend, but no additional funds from the reserve are added to general revenue. |
| 2.31% to 2.7% | 50% | Amount equivalent to 50% of year *x* PST **added to** reserve fund. | Only 50% of the PST revenue collected in year *x* is available to spend. |
| ≥ 2.71% | 0% | 100% of prior year PST **added to** reserve fund. | No PST revenue from year *x* is available to spend. |

*Note*: All figures are hypothetical and are used for illustration purposes only.

proposed here increases the odds of Albertans actually being open to discussing a sales tax because it will increase the odds that

- Alberta taxpayers will actually see the benefits of paying PST in the form of lower provincial debt costs;

- Alberta taxpayers will actually see the benefits of paying PST in the form of lower tax increases in periods of economic weakness;

- Alberta taxpayers feel more comfortable that the money they are paying in PST does not go toward spending they don't support, particularly in the good economic times; and

- the Alberta government will have access to increased PST revenues when other revenues fall during an economic decline.

The framework (shown in table 8.1) uses a lagging-year system that bases the allocation of PST revenues into the general revenues of one year (year $y$) off of the actual PST revenues of the previous year (year $x$). The PST income that goes into government revenues in any given year are determined by an objective system that would provide a degree of certainty for the government regarding its budget. Because the PST income for a given year $y$ is based on historic GDP figures and the amount of PST collected in the prior year $x$, the government does not have to guess how much PST income they have available to spend in year $y$. They already know that number at the beginning of year $y$, when they are building the budget for that year. Using the discipline and stabilization framework outlined in table 8.1, we can then see how funds might flow to and from a PST reserve fund as a jurisdiction's GDP rises and falls in table 8.2.

Tables 8.1 and 8.2 are for illustration only. Although these tables use Alberta's historic GDP data to make estimates as to where GDP trigger points could fall and what percentages of PST could be allocated to/from the PST reserve at each of these points, they present a simplified example of the proposed framework and do not represent real-world numbers. Still, we can use them to gain some important insights about how this type of framework might work. In table 8.2, for example, we see that the economy is functioning well in our hypothetical year 1: it is growing at a rate above the historic average. Based on the fiscal stabilization structure proposed in table 8.1, this means that all of the money from the PST goes into a reserve fund, and none is available for the government to spend that year. This helps constrain overspending in good times. By the time the economy has fallen into a recession in year 4 with negative 1 percent growth, the amount of PST revenue available for current-year spending has risen to $4.65 billion, or 150 percent of the PST revenue from year 3. This amounts to 100 percent of the PST revenue collected in year 4 ($3.07 billion) plus an additional $1.58 billion drawn from the PST reserve fund. The idea here is to use the reserve savings from economically prosperous times to help fill the hole that

Table 8.2. PST-GDP discipline and stabilization framework example

| | Year 1 | Year 2 | Year 3 | Year 4 | Year 5 |
|---|---|---|---|---|---|
| GDP % change, year $x$ to year $y$ | 2.8% | 2.4% | 1.51% | −1.0% | 1.0% |
| PST collected | $3 billion | $3.06 billion | $3.1 billion | $3.07 billion | $3.1 billion |
| PST allocation ratio based on year $x$ PST collected | – | 50% | 100% | 150% | 150% |
| PST available for year $y$ spending | $0* | $1.50 billion (50% of prior year PST) | $3.06 billion (100% of prior year PST) | $4.65 billion (150% of prior year PST) | $4.61 billion (150% of prior year PST) |
| PST added to / (taken from) reserve fund by end of year | $3 billion | $1.56 billion | $0 | ($1.58 billion)[†] | ($1.51 billion)[†] |
| Balance of reserve fund by end of year | $3 billion | $4.56 billion | $4.56 billion | $2.98 billion | $1.47 billion |

Note: All figures are hypothetical for illustrative purposes only.

Year $x$: previous year

Year $y$: current year

* In the first year of the PST-GDP stabilization framework, all PST revenue would be added to the PST reserve fund.

† Amount needed to top up PST collected in year $y$ to total PST available for year $y$ spending.

declining tax revenues have created without resorting to increased taxes on individuals and corporations. If effective, the result should be smoother annual revenues throughout the economic cycle.

To provide some historic context, between 1994 and 2020, Alberta has had real GDP growth below 1.5 percent five times (Statistics Canada 2021). According to our model in table 8.1, each of these instances would have triggered the 150 percent allocation of the previous year's PST revenues for government spending. In the same twenty-six-year period, the province would have triggered a 100 percent allocation another five times, and a 50 percent allocation twice. It would have had a 0 percent allocation fourteen times. Any revenue from PST in those fourteen years would have, according to our model, been allocated to the PST reserve fund.

Table 8.3 gives us a small window into how the proposed stabilization framework might have worked in Alberta over a five-year period. It also shows how this type of framework might have impacted Alberta's net debt. Like table 8.1, table 8.3 uses historical data about Alberta's revenue and GDP to illustrate how this stabilization framework could work in the province and to make estimates about key outcomes of a 5 percent PST implemented using this structure. It is imperative to remember that these

*Table 8.3.* Historic back-testing: A hypothetical example of how this provincial sales tax (PST) framework could have affected government deficits and debt if it had been implemented in 2014 ($ millions)

|  | 2014–15 | 2015–16 | 2016–17 | 2017–18 | 2018–19 | 2019–20 |
|---|---|---|---|---|---|---|
| Non-renewable resource revenue | $8,948 | $2,789 | $3,105 | $4,980 | $5,429 | $5,937 |
| Total government revenue | $49,481 | $42,619 | $42,293 | $47,295 | $49,572 | $46,224 |
| Assumed PST collected at 5% | $5,035 | $4,848 | $4,675 | $4,892 | $5,000 | $4,599 |
| GDP percentage change (calendar year) | 5.74% | −3.71% | −3.56% | 4.63% | 2.21% | −0.12% |
| PST allocation ratio | 0% | 150% | 150% | 0% | 100% | 150% |
| PST available for current-year spending | – | $7,552 | $7,271 | $0 | $4,892 | $7,500 |
| PST allocated to (drawn on) reserve fund | $5,035 | ($2,704) | ($2,596) | $4,892 | $108 | ($2,901) |

|  | 2014–15 | 2015–16 | 2016–17 | 2017–18 | 2018–19 | 2019–20 |
|---|---|---|---|---|---|---|
| Cumulative PST reserve fund surplus (deficit) | $5,035 | $2,330 | ($266) | $4,626 | $4,734 | $1,833 |
| Annual surplus (deficit) before PST allocation | $1,115 | ($6,442) | ($10,784) | ($8,023) | ($6,711) | ($12,152) |
| Annual surplus (deficit) after PST allocation | $1,115 | $1,110 | ($3,513) | ($8,023) | ($1,819) | ($4,652) |
| Net government surplus (debt) before PST reserve fund | $13,054 | $3,881 | ($8,901) | ($19,344) | ($27,477) | ($40,144) |
| Net government surplus (debt) after PST reserve fund | $18,089 | $6,211 | ($9,167) | ($14,718) | ($22,743) | ($38,311) |

*Sources*: Author's calculations based on Government of Alberta (2020); Government of Alberta, "Gross Domestic Product," Alberta Economics Dashboard, accessed 3 December 2021, https://economicdashboard.alberta.ca/grossdomesticproduct. The 5 percent PST revenue estimates are based on insights from Kenneth J. McKenzie, "Altering the Tax Mix in Alberta," *University of Calgary School of Public Policy Publications* 12, no. 25 (2019): https://doi.org/10.11575/sppp.v12i0.68390.

*Note*: This table represents a rough estimate only. It does not present real-world calculations of PST that would be collected or how spending might have changed.

are rough estimates only; they are by no means exact calculations of the true impacts that this framework might have had.

Table 8.3 suggests that the swings in the government's annual deficit or surplus should be much smaller using an approach like the one I propose. This, combined with a lower net government debt level thanks to the PST reserve fund, could give financial markets greater comfort with Alberta's fiscal situation, which may have the positive effect of lowering the province's cost of borrowing. Operating under this model, the province's PST reserve fund could also give rating agencies comfort that Alberta is better positioned to match revenues to spending through the entire economic cycle, ideally improving our credit rating and reducing the cost of debt. A lower cost of debt would result in less pressure on the government to increase tax increases for Albertans. It would also offset pressure to raise taxes or engage in dysfunctional spending cuts when the economy weakens. In those times (like 2015–16 and 2019–20 in the table 8.3), the government would have access to more revenue from the PST than they would be collecting during the year, effectively transferring funds from the good times when more revenue and spending is not necessary to the bad times when revenues have fallen well short of needs. Finally, table 8.3 illustrates how this fiscal stabilization is in part due to the enforcement of an objective spending discipline model: when Alberta's annual revenues improve, as they did in 2017–18, the funds from PST are not available for spending; they are instead saved to even out deficits in other years.

## A Disciplined PST for Alberta

The simplified examples I present in this chapter are far from complete or sufficient. Many details have not been contemplated—for example, the question of how to contain the temptation to raid the PST revenue fund; the timing when real GDP data becomes available each fiscal year; problems of revenue starvation when GDP rises from a very low level or stays for an extended period in recession; and the possibility of volatile revenue due to the large difference in amount of PST revenue for given GDP levels. It will take work to actually apply this type of framework, and that work will result in new insights not considered in this simplified presentation. The root concept, however, is the main point. In my experience as a financial manager who operated within a similar system (a credit union), I have found that cost discipline and decision making significantly improved when we applied this kind of approach to financial management. This, in turn, materially benefited the customer/owner. It has the same potential to benefit Albertans and their government. It will also increase government accountability, particularly in terms of tax increases in tough times. A government that seeks to increase taxes during a downturn is likely to face aggressive public debate of their fiscal management if people know that the PST they have been paying for years was intended to mitigate the need for such tax increases during recessions.

But again, if we wish to encourage a dialogue on what a PST could mean for Albertans, we first need to address the pervading distrust of new taxes based on the belief that increasing government tax revenue will simply lead to more ineffective and inefficient government. If we don't credibly address this distrust, a sales tax for Alberta will remain a topic of "political suicide." However, if government first demonstrates that it intends to implement a sales tax with a fiscal discipline structure that is designed to control the so-called institutional imperative and ultimately benefit the province and the taxpayer, it can build voter trust and ultimately make feasible a real conversation about sales tax in Alberta.

## Notes

1   Typically, member turnout to vote for the credit union's board of directors is very low, usually under 10 percent of members. In provincial elections, 50 to 70 percent turnout is the norm.
2   In business and government, managers may avoid implementing spending efficiencies. This is because these can be unpleasant exercises rife with pushback from small groups that stand to benefit from the status quo. If the money is available, it is often easier to keep spending it instead of engaging in confrontations with these groups.

## References

Buffet, Warren. 1990. Warren Buffet to shareholders of Berkshire Hathaway Inc., 2 March 1990. *Berkshire Hathaway Inc.* https://www.berkshirehathaway.com/letters/1989.html.

Government of Alberta. 2020. *2020 Historic Royalty Summary Revenue Workbook* (Excel spreadsheet). Available from https://open.alberta.ca/opendata/historical-royalty-revenue.

Statistics Canada. 2021. "Table 36-10-0222-01: Gross Domestic Product, Expenditure-Based, Provincial and Territorial, Annual ($\times$ 1,000,000)." Released 9 November 2021. https://doi.org/10.25318/3610022201-eng.

# 9    Join the Sales Tax Parade!
PST and the Road to Alberta's
Economic Recovery

*Kenneth J. McKenzie*

"Even talking about introducing a sales tax in Alberta would be political suicide." These words were spoken to me by Alberta Premier Ralph Klein during a personal meeting in his office in 2003. I think few would disagree that this sentiment has been taken as gospel in Alberta for a long time—but I also think the situation is changing.

To be clear, when I speak about a sales tax, I mean a broadly based tax applied to a wide range of goods and services, with few exemptions. More specifically, I mean a value-added tax: a tax that is only applied at the final consumption stage, and not on business inputs. Our federal GST is an example of this kind of tax. Therefore, when I speak about sales tax, I mean a tax that can be fully harmonized—that is, combined—with the federal GST.

The question of whether a sales tax should be part of the revenue mix has been well studied by economists, and the economic merits of sales taxation are well established. For one thing, a sales tax is significantly less costly than other forms of taxation. It's cheap to implement. In economic speak, it is less distortionary, and its marginal cost of public funds (MCF) is low. MCF measures the full economic cost of a tax "at the margin"— that is, the cost of raising one dollar in revenue by way of a given tax.

Because taxes change prices, they cause people's behaviour to change, resulting in "lost transactions" that consumers, firms, workers, and so on would have presumably engaged in were the tax not there. These lost transactions are a real economic cost to society.

In a paper written for the University of Calgary's School of Public Policy, Ferede and Dahlby (2016) measure the MCF of the three largest revenue sources for Canada's provinces: PIT, CIT, and PST. For Alberta, they calculate the MCF for PIT as $1.41, and for CIT as $2.91. This means that raising one more dollar in revenue by way of the PIT costs the Alberta economy $1.41, consisting of the $1.00 in tax revenue raised plus 41 cents. The 41 cents represent the value of the transactions lost to the tax's implementation, primarily in the form of foregone work. Though startling, this is nothing compared to the $2.91 MCF of the CIT. As Ferede and Dahlby rightly emphasize in their article's title, this makes the CIT "the costliest tax of all." In stark contrast to PIT and CIT, the MCF associated with a PST in Alberta is only $1.00. This is because the province doesn't currently have a sales tax, and no tax means no lost transactions. In the provinces that do have a PST—by which I mean every other province—Ferede and Dahlby still found the MCF to be lower than that of either of the other taxes. While this is just one study, this basic result is widely established in economics—a broadly based, value-added sales tax is the least costly way to raise revenue. The sales tax is the cheapest tax of all!

In October 2000, I wrote a paper for the Canada West Foundation entitled *Replacing the Alberta Personal Income Tax with a Sales Tax: Not Heresy but Good Economic Sense* (McKenzie 2000). In that paper, I argued that because sales taxes are economically much less costly than PIT, Alberta would be well served by eliminating the PIT altogether and replacing it with a sales tax. I calculated at the time that a sales tax of about 8 percent would largely replace the PIT in Alberta. I argued that the resulting increase in incentives to work, save, and invest would result in faster economic growth and higher living standards for Albertans. That paper garnered quite a bit of attention at the time (including a rather long and somewhat prickly interview with Mary Lou Finlay on CBC's radio show *As It Happens*). Others have since undertaken similar analyses.

For example, Mintz and Bazel (2013) argue that implementing an Alberta sales tax of 8 percent would eliminate the PIT for the majority of Albertans and generate a sizeable increase in economic activity.

A common argument against sales taxes from a social equity standpoint is that they are considered to be regressive, imposing a greater burden on low-income individuals than high-income individuals. From this perspective, a progressive tax—one that imposes a higher tax rate on those with a greater ability to pay—is more desirable. However, the regressivity of sales taxes is actually debatable. A person's ability to pay taxes is determined by their standard of living, which is often measured in terms of current income. Many economists argue that consumption is in fact a better measure of an individual's standard of living than income. This is because money that may not be captured by an income tax—inherited wealth, for example, or offshore income not reported to tax authorities—is still subject to sales tax if it is used to consume goods and services within a given jurisdiction. Moreover, increased reliance on sales taxation can shift some of the burden of taxes away from younger generations struggling to earn a living in a floundering economy to older generations who have benefited from previous periods of buoyant economic growth, and who will benefit from publicly funded health care as they age. Finally, and importantly, even if sales taxes are somewhat regressive, a refundable tax credit similar to the federal GST credit could mitigate the tax's impact on low-income earners.

The economic arguments for the introduction of a sales tax into the tax mix in Alberta are, in my view, well established and compelling. Moreover, Alberta's governments are, and have long been, well aware of these arguments. Klein, for instance, was aware of my 2000 Canada West Foundation paper. When I met with him in 2003, he even claimed to have read it. This began a lengthy conversation about the possibility of a sales tax in Alberta (so lengthy in fact that I missed my plane home, and Klein wrote a note of explanation to my wife on Office of the Premier letterhead). The premier indicated that he was personally sympathetic to the idea of having a conversation about a sales tax in Alberta, but politically he couldn't commit. Indeed, for years Alberta's premiers have considered it "political suicide" to even talk about sales tax in the province. Why is that? The answer is lack of public support. As Klein told me, he did not see a parade forming in support of a sales tax—though if he ever did, he would be happy to jump in and lead it.

As Labby (2020) says, the circumstances for such a parade are emerging. The economic environment in Alberta in 2021 is very different than it was in 2000 when I wrote my *Not Heresy* paper. Alberta has been hit by a series of body blows that have coalesced into the dual crisis of the COVID-19 pandemic and systemic challenges facing the non-renewable resource sector. Historically, we have been able to rely on non-renewable resource royalties as a major source of revenue, which has allowed the government to spend more and tax less than other provinces. This reliance has manifested in a tax mix that has not had to include a sales tax.

While resource revenues have always been volatile, their volatility has been driven home in the late 2010s and early 2020s more forcefully than ever before. Even before the onset of the COVID-19 pandemic, Alberta was dealing with the challenges accessing tidewater by way of pipelines, the associated large discounts for Alberta oil, the prospect of declining resource revenues associated with technological change (e.g., shale oil production in the United States), and looming environmental concerns. While predictions of peak oil demand are highly uncertain, some argue that structural economic changes precipitated by COVID-19 will accelerate the inevitable flattening and eventual decline in the curve. But we do know one thing for certain: regardless of what lies ahead, the Alberta of the future will not look like the Alberta of the past.

We also know that Alberta's fiscal situation is more vulnerable than it has ever been, and this is not likely to change. In its fiscal sustainability report for 2017, the federal Office of the Parliamentary Budget Officer indicated that "current fiscal policy in Alberta is not sustainable over the long term," estimating that "permanent tax increases or spending reductions amounting to 4.6 percent of provincial GDP ($14.1 billion in 2020 dollars) would be required to achieve fiscal sustainability" (72). This would amount to "a permanent 25 percent increase in the tax burden (including federal transfers) or a 20 percent reduction in program spending" (72). These findings are buttressed by Trevor Tombe (2018, 2021), who undertakes long-term projections of resource royalties, federal transfer payments, investment income, property taxes, and other sources of revenue and spending. Like the Parliamentary Budget Officer, Tombe concludes that Alberta's fiscal policies are unsustainable, and that the provincial deficit could grow to a historically high $40 billion by 2040.

Jason Kenney's UCP government has pledged to put the province on the road to fiscal sustainability. Shortly after taking office in 2019, the Kenney government established a financial review panel to report on some of these issues: the Blue Ribbon Panel on Alberta's Finances (2019). Little could be done to implement the panel's recommendations, however, before the pandemic hit. The COVID-19 pandemic changes the outlook for Alberta's economy, and not for the better. In its August 2021 fiscal update, the Alberta government announced that its deficit (including capital spending) for 2020–21 was $16.96 billion. Debt is projected to hit $105.7 billion by the end of March 2022, for a debt-to-GDP ratio of 19.6 percent. Even if the fiscal situation improves with oil prices rising as we emerge from the pandemic, this is likely to be a short-run phenomenon and does not change the underlying long-run unsustainability built in to the Alberta budget.

Since the pandemic began, the Government of Alberta (2020) has released *Alberta's Recovery Plan* to create jobs, boost investment, and grow Alberta's struggling economy. Post-pandemic economic recovery is important, but sustainable economic recovery is crucial. The province should not forget that if it wants to set itself up for a sustainable economic and fiscal future, this recovery will require more than spending cuts and hope for a jump in resource revenues. It will require adjustments to the province's revenue sources, as well. On the revenue side, in my opinion, the days of wine and roses are over. Alberta can no longer afford to be the sole province without a sales tax. Previous studies that argued for sales tax, including my 2000 paper, focussed on using it to replace or reduce existing tax revenue sources in Alberta, such as the PIT or CIT. While this remains a legitimate line of attack to explore even in the current environment, with Alberta's resource revenues on a downward trend, this model is becoming less and less feasible. The conversation is instead turning toward using a sales tax not to replace, but to supplement existing sources of revenue to address the fiscal pressures. At the time of writing, however, the Kenney government has adopted neither of these approaches. Indeed, it has done little in terms of adjusting government revenue aside from accelerating a previously announced reduction to the provincial CIT rate—something that will ultimately work to reduce the province's revenues, putting them under even more pressure in the short and intermediate terms than they already are.

In a recent paper, Daria Crisan and I argue that "the choices may be difficult, but the math is simple" (Crisan and McKenzie 2021, 21). We show that a 6 percent sales tax coupled with the repatriation of the consumer-level carbon tax (both with targeted credits for low-income households) and modest expenditure restraint that brings Alberta in line with the other provinces on a per capita basis would put Alberta's finances on a sustainable path. In light of the province's historic deficit and what is predicted by most to be a long, slow climb out of economic malaise, it is difficult to imagine how Alberta could achieve fiscal sustainability in the long run without introducing a sales tax into its revenue mix. As the public becomes more aware of Alberta's fiscal situation and more open to alternative sources of revenue, conditions may well be developing in the province for a sales tax parade to begin, whether we like it or not. The government would do well to lead it.

## References

Bazel, Peter, and Jack Mintz. 2013. "Enhancing the Alberta Tax Advantage with a Harmonized Sales Tax." *University of Calgary School of Public Policy Publications* 6, no. 29. https://doi.org/10.11575/sppp.v6i0.42441.

Blue Ribbon Panel on Alberta's Finances. 2019. *Report and Recommendations: Blue Ribbon Panel on Alberta's Finances*, chaired by Janice MacKinnon, August 2019. Available from https://open.alberta.ca/publications/report-and-recommendations-blue-ribbon-panel-on-alberta-s-finances.

Crisan, Daria, and Kenneth J. McKenzie. 2021. "Revenue Options to Close the Fiscal Gap in Alberta: Pick Your Poison." Preprint, submitted June 2021. https://www.policyschool.ca/wp-content/uploads/2021/06/AF23_Fiscal-Gap_Crisan-McKenzie.pdf.

Ferede, Ergete, and Bev Dahlby. 2016. "The Costliest Tax of All: Raising Revenue Through Corporate Tax Hikes Can be Counter-Productive for the Provinces."

University of Calgary School of Public Policy Publications 9, no. 11. https://doi
.org/10.11575/sppp.v9i0.42577.

Government of Alberta. 2020. *Alberta's Recovery Plan.* Available from https://
open.alberta.ca/publications/albertas-recovery-plan.

———. 2021. *2021–22 First Quarter Fiscal Update and Economic Statement.*
Available from https://open.alberta.ca/publications/6042188.

Labby, Bryan. 2020. "Albertans Warming to Idea of a Provincial Sales Tax,
According to Poll." *CBC News*, 12 June 2020. https://www.cbc.ca/news/
canada/calgary/alberta-pst-opinion-poll-favour-oppose-1.5603707.

McKenzie, Kenneth. J. 2000. *Replacing the Alberta Personal Income Tax with
a Sales Tax: Not Heresy but Good Economic Sense.* Calgary: Canada West
Foundation.

Office of the Parliamentary Budget Officer. 2017. *Fiscal Sustainability Report 2017.*
Ottawa: Office of the Parliamentary Budget Officer. https://www.pbo-dpb.gc
.ca/en/blog/news/FSR_October_2017.

Tombe, Trevor. 2018. "Alberta's Long-Term Fiscal Future." *University of Calgary
School of Public Policy Publications* 11, no. 31. https://doi.org/10.11575/sppp
.v11i0.52965.

———. 2021. "Fiscal Planning and Sustainability in Alberta." Preprint, submitted
May 2021. https://www.policyschool.ca/wp-content/uploads/2021/05/AF20
_Fiscal-Planning_Tombe.pdf.

# 10 Moving to a Sustainable Fiscal Future

## Addressing Alberta's Legacies of Denial

*Robert L. Ascah*

Chapter 1 started with an exclamation: "No sales tax!" By now, I hope you're asking, "*Why* no sales tax?" or even "How do we get one for Alberta?" There are, of course, arguments against a sales tax for Alberta that are worth considering. These include, perhaps most importantly, the fact that Albertans oppose a sales tax so strongly that political parties compulsively avoid even the mention of such a tax for fear that they will not get elected or re-elected. Beyond this basic cultural aversion to taxes, though, there are also some economic arguments against a sales tax. For one, a sales tax is regressive: it is applied at the same rate to everyone, regardless of how much money they earn. This means it affects lower-income individuals and families—women in particular (Lahey 2015)—to a greater degree than their higher-income counterparts. More than this, a sales tax is an additional layer of regressive taxation on top of other items such as tobacco, fuel, alcohol, and motor vehicle registration fees. Some argue, too, that implementing a sales tax risks simply giving politicians and government officials more money to waste on various pet projects that taxpayers do not necessarily support.

There are also a number of strong arguments in support of a sales tax, which we have seen in this volume. As McMillan (chapter 5) argues, although Albertans oppose increased taxation in general, Alberta could easily impose a sales tax of up to 5 percent and still remain the lowest taxed jurisdiction in Canada. McKenzie (chapter 9) notes that the marginal cost of public funds associated with sales tax is also much lower than other taxes, meaning less of the revenue from sales tax goes towards administrative costs. He also points out that a sales tax is hard to avoid: it captures revenue bases that other taxes may not, such as inherited wealth used to consume in the province and spending by visitors to the province. While Smythe (chapter 7) acknowledges that the regressive nature of a sales tax is a potential challenge, she shows how this challenge can be mitigated somewhat by not using a PST as a way to reduce CIT and by implementing a refundable tax credit directed at low-income individuals and families. And finally, as Ferede (chapter 6) and I (chapter 4) both argue from different angles, a sales tax is a far more stable source of revenue than the CIT, PIT, and non-renewable resource revenue on which the province currently relies.

Implicated in all of the reasons why a PST makes sense for Alberta is a hint at how such a tax could be introduced. For a PST to be successful, Albertans need to understand its value. This is a challenging feat in Alberta's political culture, which is historically against taxes, sales tax in particular. (As Thomson documented in chapter 2 of this volume, woe betide any senior government official who utters the words *sales tax*!) This tax-averse attitude seems to be underpinned by a political denial of the effects of Alberta's exceptionally volatile revenue mix and its over-dependence on a single resource have on its fiscal health. These effects are compounded by a denial of the serious consequences that the climate crisis and other environmental concerns will have on Alberta's economic prospects. With all of this denial, it's no wonder that Albertans are so resistant to a sales tax and, for that matter, to other policy decisions that could bolster Alberta's long-term fiscal sustainability.

It's time to turn the tide on this Albertan denialism. We need to have a frank discussion about how this province's fiscal sustainability is intimately linked to its economic sustainability, which is in turn increasingly tied to environmental sustainability.

## Fiscal Consequences of Alberta's Political Culture of Climate Denial

Despite its volatility, resource revenue is reliable in at least one way: it will decrease over the long term. The global market's response to the science of climate change means that non-renewable resources are on their way out and renewable energy solutions are coming up in a big way. Non-renewable resource revenue *will* fall over time, and a sales tax is the most efficient and obvious method to replace it.

### Alberta's Burning Economic Platform

For David Dodge, former governor of the Bank of Canada and member of Ed Stelmach's Premier's Council for Economic Strategy, Alberta is standing on a burning platform when it comes to its resource-revenue-centred fiscal policy. Speaking of his time on the Premier's Council, Dodge told me, "We had to get people to understand [...] that this essential platform on which the Government of Alberta had operated really wasn't going to be viable over the long run." For Dodge, the economic argument around resource revenue is not that the resources themselves will run out, but that "the economic value of the resource will come down because there would be alternatives developed." To maintain the income and lifestyle to which Albertans have become accustomed, Alberta needs to figure out another plan (interview with author, 7 February 2019).

The confluence of financial, economic, climatic, and technological changes in the twenty-first century does not augur well for Alberta. The "burning platform" is evident in the desperation of successive Alberta governments and fossil fuel and pipeline industries to obtain access to tidewater through projects such as the Trans Mountain pipeline. Looking through the lens of current and historical fiscal and economic policy in Alberta, the province seems to have no obvious Plan B beyond more pipelines and another oil sands plant—no other resource to extract, no rabbit to pull out of the hat. In addition to Alberta-specific questions of quickly rising debt and declining resource revenues, our planet is facing an existential crisis: the climate crisis. Among many other consequences, this has the potential to undermine Alberta's economic foundation, which has

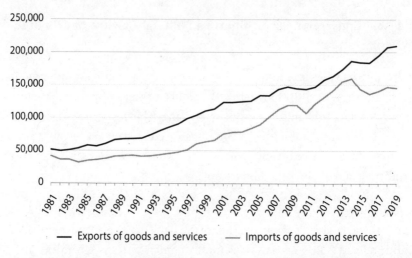

— Exports of goods and services     — Imports of goods and services

*Figure 10.1.* Alberta exports and imports, 1981 to 2019 (2012 $ millions)

*Source*: Statistics Canada, "Table: 36-10-0222-01: Gross Domestic Product, Expenditure-Based, Provincial and Territorial, Annual (× 1,000,000)," released 9 November 2021, https://doi.org/10.25318/3610022201-eng.

until now produced one of the highest standards of living on the planet. Even if Trans Mountain is completed, the inexorable and cumulative toll that greenhouse gases are occasioning upon the planet and its climates and weather, let alone the balance sheets of insurance companies and governments, will limit future economic growth in Alberta.

As the effects of global heating become more pronounced, Alberta's black gold is arguably not just losing value; it's becoming a liability.[1] Although demand for fossil fuels could grow modestly for several more decades, all Albertans should be worried about the long-term prospects for these non-renewable resources.[2] The fossil fuel industry is being challenged by some Indigenous communities and what Kenney's government calls "foreign-financed activists" (Kenney, Savage, and Schweitzer 2019), yes—but it is also feeling the pressure of strategic decisions being made in the auto industry, the courts, and the financial industry (Task Force on Climate-Related Financial Disclosures 2017).[3]

Regardless, Alberta's economy remains dominated by the extraction of three major staples or commodities—oil, bitumen, and natural gas—which it trades for manufactured goods. Indeed, from the time of the province's

Table 10.1. Alberta's major exports, 2014 to 2019 ($ millions)

|  | 2014 | 2015 | 2016 | 2017 | 2018 | 2019 |
|---|---|---|---|---|---|---|
| Mining, quarrying, and oil and gas extraction | 70,529 | 43,809 | 33,780 | 49,173 | 64,788 | 67,830 |
| Agriculture, forestry, fishing, and hunting | 693 | 655 | 648 | 580 | 550 | 614 |
| Construction | – | 302 | 137 | 173 | 433 | 400 |
| Manufacturing | 20,537 | 20,686 | 17,806 | 18,185 | 20,922 | 19,785 |
| Chemical manufacturing | 8,012 | 8,940 | 8,690 | 8,950 | 9,260 | 7,880,309 |
| Primary metal and fabricated metal manufacturing | 2,860 | 2,620 | 1,476 | 1,580 | 1,908 | 2,211 |

Source: Statistics Canada, "Table 12-10-0098-01: Trade in Goods by Exporter Characteristics, by Industry of Establishment (× 1,000)," released 18 May 2021, https://doi.org/10.25318/1210009801-eng.

first European settlers, Alberta's economy has been commodity based and trade oriented. As figure 10.1 shows, Alberta has run and continues to run a very large surplus on trade.

The dominance of the oil, gas, and mining sectors in Alberta's exports is laid out in table 10.1. The energy sector leads all sectors in terms of exports even when commodity prices fall precipitously, as they did in 2015. Agriculture, forestry, and construction exports remain relatively infinitesimal as export sectors needed to support the balance of trade. Manufacturing, Alberta's second most important export, sits at roughly one-third the value of oil and gas. Notably, the only manufacturing segment that is substantial is chemical manufacturing, mainly derived from petroleum by-products. The next largest manufacturing sectors are machinery and primary metals, which languished between 2014 and 2019. This may be explained by the fact that these sectors serve local markets. Without export markets, they do not have the scale to enter into highly competitive global markets dominated by global corporations.

How does Alberta get off this burning economic platform? The obvious answer is economic diversification. The United Nations Framework Convention on Climate Change (2016, 13) defined economic diversification as "a strategy to transform the economy from using a single source to multiple sources of income spread over primary, secondary and tertiary sectors . . . to improve economic performance for achieving sustainable growth." For governments, a diversified economy means a diversified revenue base. Alberta has intermittently been infatuated with the idea of economic diversification during periods of low oil prices. Numerous initiatives have been undertaken, studies published, and trade missions launched.

Over the years, the Alberta government has announced millions if not billions of dollars in different economic diversification incentives in the forms of tax incentives, grant programs, royalty holidays, and loan guarantees. In September 2018, the Alberta government pledged $300,000 annually to Alberta book publishers over four years. According to the news release, "the funding is from the Capital Investment Tax Credit, which helps stimulate job growth across Alberta" (Government of Alberta 2018, para 1). More recently, the Kenney government announced a $9 million "funding boost" to artificial intelligence (AI) research and development to "showcase Alberta's AI Advantage" (Alberta Advanced Education 2020). However, it is "energy diversification" that has really captured the imaginations of Alberta policy makers (see, for example, the Energy Diversification Advisory Committee's [2018] report on the topic). The government's largesse for energy diversification far exceeds its financial commitments to other diversification projects. Take, for example, the $3 billion put towards oil tanker rail cars (Government of Alberta 2019a),[4] the potential $2 billion backstop guarantee for the Trans Mountain pipeline project (Woods 2018), and the petrochemical plant being completed by Inter Pipeline in Fort Saskatchewan (Reuters Staff 2017). Not to be outdone by Rachel Notley's NDP, Kenney's UCP government has bet heavily on TC Energy's Keystone XL pipeline with a $1.5 billion equity investment and $6 billion loan guarantee. This incurred a write-down of $1.5 billion when President Joe Biden cancelled Keystone's export permit.

It should be acknowledged that such "energy diversification" projects do generate thousands of well-paid construction jobs for a few years, and perhaps a few hundred permanent jobs. The issue here is not that these projects have no positive economic impact for the province. They do. But the contrast between "energy diversification" efforts focussed on oil and gas and real economic diversification away from oil and gas (such as the publishing and AI examples cited above) is striking and invites the question: Is Alberta really diversifying in a way that will protect its economic future, or is it just deepening its reliance on the non-renewable energy sector?

Given the uncertain long-term prospects for fossil fuels, it is difficult to imagine diversification within the oil, gas, and petrochemicals sectors as an effective strategy in underwriting a sustainable and future-oriented economic and fiscal plan. Yet the province seems to have no qualms about placing billions of taxpayer dollars at risk for oil and gas projects instead of investing in real economic diversification.[5] Meanwhile, recent announcements about a strategy to use existing natural gas resources and pipelines to harvest "blue hydrogen" are being touted as having the economic potential for the province that the oil sands used to have (Varcoe 2021).

It is also worth asking how many jobs would be created if Albertans did more than just supply the labour for foreign-owned energy projects and began focussing on locally generating the engineering and design work for them. While this would clearly still be an economy reliant on the importance of oil and gas in global markets, it would at least shift Alberta away from reliance on non-renewable resource revenues and towards the accrual of royalty payments related to intellectual property rights. But Albertans should think, too, beyond the energy sector. How many jobs could be created in Alberta in book publishing, machine learning, and other intellectual-property-based sectors with $100 million, let alone the billions of dollars in incentives we currently invest in fossil fuels? Such projects don't just reduce Alberta's dependence on non-renewable energy; they shift it away from its staple-heavy, commodity-trade-based system. Unlike the late nineteenth and early twentieth centuries when great individual wealth was created from resource processing (John D. Rockefeller) and manufacturing (Henry Ford), new wealth is accruing to those individuals who develop and patent intellectual property (Bill Gates). This is why it is essential to move away from resource processing and manufacturing and tack towards development of human capital.

### Environmental Liabilities

Beyond the dim future prospects of an oil-and-gas-based economy, the provincial government also seems to be in denial about the looming unfunded environmental liabilities of the oil patch. Environmental liabilities are the by-products of and infrastructure associated with non-renewable resource development that eventually need to be cleaned up. Any serious analysis of how the economic base of Alberta impacts the provincial government's fiscal sustainability must account for these liabilities (Ascah 2021b, 12–14). There are two central questions in this regard: First, how much cleanup is there to do? And second, who is responsible for this cleanup—that is, who should pay for it?

The first question can be answered by determining the province's unfunded environmental liabilities. To do this, you must first calculate their gross value. This calculation depends on the number of oil wells, their locations, the estimated costs of their rehabilitation, the length and condition of relevant pipelines, and the size of tailings ponds. Assumptions about some of these aspects are made based on engineering studies and historic costs of similar past rehabilitation efforts. Next, the period over which the rehabilitation is to take place must be determined. Finally, a discount rate is used to determine the net present value of the gross liabilities. A suitable rehabilitation plan thus involves determining how much money must be put aside today to adequately fund environmental rehabilitation in the future. An unfunded liability is the difference between the determined liability and the actual funds that have been set aside. The question of when the liabilities are due—that is, when the rehabilitation costs must actually be paid—is central determining how much money needs to be set aside today.

Ryerson University accounting professor Thomas Schneider notes that liabilities have the potential to affect Alberta's balance sheet and credit rating (quoted in De Souza et al. 2018). As we've already seen in this book, Alberta incentivizes private control of its public energy resources. As it turns out, these same incentives encourage private abandonment of environmental cleanup responsibilities before their liabilities are due. Thus, the select few who make their fortunes off of Alberta's oil and gas are effectively incentivized to leave the cleanup costs of their operations—environmental and economic—for Alberta taxpayers. As Kevin Taft summed it up for me, there has been a transfer of "absolutely immense public wealth in the form of Alberta's oil and gas resources into private hands" and now "there's a massive transfer of private liability onto taxpayers and governments and it's systematic" (interview with author, 26 November 2018).

This problem is exacerbated when environmental liabilities are inaccurately estimated, putting the province on the hook for more than it bargained for. In 2018, investigative journalists unearthed a presentation given in February of that year by the vice-president of liability management of the Alberta Energy Regulator (AER) to a meeting of oil and gas industry historians (De Souza et al. 2018). The presentation stated that the "official" number for environmental liabilities in the province was $58 billion (Wadsworth 2018, 13). Against this sum was a security deposit of $1.6 billion: 2.7 percent of the reported liability or 0.6 percent of the "worst-case scenario," as it was officially understood. However, the investigative report revealed the presentation also said that the AER could be understating environmental liabilities by about $200 billion (Wadsworth 2018). It said, in other words, that Alberta's oil-and-gas-related environmental cleanup was going to cost vastly more than any public estimates at the time showed, making Alberta's security deposit a drop in the ocean of funds that would be required to pay for them.[6] The AER's (2018) attempt to disavow the findings and, a day later, the resignation of CEO Jim Ellis (a former Alberta deputy energy and environment minister) highlighted for the first time in the public eye the enormous costs of cleaning up oil and gas sites and tailings ponds.[7] In a few short months, the credibility of Alberta's regulatory system suffered badly.[8] Alberta's claims to be a responsible developer of energy resources have only been further damaged by the creation of the Canadian Energy Centre—better known as Alberta's "energy war room"— and the dramatic flop of the *Report of the Public Inquiry into Anti-Alberta Energy Campaigns* (Allan 2021) it commissioned.[9]

The second question—Who will pay for the cleanup?—has been a heated legal issue in Alberta. In 2015, a high-stakes litigation on exactly this issue was brought by the AER and Orphan Well Association (OWA) against another provincial agency, ATB Financial. ATB, like other lenders, provides loans to a variety of industry borrowers. The case revolved around the insolvency of Redwater Resources, a small oil and gas company that had been petitioned into receivership by ATB, its lender. Redwater's approximately one hundred inactive oil wells, which were by that time largely dry, had been licensed by the AER. Such a license requires the title owner to clean up their well sites—a process that can cost more than the land itself is worth—before they can transfer the title. When a company that holds this kind of title goes bankrupt, it leaves in question who is responsible for the cleanup. Grant Thornton Ltd., acting as receiver on behalf of ATB, attempted to disclaim the well sites in order to avoid paying the outstanding reclamation costs. Such requests normally mean the well sites would be "orphaned"—have no legal owner responsible for their cleanup—and consequently join a growing number of wells left for reclamation by the industry- and government-funded not-for-profit OWA.[10] The AER sought to prevent the receiver's renunciation of the unproductive assets to avoid further burdening the OWA. The Canadian Association of Petroleum Producers (CAPP) eventually intervened in the litigation on behalf of the OWA and the AER. CAPP was concerned that viable energy companies would face increasingly large bills from the OWA to be funded by CAPP's solvent members.

At the Alberta Court of Queen's Bench and the Alberta Court of Appeal, federal paramountcy in the field of bankruptcy and insolvency upheld the receiver's and ATB's position.[11] However, on 31 January 2019, the Supreme Court or Canada ruled 5 to 2 in favour of the OWA, affirming the AER's right to prevent receivers from disclaiming unproductive assets and the associated regulatory obligations such as reclamation costs.[12] As a consequence, ATB and other lenders to companies in either bankruptcy or financial difficulty will probably end up writing off hundreds of millions in oil and gas loans.

*Financial Implications for the Fossil Fuel Industry*

As evidence mounts that the climate crisis is a growing factor in the Alberta government's financial sustainability, it is becoming increasingly probable that the finance community will tighten further lending to the oil industry to avoid future risks of paying for environmental liabilities.[13] This would have enormous implications on energy companies attempting to finance oil sands plants.

Although the Canadian banking and oil industry are at present generally allied, the medium term is cloudy at best, especially for Canada's largest oil sands producers (Willis 2019). The biggest danger confronting Alberta's oil patch and the Alberta government's fiscal prospects is the environmental, social, and corporate governance movement (ESG). ESG has been increasingly adopted by institutional investors who have the capacity to choose where to invest. For instance, HSBC, Europe's largest bank, made a controversial decision in 2018 to scale back oil sands financing.[14] This decision, and others like it, signals a retreat by large international financial institutions and will be of great concern to Alberta's finances. At the same time, Alberta-based institutions have purchased large oil sands holdings from major international players like Chevron, Shell, and Devon Resources. Increasingly, the bet on expanding the oil sands will depend on domestic and international capital markets, which are currently revising investment policies towards oil companies. This does not mean that capital will be unavailable, but it does mean that the cost of capital will be driven higher because of ESG investment policies responding to the threat of environmental litigation. It will also mean that there will be huge and costly regulatory delays. Ultimately, these are all consequences of the existential threat of the climate crisis.[15] These shifts in global investment are already affecting Alberta's economy, as Moody's Investors Service's (2019) downgrade of the province's credit rating shows. As Moody's put it, "environmental considerations are material to Alberta's credit profile and we consider environmental risk to be elevated" (5).

More recently, the Auditor General of Alberta (2021) updated an earlier report on whether adequate systems are in place to ensure sufficient security for the rehabilitation of oil sands mines and other mines. In concluding that unsatisfactory progress was evident since the 2015 Auditor General review, the legislative auditor identified five technical loopholes that mines were employing to minimize the provision of financial security to the government for rehabilitation (33–34). The industry had been telling the government to trust them and the government was willing to pull the wool over their eyes and accept the status quo.

Taken all together, these factors raise the question of whether remaining oil sands owners (such as Suncor, Imperial Oil, and Cenovus) and the province's mine security program together have sufficient funds to meet their regulatory land reclamation obligations. In short, will these asset owners ultimately pin bondholders, lenders, shareholders, and regulators (such as the Alberta government) with the bill for a huge environmental cleanup (Olszynski 2019)? One has to ask, too, whether all of these factors presage attempts by oil sands operators to pay the government lower royalties as a way of saving money to fund their massive environmental liabilities. In these circumstances, the case for a sales tax to support a government-led transition to a low-carbon future by replacing declining resource revenue has obvious advantages.

## A Sales Tax for a Sustainable Alberta

Given the underlying economic challenges facing Alberta (which will only get more challenging), what must a government do to pay teachers' salaries, repair roads, and deliver health services?

In the face of economic pressure from climate change and shifts in global investment away from fossil fuels, there are some clear advantages to Alberta using a sales tax as a tool to move away from declining resource revenue, to fund these environmental liabilities, and ultimately to support a transition away from non-renewable resource extraction. As I show in chapter 4 of this volume, resource revenue is volatile; as Ferede shows in chapter 6, a sales tax is a more stable tax revenue base than both CIT and PIT. Fiscal sustainability in Alberta therefore calls for the addition of a sales tax to stabilize provincial government revenue.

*Sales Tax as a Means of Reducing Income Tax Rates?*

Still, there is the challenge of making a sales tax a palatable option to tax-averse Albertans. Increasingly, this is being done by advertising a sales tax as a means to lower taxes on personal and corporate incomes—an argument advanced in Ferede's and Dahlby's (2019) analysis of the positive economic effects of reducing CIT, which has been widely cited by Jason Kenney's UCP government. This approach is tantamount to "softening" the blow of a new set of taxes. In their study, Ferede and Dahlby use historical data such as growth rates of GDP and CIT rates to estimate the effects that changes to CIT rates might have on GDP and employment growth. The authors find that "a one percentage-point reduction in a provincial government's statutory CIT rate increases the growth rate by 0.12 percentage points four years after the initial CIT rate cut and increases real per capita GDP by 1.2 percent in the long run" (Ferede and Dahlby 2019, 19). While acknowledging that many factors can influence long-term economic growth rates, Ferede and Dahlby subject the regression results to robustness checks by including additional variables such as commodity prices, US GDP growth, population growth, and export price indices. Using these tests, the authors conclude that these other factors do not support objections that commodity prices or US economic growth are more deterministic than CIT rate changes for Alberta (18–23).

While such positions on sales tax may well make a new sales tax conceptually easier to swallow, they also invite, from the perspective of fiscal sustainability, some pressing questions: Does using a sales tax in this way actually achieve the goal of fiscal sustainability that we need to be aiming for? Can we know with certainty that lowering CIT rates will increase long-term economic growth? And how much difference would a 1.2 percent long-term rise in Alberta's GDP make for an average Albertan, anyway?

It is not, in fact, a foregone conclusion that reducing CIT stimulates the economy, and there are several criticism worth mentioning of studies that assume it is. First, although the results of empirical tests do show small increases in GDP, it is difficult to conclusively determine that lowering

CIT is the variable most responsible for these increases. Since 2000, federal and provincial governments have been lowering CIT rates in response to arguments made by Ferede, Dahlby, and other economists (Bazel and Mintz 2013; McKenzie 2019). Up until 2015, when the New Democrats took office, Alberta had been the most aggressive of the big four provinces in lowering CIT rates. That said, taxation economists have observed that the provincial CIT rates are kept stable for long periods of time and that the most intensive forms of tax competition may be tax incentives for research and development, television and film, and oil and gas royalties (Dahlby and Ferede 2019, 10). Another factor noted by Dahlby and Ferede is the role played by allocation formulae by which the provincial CIT of companies operating interprovincially is computed according to provincial weightings that are based on in-province sales and payroll costs. This tax allocation formula "has greater impact on the marginal cost of hiring labour than the tax rate differential between the provinces" (11). These other factors affecting corporate taxes payable could make promised growth rates under CIT reductions difficult to quantitatively separate out from these individual effects.

A second criticism of this type of study is the value structure embedded in the models created. One of Ferede's and Dahlby's (2019, 11) foundational beliefs is that "tax bases almost always shrink in response to a tax rate increase because taxpayers have an increased incentive to alter their labour, savings and investment decisions." This assumption is canon for the neoclassical idea that the world is made up of economically rational actors. The real world is, arguably, different. Most individual taxpayers and many small corporate taxpayers have no time to pay attention to differential tax rates since their mobility is theoretical, not real. The claim that "shrinkage of the tax base is a measure of the *harmful distortion* in the allocation of resources caused by taxation" (Ferede and Dahlby 2019, 11, emphasis added) is a normative judgment. Moreover, many workers and small businesses, heavily indebted to financial institutions, do not have the choice to withdraw their labour or reduce business hours if they are to avoid bankruptcy. As Himmelfarb and Himmelfarb (2013) argue, the assertion that taxation is a "dirty word" because experts say so is a belief, not a fact.

A third criticism that may be levelled at these analysts is their acceptance of the Laffer curve. Developed by economist Arthur Laffer, this model is used to show that, in certain circumstances, lowering tax rates can lead to increased tax revenue. Ferede and Dahlby (2019, 12) argue exactly this: by reducing CIT, they can increase tax revenue in the long run. Indeed, much of the neoliberal school puts great faith in the view that, over the long run, the revenue growth estimated by Laffer curve models will come true. This argument can be refuted in two ways. The first refutation consists simply in discounting the Laffer curve as an unprovable article of faith of the neoliberal school. The second refutation follows the first and is more potent. The belief that the Laffer curve projections will come true is belied by evidence that long-term economic growth is slowing in modern industrialized economies (Piketty 2014, 93–95). Many of these now-slowing economies have, since the 1990s, been the subjects of neoliberal economic experiments.

There is also the question of technological progress as a factor in overall economic growth. Ferede and Dahlby (2019, 4) posit that higher CIT rates "reduce economic growth by reducing productivity and by lowering investment." It is not clear from the context whether this statement is a fact, an assertion, or an assumption. While plausible, there are many other factors that may reduce investment and hence productivity growth. One of the central factors currently afflicting investment in Alberta is the desire by institutional investors to reduce their exposures to fossil fuel production, which has nothing to do with relative corporate tax rates. Rather, as Mark Carney (2019, 8), former Governor of the Bank of England, has said, "*every* financial decision must take climate change into account."

### Sales Tax and Alberta's Tax Policies

In Kathleen Lahey's (2015) persuasive report *The Alberta Disadvantage*, she argues that if a sales tax were introduced into Alberta's current taxation system, it would contribute to social and income inequality and to the precarity of Alberta's fiscal future. A key part of her position is that recommendations for a sales tax come from arguments, like those presented above, that support low taxes on capital (76).

For Lahey, such arguments are based on "detaxation" policies in Alberta that have reduced tax revenue overall, including taxation on the wealthiest income earners. Yet these same policies have resulted in tax *increases* for Alberta's poorest. By reducing overall tax revenue, these same policies have also increased the province's dependence on non-renewable resource revenues to make up the gap in funding for government services.

Importantly, it is not necessarily sales tax as such that would exacerbate these problems, but a sales tax in the context of detaxation. Sales taxes are regressive—their rate is not adjusted based on a taxpayer's wealth or income. This means that all consumers will be taxed at the same rate regardless of how much they consume, whether they're able to pay the tax, or how much they earn; a millionaire would pay the same percentage tax or mark-up on a case of beer as minimum-wage worker. If a regressive sales tax were introduced into Alberta's current system as a way of further reducing income taxes, the province would saddle its lowest income earners with a heavier tax burden, and saddle itself with ever-greater reliance on non-renewable resources.

Lahey (2015) observes that many taxes and fees that the Alberta government already collects are regressive. These include major sources of revenue for Alberta such as fuel taxes, tobacco tax, insurance taxes, carbon taxes, vehicle licenses, tuition and school fees, and markups from the Alberta Gaming, Liquor and Cannabis Commission.[16] Her empirical research shows that Alberta's shift from a progressive PIT system to a flat 10 percent income tax (which began in Alberta at the beginning of the 2000s) placed a disproportionate burden on the province's lowest income earners (76–78). She proposes implementing a new progressive PIT, estimating that an extra $1.6 billion of revenue could be obtained without imposing any tax increases on the bottom five deciles of income groups.[17] Unlike a progressive PIT, however, a retail sales tax would place a burden on all income groups (although the highest earner is also likely to be the higher consumer, and would end up paying about twelve times the consumption tax as the lowest).

Lahey notes that refundable consumption tax credits would reduce "some of the regressive incidence" of these taxes, but they would not really solve the problem. Even if the province instituted a refundable PST credit, Lahey finds that the overall share of the additional tax collected by each of the lower deciles would still be unfair from an equity and gender perspective. Other low-income measures don't solve this problem, either. If the calculations of taxes payable, social assistance, rent and housing supplements, and special income programs for First Nations are becoming too complex and expensive to efficiently administer and do not ameliorate a sales tax's regressive nature, then the time for more tinkering to would seem to be over. A sales tax as a means of reducing income tax is, from Lahey's perspective, untenable.

Instead of introducing a sales tax to reduce income tax, Lahey (2015, 80) says that

> the main focus [of building a less regressive tax system] should be on developing robust fiscal progressivity and a diverse array of stable taxes and economic sectors in order to move away from heavy reliance on resource revenues and begin the slow process of saving and sterilizing resource receipts for use as the capital assets they represent. Once Alberta reaches that level of fiscal development, it would then be time to begin the discussion of whether sales taxes with a robust low-income credit feature would enhance the overall tax mix.

In other words, Alberta doesn't need another regressive tax right now. What it *does* need is a complete overhaul of its taxation system.

While a system of refundable tax credits would not completely solve the problem, improvements to the rebate or an aggressive overhaul of all social assistance programs would help. Moreover, creating a more stable, sustainable revenue structure with a sales tax would improve the periodic spending cuts that have afflicted public services for all citizens, but especially lower-income families. A key goal of fiscal reform is to balance efficiency in collecting consumption taxes with a simplification in the administration of social assistance and eventually, ideally, basic annual income for low-income individuals and families. The solutions are technical ones—ones that necessitate a thorough review of Alberta's current system of personal and corporate income taxes.

From our examinations of Ferede, Dahlby, and Lahey, we are left with competing versions of not only how Alberta's economy does run, but how it should run, and specifically whether and how it should integrate a sales tax. To be clear, I believe it would be in the long-term interest of neither the Alberta economy nor Albertan society to implement a sales tax simply to lower PIT or CIT. I do, however, agree with Glassford's emphasis in chapter 8 of this book that PST can reduce the need to raise taxes in a recession. Along the same lines, I believe a sales tax is ultimately necessary to Alberta's long-term plan if we hope to sustainably fund our public programs and maintain our quality of life. This is especially true considering the serious revenue shortfalls witnessed in fiscal years 2019–20 and 2020–21 and the diminished future investment and employment prospects in Alberta's energy sector.

## A Process for Sustainable Change

If relying on the allure of lower CIT and PIT rates is out, how *could* a future Government of Alberta successfully adopt a sales tax and begin to move towards a more fiscally sustainable future? How could they adopt sustainable policy in a way that is itself sustainable—able, that is, to survive more than one government term? In order to have a sustainable fiscal policy stick around long enough for us to begin to reap its rewards, it needs to be publicly accepted and supported. Politicians must be ready to leave behind their habits of economic and climate change denialism and be ready to sell the virtues of a sales tax to voters. Albertans need to understand why a sales tax is needed and believe in its value. As Al O'Brien, former deputy finance minister, put it, "It has to be something that Albertans believe is appropriate and good government. If you're not prepared to sell that to Albertans on a vote, it isn't going to happen" (interview with author, 3 November 2018).

Interviews with O'Brien and fellow former deputy finance minister Robert Bhatia also emphasize the fundamental importance of appropriate and robust consultative processes that actually engage the public in informed conversations about proposed policy changes before those changes are implemented. "In some fashion," Bhatia told me, "there needs to be a broad engagement with elected officials outside of the normal process of the budget and legislation." To get Albertans to really care about these discussions, Bhatia noted, it's important that they emphasize not just the "technical merits" of a sales tax, but the way in which such a tax might support the welfare and well-being of Albertans in general. The consultations must, that is, be framed "in terms of sustainability of public service, the financial costs and benefits to individual Albertans, the economy [...] and then ask the question: Does the sales tax fit into that?" (interview with author, 7 December 2018). As O'Brien summarized, first a government needs to get Albertans to understand *that* the province needs revenue, and then they have to involve Albertans in the process of deciding how to acquire that revenue (interview with author, 3 November 2018). To begin this consultation on good footing, though, Albertans must be ready to have the conversation. Public education around the long-term (un)sustainability of provincial finances is crucial to facilitating a balanced and more nuanced understanding of taxes by the electorate and to dispel the public's fear of discussing provincial finances.

Recent conversations on the matter have been dominated by policy elites from business, academic specialists, provincial officials, lawyers, regulators, and professional lobbyists who speak a language inaccessible to the general population. This chain can only be broken through a political willingness to recruit persons outside the "usual suspects"—experts in a chosen field—into the discussion, and a willingness to resist controlling outcomes. In short, politicians must reinvigorate policy discussions by challenging the status quo, providing Albertans with all of the necessary information, engaging them in the political process, and trusting them to make the tough decisions.

Below, I offer some suggestions about what this process could look like. While it is by no means an exhaustive how-to guide, I hope it functions as a productive starting point.

### Consultation and Education

Public education and debate must be led by a third party who both politicians and the public trust, and who the public is confident will listen to them. This third party could take the form of, for instance, a financial sustainability commission. To gain the public's trust, such a commission must be carefully appointed to accurately represent the diversity of people and perspectives in Alberta today. A starting point, then, would be to appoint at least two co-chairs to this commission: one who represents the interests of the business sector and the other the broad consumer and public interest. Committee selection would be by open competition with final decisions made by the government, and should include representatives of various stakeholders, public and private, from across the socioeconomic spectrum. This would be a shift away from status quo committee selection, which tends to be driven by the elites of the area under review. For example, the Blue Ribbon Panel chaired by Janice MacKinnon had no one to represent the day-to-day users or front-line providers of government services.[18]

Before consultations get underway, commissioners should recommend a program of research and a process for engagement by publicly communicating these recommendations to the government. Kevin Taft suggested in an interview that "the very first thing that needs to be done is a comprehensive assessment of the province's assets and liabilities" in order to assess "the size of the problem" and better understand how much revenue would have to be raised through taxes, or how much spending would need to be cut (interview with author, 26 November 2018). Regardless of the starting point, though, the commission's program and process should be approved with or without revisions by the government in a transparent manner. This transparent method would also help ensure that recommendations are implemented by the government. It would also help generate buy-in from government caucus members, making the commissioners and staff become agents of the elected representatives. Should the governing party seek to "guide" the process in a particular manner (e.g., try to suggest that the province has a one-sided revenue or a spending problem), this guidance would be transparent to the opposition and the public, and the government could be held accountable for making decisions to narrow or broaden the mandate.

The commission would then invite submissions on research projects. The results of accepted projects would be made public. The government would have a veto on topics studied, but the commission would have a free hand in selecting researchers for approved topics. Merit, including experience, would be the primary factors in researcher selection. The research team would benefit from being interdisciplinary, not dominated by economists and accountants. Widening the net beyond finance and economics would allow fiscal problems to be examined in a more wholistic way and hopefully produce innovative solutions.

## Engagement

For too long, Alberta politicians had the luxury of relying on bonus royalty revenue to smooth over various constituencies' demands for better public services and more capital infrastructure. Today, in the midst of the worst economic and fiscal situation since the Great Depression, spurred on in part by the concurrent COVID-19 pandemic, Alberta politicians and members of the public no longer have the luxury of remaining silent or complacent. Everyone in the province has a stake in the quality of provincial financial management. A robust engagement campaign must, therefore, be part of this process.

*Developing accessible and interactive channels of communication.* After the research program has been completed and published, the commission staff would prepare a summary of key research findings. The information would be available online through a special commission portal. In the interests of transparency, the portal would also disclose the commission's expenses and those of its staff and researchers. In addition, there would be a public log of who commission members and staff met with to ensure transparency and build trust in the engagement process.

One bright spot of the COVID-19 pandemic is that, because we have all had to stay home, more people than ever are comfortable using online methods of engagement. Virtual townhalls can be, and have already been, successfully organized to receive submissions and to foster interest and public debate. We have incredible capacity to bring together large numbers of people into a consultative dialogue—a mutual or collective learning process—at relatively low cost, and with impressive results. Engagement efforts in the mid-2010s by the Royalty Review Advisory Panel and the Climate Leadership Panel used online portals, surveys, open houses, technical engagement with experts, and submissions, including email and online articles and reports. The Royalty Review Advisory Panel received over 7,200 submissions through its web portal; the Climate Leadership Panel received 25,000 responses to its online survey. Both reports are remarkable for the alacrity by which the panels accumulated and digested information and reported on it (Mowat et al. 2016, 15–16, appendix B; Leach et al. 2015, 14–15).

These public consultation approaches are mechanisms by which a commission could find areas of public consensus by engaging a wide audience and providing opportunities for Albertans to comment on issues confronting government.

Obviously, not all Albertans participate in public forums of this type. For this reason, the media must also play an important role in public engagement. Especially given the mistrust of media that exists in some communities particularly since the Trump presidency, it is imperative that the commission invoke participatory channels of media communication. Again, it is necessary for the public to trust that they are being listened to. Although a bit passé, the call-in radio talk show provides a template on which such interactive media channels could be developed. On these call-in shows, experts are invited to discuss a particular topic with the host as callers share their perspective with or questions for the expert, who is then given a chance to respond. While not all Albertans will directly participate in such media events, these publicly broadcast forums have the benefit of reaching broader audiences of listeners or viewers. They could thus be tapped to widen the public's engagement in and understanding of the topics at hand—in this case, the province's finances.

There are a number of experts that the public could speak to through these outreach and engagement strategies to educate themselves about the provincial government's fiscal situation. In no particular order, such individuals would include the premier; finance, health, energy, and education ministers; credit rating analysts; economists; political scientists; and finance and accounting professors. Other viewpoints that should be heard on various topics include the Canadian Association of Petroleum Producers, Greenpeace, the Alberta Chambers of Commerce, the Canadian Taxpayers Federation, the Alberta Federation of Labour, and First Nations groups. Leaders in the not-for-profit sector, education, and health care should also be invited to provide context and understanding on critical issues of service delivery and effectiveness of government programs. Another benefit of participatory townhalls and media is that members and staff of the proposed financial sustainability commission could also be participant listeners or guests, allowing them to listen directly to the spectrum of values held by Albertans and their understanding of the province's fiscal challenges. It should also be mandatory for all MLAs, as ultimate decision makers, to listen to townhalls and forums either live or in recorded form.

*Exploring values, principles, and biases.* An open, transparent process that reaches out for diverse views will make for better, long-term fiscal policies and a greater acceptance by a more informed public. Of course, voters' understandings of the current fiscal and economic situation in the province vary and most bring their own set of values, principles, and biases to the table. In reaching out to Albertans, a financial sustainability commission would need to gauge Albertans' understandings of the current situation and gain an understanding of the broad values and principles that the majority would accept to guide a new fiscal framework.

The commission must demonstrate to the public that its study is not simply a ruse to obtain buy-in for a sales tax. To be effective, the channels of communication chosen by the commission should be designed to seek areas of consensus—that is, guiding principles that the majority find acceptable—by exploring particular issues on which there are fundamental disagreements. They should then explore how a sales tax might help or hinder in each case. Issues could include, to name a few, regulatory reform; pay and benefits in the public sector, including the use of performance pay for executives; private versus public delivery of health care; how resource royalties are used; the issue of balancing spending against revenue; the role of borrowing and savings in government fiscal policy; the use of technology in service delivery; reviews of government programs; and the impact of environmental liabilities on the province's balance sheet.

At the end of this process, the commission would issue a final report, which would be made public at the same time as it is sent to cabinet members and all MLAs. The report would identify areas of consensus and a set of actionable recommendations. The government would then decide how best to implement a program to support long-run fiscal sustainability. The public would have a role here in holding the government accountable to the program's correct implementation.

For any of this process to work, it must be based on a foundation of willingness on the part of politicians to engage honestly with Albertans about the province's precarious fiscal situation and the role a sales tax could play in remedying it. Only then will it be possible for Alberta to shed the fiscal and environmental denial of governments past and begin implementing a fiscal sustainability program that makes sense for Albertans.

## Some Policy Suggestions

A financial sustainability commission might also wish to consider two specific policy ideas, alongside the implementation of a sales tax. The first has to do with the Heritage Savings Trust Fund: a shining example of Alberta exceptionalism that feeds into antitax sentiment. I suggest that the commission may wish to examine the continuing utility of managing this pool of assets while Alberta's debt continues to rise. The second policy idea relates to the existential crisis of climate change, and asks politicians to consider: Is the current policy of Alberta allowing the federal government to collect carbon taxes and to redistribute the moneys back to Albertans appropriate when the province is running large deficits?

*Eliminate the vestiges of a "have" province.* The Heritage Fund's investment returns are typically higher than the cost of Alberta's debt. However, as we saw in chapter 4, investment income is subject to wide fluctuations and exposes the province to risks outside its control—principally, the risk of a prolonged downturn in global equity and financial asset markets. To simplify the province's finances, the liquidation of approximately $17.8 billion of the Heritage Fund's assets (as of 31 March 2021) would be both a concrete measure and a symbolic move. It would be a concrete measure in terms of removing a complex administrative and policy process that costs the province millions of dollars.[19] The proceeds of liquidation could be used to purchase some of the province's outstanding debt in the open market. This would put an end to the arbitraging of the province's assets and liabilities,[20] and reduce balance sheet complexity. A liquidation would be a symbolic act in terms of underlining that the province is no longer "special" in any financial or economic sense—it is no longer a have province. The burial of the Heritage Fund would signal that the government is no longer in denial about the fiscal challenges lying ahead. To the public, there would no longer be any debate about the virtues of the Heritage Fund and net debt would essentially be the same as debt outstanding.

*Reinstate the carbon tax.* The carbon tax has become a highly charged and polarizing tax. As economist Mark Jaccard (2018) notes, a common complaint is that the money raised through this type of tax is not put to good use or does not effectively reduce the carbon footprint. It is widely accepted that at the current rate, and even at proposed higher rate of $170 per tonne of $CO_2e$ (carbon dioxide equivalent) by 2030—compared to the $50 per tonne rate in 2022—carbon emission reduction goals will be hard to achieve. Given the way current political winds are blowing, a stronger rationale is required to buttress support for the continuation of carbon tax.

As noted above, the oil and gas industry has created vast environmental liabilities that will take many generations to clean up, assuming they can be cleaned up at all. Instead of using the carbon tax to redistribute income, a large-scale program could be undertaken to clean up orphan wells and pipelines, return farmland to productive use, explore ways to use wells for geothermal power, and commence a massive project focussed on cleaning up the vast oil sands tailings ponds. Such a multibillion-dollar, multidecade program would employ thousands of former oil industry workers for a just cause—a clean environment. This bold proposal has already been made in an Alberta Liability Disclosure Project report (Boychuck et al. 2021).

Some may object that this is an unwise use of public funds and amounts to cover up market and regulatory failures. However, regulatory measures could still be undertaken to bill licensees for cleanup costs, forcing large producers to book the liability adequately. This process would provide greater comfort to investors on the grounds that (1) the liabilities are being addressed; (2) companies are disclosing fairly the estimated costs incurred and future costs companies must face; (3) rating agencies can better evaluate the scope of environmental liabilities; and (4) the provincial government is seen to be an honest broker in dealing with these massive liabilities.

Alberta, as a political jurisdiction with a stand-alone credit rating, is now facing staggering environmental liabilities that, in a "worst-case scenario," are almost equal to the province's GDP. This does not include the provincial government's debt of approximately $110 billion nor the $8.6 billion in unfunded pension liabilities (Government of Alberta 2021b, 22, 64). This situation should command the attention of all Albertans.

## Political Conditions Enabling a Sales Tax

Speaking on panel discussion regarding a sales tax for Alberta at The University of Alberta in January 2015, Graham Thomson outlined four conditions to justify a sales tax to the public. These conditions are: (1) fiscal crisis, whether real or created; (2) limited options to sustain needed public services; (3) an opposition party in disarray; and (4) the sales tax tied to a common societal objective, for example, health care.

The first condition is arguably satisfied in Alberta in 2021. In spite of an improving oil and gas sector, and in spite of the fact that the province's revenue capacity can be substantially increased by bringing in a sales tax, public services are being degraded. We've seen provincial governments regularly take advantage of these moments to change the direction of fiscal policy, though they have usually changed it towards spending cuts. In chapter 1, I described the carefully crafted report of the Alberta Financial Review Commission (1993), which stressed the near-catastrophic nature of Alberta's fiscal situation. This crisis created an opportunity for the Klein administration to propose gearing down spending in a drastic fashion. With mainstream media agreeing with the report's conclusions and recommendations, the June 1993 election was framed around this issue. It was merely a matter of which political party would carry out the program. The province has seen Jason Kenney's government introduce similarly drastic cuts to public services after his own financial commission, the Blue Ribbon Panel on Alberta's Finances (2019) controlled the narrative. A sales tax requires a different approach because it opposes Alberta's exceptionalism and tax aversion. As suggested above, politicians are just going to have to trust Albertans to make the difficult choices for them.

The second condition may also already be satisfied. At the time of writing, freezes on spending are beginning to have a deleterious effect on the lives of Albertans, the vulnerable and well-heeled alike. There is little evidence that vast stores of wasted dollars and new revenue have been or will soon be unearthed. Thus, the government might use the fear of lost public services to explore its revenue alternatives. Indeed, Premier Kenney suggested as much in comments at the press conference announcing the Blue Ribbon Panel. Finance Minister Travis Toews did the same during a press conference in August 2021. It seems even the UCP government may be forced to study alternatives on the revenue side. That said, oil and natural gas prices have reached five-year highs in 2021. This may relieve the pressure from rating agencies worried about Alberta's rising debt levels and allow the UCP to persist with their agenda to reduce or freeze government spending.

The third condition is an opposition in disarray. Rachel Notley's leadership is not under siege and she retains near saint-like status among rank-and-file New Democrats. With a united opposition still opposed to even publicly discussing a sales tax, it is very uncertain that a conservative government led by Kenney, a former Alberta director of the Canadian Taxpayers Federation, would dare fight an election on bringing in a sales tax.

Still, what if the public could, through a public consultation and education process like the one outlined above, come to a consensus that there is no other viable option? This is the fourth condition. In order to prepare Alberta for a transition to a world without oil, bitumen, and natural gas, a sales tax could be framed by leaders in the province as a medicine that will protect against future fiscal disasters, a sustainable and necessary solution to enhance economic growth, fund a transition to a cleaner environment, eliminate the deficit, pay down debt, and preserve fundamental public services such as health care and education. As David Dodge put it, "We can think of the harmonized sales tax as a health services budget" or attach it to other spending functions. We can "rechristen it" (interview with author, 7 February 2019). If Alberta can thoughtfully retain progressivity in the

PIT system, mitigate the regressive nature of a sales tax, preserve essential public services, and earmark sales tax revenue for health and education, this might just be a campaign that could be won.

As a final word, readers should not think that the implementation of a PST, or a tax harmonized with the federal GST, is a cure-all for Alberta's fiscal woes. Alberta is facing a fiscal crisis that has arisen out of historical reliance on non-renewable resource revenue and a culture of tax aversion. Volatile resource revenue has encouraged more government spending based on a public's experience such services could be afforded at low rates of taxation. In addition, Alberta's economy—its burning platform—is facing its most difficult challenge, with previously economically viable resources becoming stranded as the world weans itself off fossil fuels. Without an open public debate on the difficult choices to be made about taxing and spending, rising oil prices may encourage politicians to kick the can down the road once again.

## Notes

1   In May 2019, the *Guardian* changed its style guide to indicate that the terms *climate crisis, climate breakdown,* and *global heating* are preferred over *climate change* and *global warming* in their publications. The change was made as a way of being "scientifically precise, while also communicating clearly with readers on this very important issue." I agree with *Guardian*'s logic and apply the same vocabulary here. See Carrington (2019) and Marsh and Hodsdon (2021).

2   BP's (2020) forecast for global demand of liquid fuels argues that under a "rapid" or "net zero" scenario, liquid fuels demand peaked in 2019. Under a "business as usual" scenario, demand will marginally increase through 2030, after which demand will fall slowly. The net zero scenario would see only thirty-five million barrels per day production, the rapid scenario about fifty million, and the business as usual scenario about ninety-three million. The forecast also notes that "differences in operational carbon intensity of crudes have an increasing impact as carbon prices increase" (sec. 4). While BP acknowledges some room for reducing carbon intensity for onshore projects, it reports Canada as having the third highest carbon intensity for crude production.

3   An important example of this type of decision was the 8 March 2019 announcement by Norway's finance minister that its huge public pension fund

would reduce its exposure to exploration and development companies. See Davies (2019).

4 This contract is to be reversed by the Kenney government through the sale of contracts with a potential write-down in the hundreds of millions of dollars. The Government of Alberta's (2020, 3) first quarter fiscal update reported a provision for losses of $1.25 billion on top of an actual provision of $866 million for fiscal 2019–20. Another example of the Alberta government's penchant for energy value-added processing is the ill-fated North West Redwater Partnership on which the Alberta Petroleum Marketing Commission has taken a $2.758 billion charge. It remains to be seen over the thirty-year term how much the province may gain or lose or whether the United Conservative Party will "crystallize" these losses, believing that they will never be recouped. The North West Redwater Partnership Monthly Toll Commitment, negotiated mainly under Ed Stelmach, may be a major boondoggle as well. Future toll commitments as of 31 March 2019 were $26.7 billion, according to a Government of Alberta (2019b) report. The report further stated that Alberta Petroleum Marketing Commission's own analysis "determined the agreement has positive net present value of future cash flows and no provision is required" (51). These financial blunders exceed those of the Don Getty government in the late 1980s—an already very bad precedent.

5 See, for example, the Government of Alberta (2019c) news release in which it announced it is providing a loan guarantee up to $440 million to support the Value Chain Solutions Inc. upgrader in the "Alberta Industrial Heartland." This move is consistent with the United Conservative government's continuing bet on the energy industry. This tendency also persists with various stopgap programs to grant struggling gas producers relief from municipal taxes. See, for example, Government of Alberta (2019d), a news release entitled "Reducing Assessment to Protect Jobs, Communities."

6 Later revelations from the same 2018 presentation suggested that Alberta's oil patch cleanup could take 2,800 years. See McIntosh and De Souza (2019).

7 As a side note, shortly after the news broke about Ellis's departure, David Swann, then the Alberta Liberal Party's sole MLA, requested an emergency legislative debate on the liability issue. The New Democrat Speaker of Alberta's Legislative Assembly refused to allow the debate. So much for the urgency of addressing this issue, which has been building for decades.

8 Not only was the Alberta Energy Regulator defective in regulating the energy industry, but the agency culture was one of intimidation and self-interest, as recorded in reports from the Auditor General of Alberta (2019), Office of the Ethics Commissioner (2019), and Public Interest Commissioner (2019).

9  In an irony of ironies, Commissioner J. Stephens Allan (2021) commented in his report that in his private conversations he was told that the Canadian Energy Centre's governance had probably been damaged beyond repair. See also Johnson (2021).

10 In May 2017, the Alberta government agreed to lend the OWA $235 million to help with the backlog of orphan well reclamation. In March 2020, the province contributed another $100 million in loans to the OWA. Contrast this frugality with $1 billion in grants from the federal government through the Alberta government in April 2020 to address Alberta's orphan wells issue. See Government of Canada (2021) and the amended loan agreement between the Government of Alberta and OWA (2021).

11 See Redwater Energy Corporation (Re), 2016 ABQB 278; Orphan Well Association v. Grant Thornton Limited, 2017 ABCA 124.

12 See Orphan Well Association v. Grant Thornton Ltd., 2019 SCC 5, [2019] 1 SCR 150. For more context on this case, see Ascah (2016, 2017, 2018a, 2018b, 2019, 2021a).

13 There have already been several decisions in this direction. For instance, on 8 March 2019 the Government of Norway expressed in a news release its commitment "to reduce the vulnerability of our common wealth to a permanent oil price decline. Hence, it is more accurate to sell companies which explore and produce oil and gas, rather than selling a broadly diversified energy sector . . . A permanent reduction in the oil price will have long-term implications for public finances. An exclusion of energy stocks in the GPFG will serve to further reduce the oil price risk, but the effect appears to be limited." Canadian integrated oil sands producers were not immediately affected by this decision. However, in October 2019, Norges Bank announced it was divesting its interests in oil sands producers CNRL, Suncor, and Cenovus. A few months later, on 23 February 2020, Teck Resources withdrew its application for the massive Frontier oil sands mine project, writing off $1.13 billion in value in the process. In a letter to Environment Minister Jonathan Wilkinson, Teck Resources president Don Lindsay wrote, "Global capital markets are changing rapidly and investors and customers are increasingly looking for jurisdictions to have a framework in place that reconciles resource development and climate change, in order to produce the cleanest possible products. This does not yet exist here today and, unfortunately, the growing debate around this issue has placed Frontier and our company squarely at the nexus of much broader issues that need to be resolved." See Government of Norway (2019), Sharp (2019), and Teck Resources (2020).

14 HSBC bore the contempt and ridicule of Jason Kenney for this decision several days before he was sworn in as premier. See Morgan (2019) and Reuters
Staff (2018).

15 Such obstacles have already been responsible for companies pulling out of
projects in Alberta. See, for example, Friedman (2020) and Fife and Marieke
(2020).

16 In 2020–21, the Alberta Gaming, Liquor and Cannabis Commission accounted
for about 14 percent of government revenue (Government of Alberta 2021b, 43).

17 In October 2015, the NDP government did, in fact, announce it was adopting
a new progressive system of income taxation with three tax brackets. See An
Act to Restore Fairness to Public Revenue, Bill 2, 29th Legislature, 1st Session
(2015).

18 In the Blue Ribbon Panel, there was no open competition for the panel's positions. Women were out-numbered four to two. The panel had no Indigenous,
small business, labour, municipal government, health, or education representation or the consumer of public services. There was one non-Caucasian
on the committee, a former Alberta deputy minister.

19 Investment costs for the Heritage Fund were $167 million in 2020–21—a
significant amount (Government of Alberta 2021a, 23). Danielle Smith (2020),
former Wildrose Party leader, made a similar recommendation to liquidate
the fund, arguing that it could be used to pay for the province's COVID-19
expenses.

20 Arbitraging means that a government borrows to invest. The logic is that the
province can borrow at lower rates and earn a higher investment return on the
borrowed money with a net profit to the province after expenses.

## References

Alberta Advanced Education. 2020. "Showcasing Alberta's AI Advantage."
New release, 18 September 2020. https://www.alberta.ca/release.cfm?xID=
7325353A14DB9-C847-DC89-7F952CABE75AF1CF.

Alberta Energy Regulator. 2018. "Statement from the Alberta Energy Regulator."
News release, 1 November 2018. https://www.aer.ca/providing-information/
news-and-resources/news-and-announcements/news-releases/public
-statement-2018-11-01.

———. 2021. *Liability Management Programs Results Report*, 6 March 2021.
https://www.aer.ca/data/facilities/LLR_Report_03.pdf.

Alberta Financial Review Commission. 1994. *Report to Albertans,* chaired by
Marshall Williams. Calgary: Alberta Financial Review Commission.

Allan, J. Stephens. 2021. *Report of the Public Inquiry into Anti-Alberta Energy Campaigns*, 30 July 2021. Available from https://open.alberta.ca/publications/public-inquiry-into-anti-alberta-energy-campaigns-report.

Ascah, Robert L. (Bob). 2017. "Redwater Resources." *AB Pol Econ*, 1 July 2017. http://abpolecon.ca/2017/07/01/redwater-resources/.

———. 2018a. "Docket 37627 Orphan Well Association, et al. v. Grant Thornton Limited, et al. (Redwater Resources contd)." *AB Pol Econ*, 13 January 2018. http://abpolecon.ca/2018/01/13/docket-37627-orphan-well-association-et-al-v-grant-thornton-limited-et-al-redwater-resources-contd/.

———. 2018b. "Redwater Supreme Court Hearing—Part 1." *AB Pol Econ*, 30 October 2018. http://abpolecon.ca/2018/10/30/redwater-supreme-court-hearing-part-1/.

———. 2019. "Further Reflections on Orphan Well Association v. Grant Thornton (Redwater)." *AB Pol Econ*, 28 February 2019. http://abpolecon.ca/2019/02/27/further-reflections-on-orphan-well-association-v-grant-thornton-redwater/.

———. 2021a. "Alberta's Environmental Bills Coming Due. Who will Pay?" *AB Pol Econ*, 4 July 2021. http://abpolecon.ca/2021/07/04/albertas-environmental-bills-coming-due-who-will-pay/.

———. 2021b. "Bring In a Sales Tax." *Alberta Views* 24, no 3 (April 2021).

Auditor General of Alberta. 2019. *An Examination of the International Centre of Regulatory Excellence (ICORE)*, October 2019. Edmonton: Office of the Auditor General.

———. 2021. *Processes to Provide Information About Government's Environmental Liabilities: Report of the Auditor General*, June 2021. Edmonton: Office of the Auditor General.

Bazel, Peter, and Jack Mintz. 2013. "Enhancing the Alberta Tax Advantage with a Harmonized Sales Tax." *University of Calgary School of Public Policy Publications* 6, no. 29. https://doi.org/10.11575/sppp.v6i0.42441.

Blue Ribbon Panel on Alberta's Finances. 2019. *Report and Recommendations: Blue Ribbon Panel on Alberta's Finances*, chaired by Janice MacKinnon, August 2019. Available from https://open.alberta.ca/publications/report-and-recommendations-blue-ribbon-panel-on-alberta-s-finances.

Boychuk, Regan, Mark Anielski, John Snow Jr., and Brad Stelfox. 2021. *The Big Cleanup: How Enforcing the Polluter Pay Principle Can Unlock Alberta's Next Great Jobs Boom*, June 2021. Calgary: Alberta Liabilities Disclosure Project. Available from https://www.aldpcoalition.com/thebigcleanup.

BP. 2019. "BP Energy Outlook 2020 Edition." BP Energy Economics. Accessed 11 May 2022. https://www.bp.com/en/global/corporate/news-and-insights/press-releases/bp-energy-outlook-2020.html.

Carney, Mark. 2019. "Après Benoît le déluge?" Speech given by Mark Carney, Governor of the Bank of England, at the European Central Bank in Frankfurt, DE, 17 December 2019. Available from https://www.bankofengland.co.uk/ news/speeches.

Carrington, Damian. 2019. "Why the Guardian Is Changing the Language It Uses About the Environment." *Guardian*, 17 May 2019. https://www.theguardian .com/environment/2019/may/17/why-the-guardian-is-changing-the-language -it-uses-about-the-environment.

Dahlby, Bev, and Ergete Ferede. 2019. "Simulating the Growth Effects of the Corporate Income Tax Cuts in Alberta." *University of Calgary School of Public Policy Publications* 12, no. 30. https://doi.org/10.11575/sppp.v12i0.69131.

Davies, Rob. 2019. "Norway's $1tn Wealth Fund to Divest from Oil and Gas Exploration." *Guardian*, 8 March 2019. https://www.theguardian.com/world/ 2019/mar/08/norways-1tn-wealth-fund-to-divest-from-oil-and-gas-exploration.

De Souza, Mike, Carolyn Jarvis, Emma McIntosh, and David Bruser. 2018. "Alberta Regulator Privately Estimates Oilpatch's Financial Liabilities Are Hundreds of Billions More than What It Told the Public." *National Observer*, 1 November 2018. https://www.nationalobserver.com/2018/11/01/news/ alberta-regulator-privately-estimates-oilpatchs-financial-liabilities-are -hundreds. Accessed 3 January 2018.

Energy Diversification Advisory Committee. 2018. *Diversification, Not Decline: Adapting to the New Energy Reality*. Available from https://open.alberta.ca/ publications/9781460136867.

Fife, Robert, and Marieke Walsh. 2020. "Teck Shelves Frontier Oilsands Projects." *Globe and Mail*, 20 February 2020.

Friedman, Gabriel. 2020. "What Teck gave Up on Its Controversial Project." *Edmonton Journal*, 25 February 2020.

Government of Alberta. 2018. "A New Chapter for Alberta's Book Publishers." News release, 14 September 2018.

———. 2019a. "Alberta Takes Decisive Action to Get More Oil to Market." News release, 19 February 2019.

———. 2019b. *2018–19 Government of Alberta Annual Report*. Available from https://www.alberta.ca/budget-documents.aspx.

———. 2019c. "Made-in-Alberta Plan Moves $2-Billion Investment Forward." News release, 22 January 2019.

———. 2019d. "Reducing Assessment to Protect Jobs, Communities." News release, 19 December 2019.

———. 2020. *2020–21 First Quarter Fiscal Update and Economic Statement*. Available from https://www.alberta.ca/budget-documents.aspx.

———. 2021a. *Alberta Heritage Savings Trust Fund: Annual Report 2020–21.* Available from https://open.alberta.ca/publications/0702-9721.

———. 2021b. *Annual Report: Government of Alberta 2020–21.* Available from https://www.alberta.ca/budget-documents.aspx.

Government of Alberta and OWA (Orphan Well Association). 2021. Further amended and restated loan agreement between the Province and the OWA, 1 March 2021. https://www.alberta.ca/assets/documents/energy-owa-loan -agreement.pdf.

Government of Canada. 2020. "Prime Minister Announces New Support to Protect Canadian Jobs." News release, 17 April 2020. https://pm.gc.ca/en/ news/news-releases/2020/04/17/prime-minister-announces-new-support -protect-canadian-jobs.

Government of Norway. 2019. "Excludes Exploration and Production Companies from the Government Pension Fund." News release no. 6/2019, 8 March 2019. https://www.regjeringen.no/en/id2631707/.

Himmelfarb, Alex, and Jordan Himmelfarb, eds. 2013. *Tax Is Not a Four-Letter Word: A Different Take on Taxes in Canada.* Waterloo: Wilfrid Laurier University Press.

Jaccard, Mark. 2018. "Divisive Carbon Taxes are Much Ado About Nothing." *Globe and Mail*, 15 December 2018.

Johnson, Lisa. "Allan Inquiry's Report Triggers War of Words with Alberta's Energy War Room." *Edmonton Journal*, 22 October 2021. https:// edmontonjournal.com/news/politics/allan-inquirys-report-triggers-war-of -words-with-albertas-energy-war-room.

Kenney, Jason, and Travis Toews. 2019. "Premier Kenney Introduces the Blue Ribbon Panel." Press conference, recorded 7 May 2019. YouTube video. https://www.youtube.com/watch?v=-MFYXjKcbEo.

Lahey, Kathleen. 2015. *The Alberta Disadvantage: Gender, Taxation, and Income Inequality.* Edmonton: Parkland Institute. https://www.parklandinstitute.ca/ the_alberta_disadvantage.

Leach, Andrew, Angela Adams, Stephanie Cairns, Linda Coady, and Gordon Lambert. 2015. *Climate Leadership: Report to Minister*, 20 November 2015. Available from https://open.alberta.ca/publications/climate-leadership -2015.

Marsh, David, and Amelia Hodsdon, eds. 2021. "Guardian and Observer Style Guide." *Guardian*, last updated 21 May 2021. https://www.theguardian.com/ guardian-observer-style-guide.

McIntosh, Emma, and Mike De Souza. 2019. "How Long Could It Take to Clean Up Alberta's Oilpatch? 2,800 Years, Alberta Energy Regulator Official Warns."

*Star Calgary*, 3 June 2019. https://www.thestar.com/calgary/2019/06/03/how
-long-could-it-take-to-clean-up-albertas-oilpatch-2800-years-alberta-energy
-regulator-official-warns.html.

McKenzie, Kenneth J. 2019. "Altering the Tax Mix in Alberta." *University of
Calgary School of Public Policy Publications* 12, no. 25. https://doi.org/10.11575/
sppp.v12i0.68390.

Moody's Investor Services. 2019. "Province of Alberta (Canada): Update
Following Rating Downgrade." Credit opinion, 9 December 2019. https://www
.alberta.ca/assets/documents/investor-relations-credit-report-moodys.pdf.

Morgan, Geoffrey. 2019. "HSBC Defends Itself after Months of Jabs from Jason
Kenney over Its Oilsands Lending Policy." *Financial Post*, 29 April 2019.
https://financialpost.com/commodities/energy/hsbc-defends-itself-after
-months-of-jabs-from-jason-kenney-over-oilsands-lending-policy.

Morton, Ted. 2018. "Why Alberta Needs a Fiscal Constitution." *University of
Calgary School of Public Policy Publications* 11, no. 25. https://doi.org/10.11575/
sppp.v11i0.56861.

Mowat, Dave, Leona Hanson, Peter Tertzakian, and Annette Trimbee. 2016.
*Alberta at a Crossroads: Royalty Review Advisory Panel Report*. Available from
https://open.alberta.ca/publications/9781460126882.

Office of the Ethics Commissioner. 2019. Report of the Investigation Under the
Alberta Energy Regulator Conflict of Interest Policy and Procedures, 14 June 2019.

Olszynski, Martin. 2019. "Alberta Ignores the Ticking Time Bomb of Orphaned
Oil and Gas Wells at Its own Peril." *Globe and Mail*, 9 December 2019.

Piketty, Thomas. 2014. *Capital in the Twenty-First Century*. Translated by Arthur
Goldhammer. Cambridge, MA: Harvard University Press.

Public Interest Commissioner. 2019. A Report of the Public Interest
Commissioner in Relation to Wrongdoings Within the Alberta Energy
Regulator, 3 October 2019.

Reuters Staff. 2017. "Inter Pipeline to Build $2.7 billion Alberta Petrochemical
Plant." *Reuters*, 18 December 2017. https://www.reuters.com/article/
idUSL1N1OI1HU.

———. 2018. "HSBC Joins Banks' Fossil Fuel Exodus; Will Stop Funding
Most New Developments." *Globe and Mail*, 20 April 2018. https://www
.theglobeandmail.com/business/industry-news/energy-and-resources/article
-hsbc-to-stop-funding-most-new-fossil-fuel-developments/.

Sharp, Alistair. 2019. "Norway Public Pension Fund Severs Final Link with
Canada's Oilsands." *National Observer*, 7 October 2019. https://www
.nationalobserver.com/2019/10/07/news/norway-public-pension-fund-severs
-final-link-canadas-oilsands.

Smith, Danielle. 2020. "Alberta Is a Financial Disgrace. We Need to Hit the Reset Button." *Calgary Herald*, 4 September 2020.

Task Force on Climate-Related Financial Disclosures. 2017. *Recommendations of the Task Force on Climate-Related Financial Disclosures*, chaired by Michael R. Bloomberg, written for the Financial Stability Board, June 2017. https://www .fsb-tcfd.org/.

Teck Resources. 2020. "Teck Withdraws Regulatory Application for Frontier Project." News release, 23 February 2020. https://www.teck.com/news/news -releases/2020/teck-withdraws-regulatory-application-for-frontier-project.

Thomson, Graham. 2015. "Roundtable on Provincial Sales Tax." Presentation at the University of Alberta, Edmonton, Alberta, 12 January 2015. https://sites .ualberta.ca/~ipe/IPE/Policy-events.html.

Toews, Travis. 2021. "2021–22 First Quarter Economic and Fiscal Update." Alberta Legislature. Recorded 31 August 2021. YouTube video. https://www.youtube .com/watch?v=5sNiSNEuhDU.

United Nations Framework Convention on Climate Change. 2016. *The Concept of Economic Diversification in the Context of Response Measures*. UNFCCC technical paper by the secretariat, 6 May 2016. https://unfccc.int/documents/ 9179.

Varcoe, Chris. 2021. "Hydrogen Has the Potential to Be Alberta's Next Oilsands in Importance." *Edmonton Journal*, 5 November 2021. https://edmontonjournal .com/opinion/columnists/varcoe-hydrogen-has-the-potential-to-be-albertas -next-oilsands-in-importance/wcm/9f204295-431b-4e7a-bfa1-41e349c86a6e.

Wadsworth, Robert. 2018. "Liability Challenges." PowerPoint presentation to the Alberta Energy Industry Historical Association, 28 February 2018.

Willis, Andrew. 2019. "Oil-Loving Banks Must Reckon with the Future." *Globe and Mail*, 1 June 2019.

Woods, James. 2018. "Alberta Ready to Pony Up $2 Billion for Trans Mountain, but Details Are Scarce." *Calgary Herald*, 29 May 2018. https://calgaryherald .com/news/politics/alberta-ready-to-pony-up-2-billion-to-move-trans -mountain-forward-but-details-are-scarce.

# Afterword

*Trevor W. Harrison*

This is an important book—one long overdue. There is widespread agreement that Alberta's financial situation is a mess. Things were bad enough before COVID-19 came along; the price of oil, upon which Alberta has overly relied, has fallen steadily since 2014, along with investment in the oil sector. The pandemic has only added to the province's accumulating fiscal difficulties.

But while the pandemic's effects will diminish with time, the deeper structural problems facing Alberta's finances will continue and predictably get worse given global economic and environmental challenges. On this point, there is also general agreement. While Alberta's debt-to-GDP ratio remains enviably low compared to other provinces, the trajectory of deficits and debt is not positive. What is the cause of Alberta's fiscal problems? More importantly, what should we do about it? This book offers one specific, if partial, solution: a sales tax.

## Competing Schools, Confronting Myths

There is no single interpretation of the cause of Alberta's fiscal problems. From the collection of different explanations, however, two distinct (and opposing) views can be discerned. One school of thought focusses on government spending—or, as some aver, overspending. Because the definition of any problem conceals its own solution, this argument's proponents contend that the solution to Alberta's fiscal woes lies in major, if not brutal, cuts in public expenditures—a phrasing with which Albertans of a certain age are themselves majorly and brutally familiar, having lived through the Klein government's cuts in the early 1990s. The policies of the so-called Klein revolution—corporate tax cuts, public sector layoffs, privatization, and deregulation—mirrored similar actions taken by New Right politicians elsewhere at that time, especially in the United States and Britain. Within Alberta, at least, the impact of these cuts has since taken on a mythic status.

A second school of thought focusses on government revenues, specifically Alberta's lagging tax effort, including, as this volume underlines, the absence of a sales tax. While there are valid points on both sides, I suggest that this second school forwards the more empirically defensible argument. The smoking gun for this argument is the well-known Alberta Tax Advantage figure from Alberta Treasury Board and Finance, replicated by Robert Ascah in chapter 1 (figure 1.1). It shows that Alberta collects over $14 billion less in revenue than Canada's next-lowest-taxing province, Ontario. Even Alberta's conservative-minded next-door neighbour, Saskatchewan, taxes an equivalent of $15.1 billion more than Alberta. One can still argue the need for responsible and accountable spending, but the idea that Alberta can cut its way to prosperity is a beggar's belief, and indeed will continue to beggar the province.

Having a frank discussion about Alberta's revenues, and the need for a sales tax specifically, first requires the sweeping away of some deeply held beliefs—particularly, as both Kevin Taft (foreword) and Ascah (chapter 1) articulate, the belief that Alberta is somehow exceptional compared to other provinces, and that taxes are an insult. These beliefs, ensconced within a broader subscription to small government—even while deferent to Alberta's Big State (Harrison 2005)—have a long history, going back to the province's founding in 1905. But, as Ascah shows (chapter 3), Alberta's low tax regime has been possible only because of revenues from nonrenewable natural resources. As Taft (foreword) notes, in recent decades, as much as 40 percent of Alberta's economy has directly or indirectly depended on the petroleum industry.

Indeed, Ascah's figures in chapter 3 show that, except for resource revenues, Alberta's books have not balanced since the mid-1960s. The mantra of low taxes—christened as the "Alberta Advantage" during Klein's 1993 election run—took on a mythic status after the Klein years in part by ignoring this reality. It is factually correct that, a couple of years after Klein's election, Alberta eliminated both its deficits and its trifling debt. Indeed, the province sported a series of healthy surpluses while continuing to boast of the lowest taxes in Canada. The thing is, Alberta's low tax "advantage" had little to do with these outcomes. The self-congratulatory boosterism built around the Alberta Advantage myth specifically ignores the role of non-renewable resource revenues in Alberta's fiscal turnaround after 1997—a turnaround resulting largely from increased demand for, and thus a rise in the global price of, oil. In this equation, Alberta is a price taker, not a price setter. During the Klein years, Alberta merely rode the boom to the top before falling (again) during the next inevitable bust. This is a cycle familiar to all staples-driven economies.

The mythology of the Alberta Advantage has interfered with an honest and critical evaluation of economic policy within Alberta, specifically the role of taxes in this policy. It has inverted the causal relationship between Alberta's prosperity and its taxes. Low taxes have often been cited as a major cause of Alberta's prosperity, but in reality their contribution to the province's wealth is largely incidental—a minor cause at most. It is more correct to see them not as a cause, but as a *consequence* of the province's prosperity. Inverting this causal relationship has had the unfortunate result of delaying a serious long-term discussion of the role of non-renewable resource revenues in Alberta's future.

## Taxes and the Resource Curse

Harold Innis was writing about the problems faced by staples-based economies such as Alberta's as early as the 1930s. He argued that such economies risk getting caught on the rollercoaster of boom and bust—something that Melville Watkins (2014, 151) later called the "staples trap"—but that this need not be their inevitable fate. Escaping the trap, Innis said, was possible with good political stewardship.

Alberta had a chance to make its escape years ago, when the province tried to take a different approach to both saving and investing for the future. After 1971, the newly elected government of Peter Lougheed employed the powers of the state to develop the oil sands. (They did so, Albertans tend to forget, with the help of the federal government.) Lougheed said Albertans should act like owners of the resource, and not as mere passive rentiers, as had been the practice under the previous Social Credit government. Lougheed's Progressive Conservative government engaged in an aggressive policy of "province building." Especially important to the issue of tax policy was the creation of the Alberta Heritage Savings Trust Fund. Lougheed argued for a royalty take of at least 35 percent, a large portion of which would go into the fund.

Unfortunately, the best laid plans of politicians go awry when faced by a recession. This was certainly true in the early 1980s, when the Lougheed government strayed from its original dictum. After that decade's midpoint, as Melville McMillan notes (chapter 5), the percentage of resource revenues contributing to government revenues sharply declined. Fearful of asking voters to fill the fiscal hole with tax money, Alberta governments beginning with Lougheed instead began dipping into the sacred Heritage Fund. Common sense would dictate that this habit be reversed when good times returned, switching from draining the fund to replenishing it, but common sense has not prevailed. The temptation to use resource revenues to appease the appetites of voters has been hard for Alberta's politicians to resist.

There are two important points to note here. The first is that Alberta's governments since the Klein years have engaged in a policy of procyclical spending—that is, spending like drunken sailors when the revenue ship comes in, but throwing passengers overboard without life jackets when the ship leaves again. This policy is precisely the reverse of what economists going back to John Maynard Keynes would recommend for dealing with volatility in the economy. The second point is related to the first, and deals with arguments made in the MacKinnon Report (Blue Ribbon Panel on Alberta's Finances 2019). The report focusses on government expenditures—specifically public sector wages, which tend to be high in comparison with workers in other provinces—as the root of all Alberta's fiscal woes. This is an argument seconded by some of this book's authors, and is correct as far as it goes. But there is an important codicil to this argument that needs some attention: just because a jurisdiction's economy is reliant on resource revenues does not mean that the government must be, too.

Take Norway, for example. As Ergete Ferede notes in chapter 6, Norway—which, like Alberta, has a resource-based economy reliant upon oil revenues—has both a sales tax (a value-added tax) and a revenue stabilization fund. In fact, Norway's Government Pension Fund Global, established in 1990, was modelled in part on the Alberta Heritage Savings Trust Fund. As of August 2021, the value of the Norwegian fund is US$1.4 trillion; Alberta's Heritage Fund, meanwhile, is sitting at US$14.7 billion. The crucial difference between Norway's fund and its Albertan counterpart is that Norway's government spends little of its resource revenues, instead adding them to the fund's earnings and reinvesting them abroad in nine thousand companies across seventy-four countries (Norges Bank, n.d.). This practice hasn't changed since the fund was established. Norway thus doesn't spend its resource revenue dollars to pay for public programs within the country, relying instead on tax revenues. By doing this, the country effectively exports its inflation. By contrast, Alberta has kept inflation at home by spending its royalty windfall within the province rather than investing it abroad. A by-product of this practice, to the chagrin of many Albertan employers, is the need to pay workers very high wages: workers, whether in the private or public sectors, must negotiate high wages in order to cope with Alberta's high—and volatile—cost of living. But this is not inevitable. The Norway model shows how resource-dependent governments can get around chasing the inflation tail: invest non-renewable resource revenues abroad and tax appropriately for necessary, and predictable, government services at home.

Despite obvious counterexamples such as Norway, the myth that Alberta's low taxes are the source of the province's prosperity remains strong. Immediately after coming to power in 2019, Premier Kenney's UCP government commissioned the Blue Ribbon Panel on Alberta's Finances. The panel's mandate was to examine government expenses only, not revenues. Not surprisingly, then, its final report did not focus on revenues either, and concluded that Alberta had a spending problem that could, once again, be cured by a heavy dose of public sector cuts (Blue Ribbon Panel on Alberta's Finances 2019).

The report also states, however, that the level of cuts needed to eliminate Alberta's deficit would go far beyond anything seen during the Klein era, and would raise the question of how much pain Albertans are willing to endure. Beyond the raw politics of austerity, one needs to consider the larger socioeconomic implications of severe cuts in further depressing aggregate demand in the short-term and causing irreparable harm to the economy's chances in the long-term. Already, anecdotal evidence suggests Alberta's best, brightest, and youngest are fleeing to locales where services and opportunities are better. Moreover, such cuts can only exacerbate the severe social deficits faced by the most vulnerable in the province.

The school of through that perpetuates the myth of government over-spending as the source of Alberta's fiscal ills remains powerful. Though perhaps not entirely believed by its purveyors, it nonetheless constitutes a psychological and, more importantly, political barrier to arguments presented by a second school of thought. This school, while not arguing against efficiencies in government spending—who would?—contends that Alberta's fiscal difficulties stem from instabilities, and even insufficiencies, in its revenue streams, which have drawn over many years upon the non-renewable resource sector.

What, then, is to be done?

## The Benefits of a PST—and How to Get There

If, as the assembled authors in this collection argue, relying on spending cuts alone will not solve Alberta's fiscal problems and will risk damage in the short and long term, the question then turns to revenue reform. As this book argues, a necessary part of this solution is a PST. None suggest, however, that a PST is the only solution. Elizabeth Smythe (chapter 7) specifically states it is not "a panacea" to Alberta's fiscal ails. Ascah similarly suggests a range of other forms of revenue, a sales tax being only one arrow in the fiscal quiver.

The array of sales tax proponents, including myself, span the political spectrum. Such wide-ranging agreement is rare on any issue—so why the unanimity? The authors in this volume note several positive benefits of a sales tax. First, sales taxes offer both predictability and stability of revenue. Second, sales taxes are efficient and less prone to tax avoidance than other measures—an efficiency that is enhanced when harmonized with the federal GST. Third, sales taxes are fair as they require temporary workers and visitors to pay for services they use while in the province, and also capture inherited wealth. Fourth, as Smythe argues in chapter 7, a sales tax would be "a small step toward restoring democracy" by freeing Alberta from its dependence on, and thus its subservience to, the oil and gas industry. Finally, a sales tax would broaden the sources of provincial revenues. Ultimately, a sales tax would make Alberta more resilient to economic circumstances beyond its immediate control.

These are good, rational arguments. They provide fodder for the notion that a sales tax might offer at least a partial solution to Alberta's fiscal dilemma. What, then, are the barriers—psychological, practical, and political—to bringing in a PST for Alberta?

The most immediate alleged barrier is what critics refer to as Alberta's "political culture." Although the term is imprecise, it broadly refers to the manner in which people come to define problems and identify solutions—including some, excluding others. Albertans, it is said, are too viscerally opposed to a sales tax or, as Graham Thomson (chapter 2) colourfully describes it, a "political suicide tax."

However, like so many other things discussed here, the barrier of political culture is not inevitable. No culture is static, especially in the face of obdurate political realities. Both Smythe (chapter 7) and Kenneth McKenzie (chapter 9) suggest public attitudes towards a sales tax may be mellowing. People may not like paying taxes—who does?—but most also recognize there are positive, collective benefits that accrue from paying taxes, such as having the vast array of public services upon which Albertans have come to rely.

To get to "yes" on the issue of sales tax, then, at least two related issues must be addressed. The first issue, as Ian Glassford (chapter 8) argues, is one of trust. Many Albertans are ideologically conservative.

As such, they support the notion of small government; a few are even antigovernment. They believe that governments are both incompetent and wasteful, and that only private markets are capable of instilling fiscal discipline—a curious argument given the record of market failures since the late 1990s, topped off by the great recession of 2008–10, but I digress. This lack of trust can only be resolved through a clear and reasoned laying out of Alberta's fiscal dilemma, the options for dealing with the problem (and the consequences), and how a sales tax must be part of any solution.

The second issue is one of fairness. There is no escaping it: a sales tax is regressive. Those at the bottom of the income scale have less disposable income than those at the top, but would pay the same proportion of tax on each purchase. As Ascah (chapter 10) points out, though, a sales tax is potentially less regressive than many other taxes and charges that Albertans already pay, such as licensing and school fees. For reasons of both political acceptability and social fairness, refundable tax credits such as those suggested by Smythe (chapter 7) and McKenzie (chapter 9) would need to be included in any proposal of a PST in Alberta. Low-income earners would receive an additional indirect benefit from the stabilizing of government programs upon which many depend. A sales tax with built-in tax credits would also assist low-income groups.

In other words, getting a "yes" on sales tax requires convincing Albertans of the benefits of sales tax; the sales tax must be sold. Unfortunately, the primary purpose of sales tax—to correct the imbalance between the services Albertans need (and demand) and the revenues to pay for them—too often gets lost, as does the sales pitch's appeal. For instance, a lack of focus can be seen in arguments that a sales tax should be revenue neutral; that is, that money obtained through a PST should be used to lower corporate taxes (as Ferede argues in chapter 6) or personal taxes (as McKenzie argues in chapter 9). Such arguments largely ignore the immediate and serious problems that Alberta's fiscal hole implies. In the case of corporate taxes especially, there is another problem: further reducing CIT is politically unsaleable, as Alberta's corporate tax rates are already the lowest in Canada. If Albertans are to be convinced to accept a sales tax, the idea of lowering corporate taxes is a political nonstarter. It comes down to fairness again. As Ascah further notes in chapter 10, these arguments are based on the hope that higher revenues will, in the long run, result in increased corporate investment and personal spending—the so-called Laffer curve. While many mainstream economists continue to voice this (neoliberal) argument, the evidence from nearly forty years of practice is not persuasive; instead, one is reminded of Keynes's (1923, 94) quip that, in the long run, "we are all dead."

Glassford (chapter 8) makes a different pitch, suggesting that a PST be used to build up a cash reserve, the money from which would go into general revenues only when the economy was weak. But this, too, is currently, in my opinion, a political nonstarter. Private businesses are expected—and need—to build up cash reserves. However, the public expects governments, unlike private businesses, to take in only as much money as they need to provide services; anything else would be viewed as a form of hoarding that results in lessening aggregate demand. The howls of private business and regular taxpayers would be deafening. Indeed, a major problem of the Heritage Fund has been that too many Albertans—unlike Norwegians—have ignored the value of making long-term investments, and viewed the fund as nothing but a piggy-bank for satiating immediate needs—a view that politicians have been only too happy to nurture.

How, then, to really get to a "yes" on a sales tax? The path, as Ascah (chapter 10) suggests, is surely through education. In this regard, the establishment of a broad-based commission to look at Alberta's fiscal situation in its entirety—that is, from both an expenditure *and* a revenue point of view—would be a good starting point. While a sales tax offers only a partial solution, it is nonetheless an important one that must be part of the commission's deliberations. In the end, however, the biggest hurdle to overcome in implementing a sales tax is political will—the will, that is, of the general public to make this change. Most politicians are not leaders, but followers of their constituents—a fact McKenzie alludes to in chapter 9. To get sales tax through the Legislature doors, the general public must show elected officials that Alberta's political culture is changing—that, all things considered, a sales tax is an acceptable alternative to an endless rollercoaster ride of funding for important services.

Changing Alberta's political will towards sales tax may feel to many like a pipe dream. As Sherlock Holmes famously says, however, "When

you have eliminated the impossible whatever remains, HOWEVER
IMPROBABLE, must be the truth" (Doyle [1890] 2009, 71). So it is in
Alberta's long-standing fiscal dilemma. Our fiscal experience and projections have identified certain expenditure-related solutions to be
impossible. What remains are solutions based in revenue reform, including
the introduction of a sales tax. Although this solution, politically speaking,
has long been viewed as an improbable, if not untenable, choice in the
province, it is among the only reasonable choices that remain. Indeed, as
McMillan (chapter 5) states, a sales tax is not just reasonable; it is "inevitable." This book can only serve to speed on the inevitable.

## References

Blue Ribbon Panel on Alberta's Finances. 2019. *Report and Recommendations:
Blue Ribbon Panel on Alberta's Finances*, chaired by Janice MacKinnon,
August 2019. Available from https://open.alberta.ca/publications/report-and
-recommendations-blue-ribbon-panel-on-alberta-s-finances.

Harrison, Trevor. 2005. "Introduction." In *The Return of the Trojan Horse: Alberta
and the New World (Dis)Order*, edited by Trevor Harrison, 1–20. Montréal:
Black Rose Books.

Innis, Harold A. 1933. *Problems of Staple Production in Canada*. Toronto: Ryerson
Press.

Keynes, John Maynard. 1923. *A Tract on Monetary Reform*. London, UK:
Macmillan.

Norges Bank. n.d. "About the Fund." Accessed 22 October 2021. https://www
.nbim.no/en/the-fund/about-the-fund/.

Doyle, Arthur Conan. (1890) 2009. *The Sign of the Four*. Reprint, Auckland: The
Floating Press.

Watkins, Melville. 2014. "A Staple Theory of Economic Growth." *Canadian
Journal of Economics and Political Science* 29, no. 2, 141–58. https://doi.org/10
.2307/139461.

# Contributors

**Robert L. (Bob) Ascah** holds degrees in commerce and public administration from Carleton University. He completed his PhD in political science at the University of Alberta in 1984. After graduating, he joined the Alberta public service, beginning in Federal and Intergovernmental Affairs, then moving to Alberta Treasury in 1986. At Treasury, he was responsible for financial sector policy, foreign borrowing, and liaising with credit rating agencies. In 1996, he joined Alberta Treasury Branches, becoming responsible for government relations, strategic planning, and economic research. In August 2009, he was appointed director of the Institute for Public Economics at the University of Alberta, where he served for four years. Ascah is the author of *Politics and Public Debt: The Dominion, the Banks and Alberta's Social Credit* (University of Alberta Press, 1999). His current research interests include Alberta fiscal history, the history of ATB, and appointments to Alberta agencies. Find more of Ascah's work on his blog, abpolecon.ca.

**Ergete Ferede** is a professor of economics at MacEwan University in Edmonton, Alberta, and a senior fellow at the Fraser Institute. He has taught at Addis Ababa University (Ethiopia), University of Alberta, and University of Windsor. His research has been published in the *National Tax Journal*, *International Tax and Public Finance*, *Public Finance Review*, and *Small Business Economics*. He is also currently pursuing various research projects on corporate income tax policy, intergovernmental grants, marginal cost of public funds, and tax reform.

**Ian Glassford**, before he retired, worked as the chief financial officer of Servus Credit Union, a $15-billion financial institution serving Alberta. His career has included roles as a foreign exchange and money market trader, serving on the board of a Canadian investment dealer, and taking on professional responsibilities in areas from wealth management to strategy. He has collected the usual range of alphabet soup, including a BComm from the University of Alberta, an MBA from the Richard Ivey School of Business, and an ICD.D.

**Trevor W. Harrison** is a professor of sociology at the University of Lethbridge. From 2011 to 2021, he served as the director of the Parkland Institute, an Alberta-wide research organization, of which he was also a founding member. Harrison is best known for his studies in political sociology, political economy, and public policy. He is the author, co-author, or co-editor of nine books, as well as numerous journal articles, book chapters, and reports, and is a frequent contributor to public media, including radio and television.

**Kenneth J. McKenzie** is a professor in the department of economics and distinguished fellow in the School of Public Policy at the University of Calgary. He has published extensively in public economics, with an emphasis on taxation. He has received several research awards, including the Harry Johnson Prize for the best article in the *Canadian Journal of Economics*, and is a two-time recipient of the Douglas Purvis Memorial Prize from the Canadian Economics Association. He has served as editor of *Canadian Public Policy*, and as a member of the editorial board for the *Canadian Journal of Economics* and the *Canadian Tax Journal*.

**Melville McMillan** is professor emeritus in the Department of Economics and a fellow of the Institute of Public Economics at the University of Alberta. His BA and MSc are from the University of Alberta, and his PhD from Cornell University. After a brief stint at the University of Wisconsin (Madison), he joined the University of Alberta as a faculty member in 1975. McMillan's research and teaching interests are in public economics and, in particular, public finance, fiscal federalism, urban and local economics, and the demand for and supply of public goods and services. He has published in these areas and has advised governments and organizations nationally and internationally (e.g., the World Bank). Although "retired," McMillan remains engaged in academic and policy matters.

**Elizabeth Smythe** is professor of political science at Concordia University of Edmonton where she teaches international and comparative politics courses as well as Canadian public policy. Her research interests include international trade and investment agreements, food standards, social movements, and global justice. Her most recent publications are *The Role of Religion in Struggles for Global Justice* (Routledge 2018) co-edited with Peter J. Smith, Katharina Glaab, and Claudia Baumgart-Ochse; and "Food for Thought: How Trade Agreements Impact the Prospects of a National Food Policy" (*Canadian Food Studies* 5, no. 3 [2018]).

**Graham Thomson** has covered Alberta politics for more than thirty years, starting with his work as Legislature correspondent for the CBC and later becoming the political editor of the *Edmonton Journal* before spending sixteen years as the paper's political affairs columnist. Among his awards are a National Newspaper Award for his reporting, and a nomination for his columns. Graham spent eight months at the University of Toronto in 2008–09, where he studied environmental law and climate change after being awarded a Canadian Journalism Foundation fellowship.